# "I Am My Brother's Keeper"

## Journal of a Gunny in Iraq

### J. K. Doran

Caisson Press

"I Am My Brother's Keeper"
Journal of a Gunny in Iraq

Caisson Press / January 2005

Book Jacket design by Gary Livingston and Jason Doran
Cover photo provided by Jason Doran

Library of Congress Catalog number: 2004113530
ISBN: hardcover 1-928724-05-1

Caisson Press, North Topsail Beach, North Carolina

Manufactured in the United States of America

*This book is dedicated to my daughters*
*Addie and Jennifer*

# IF

## Rudyard Kipling

If you can keep your head when all about you
Are losing theirs and blaming it on you;
If you can trust yourself when all men doubt you,
But make allowance for their doubting too;
If you can wait and not be tried by waiting,
Or being lied about, don't deal in lies,
Or being hated don't give way to hating,
And yet don't look too good, nor talk too wise.

If you can dream- and not make dreams your master;
If you can think- and not make thoughts your aim;
If you can meet with Triumph and Disaster
And treat those two imposters just the same;
If you can bear to hear the truth you've spoken
Twisted by knaves to make a trap for fools,
Or watch the things you gave your life to broken,
And stop and build 'em up with worn out tools.

If you can make one heap of all your winnings
And risk it on one turn of pitch-and-toss,
And lose, and start again at your beginnings
And never breathe word about your loss;
If you can force your heart and nerve and sinew
To serve your turn long after they are gone,
And so hold on when there is nothing in you
Except the Will in which says to them "hold on!"

If you can talk with crowds and keep your virtue
Or walk with Kings- nor lose the common touch,
If neither foes nor loving friends can hurt you
If all men count with you but none too much;
If you can fill the unforgiving minute
With sixty seconds worth of distance run
Yours is the Earth and everything that's in it,
And- which is more- you will be a man my Son!

What I write is written more for us than for you. I write only what I felt and saw, and this is personal to me. Personal not only to me, but to those who served with me. I leave unwritten a lot of what I saw or heard that may bring up scars to my brothers. If I fail at this, I apologize.

I wrote in a letter once about the emotions I knew I would feel during the battles and firefights. These emotions can overlap each other or be distinctly different. In the beginning of the fight, there is the excitement and rush of the unknown. Then, as the fight starts and carries through, the excitement turns to chaos and the chaos mixes with fear. This fear within divides you. It is like a two-edged sword fighting itself. One side of the blade is the selfish side, the fear of dying. The other side of the blade is the unselfish side, the fear of not doing what is required and letting those that are there with you down, or worse, letting them die. The leadership that has been developed in the Marine Corps is keen on keeping the unselfish side of the blade sharp through peer pressure and hard discipline. When the fight is over, the adrenalin still remains. When this adrenalin does end, it ends hard and all the curses that come with the lack of sleep and stress follow: irritability, rash thought, and erratic behavior. Then after this comes the sadness and regret. Everyone is different, but I believe the sadness to be the worst of all -- sadness over what you saw, the killing that you did or even failed to do, decisions that were or were not made, the wounded, and of course, the dead. Somewhere in all of these feelings, blame comes in.

Who was at fault? Why did all this just happen? Was it justified? What did we accomplish? There are a thousand more questions that I know come to mind. Nevertheless, "Was it worth it?" comes to be the one true question. More often than not, the answer at that time is no. Only with the time, patience, and understanding that comes with age will the answer change to "yes, it was."
Usually in all this, the one person who is dealt the blame immediately is whoever was in charge. No one really understands though, that no matter what his rank or position, he is given orders. Ultimately, just as no one refuses the orders they are given, neither does he refuse his. He, as we all did that day, did the best with what he had.

At the end of the day he must be able to look in the mirror and truly be judged, by himself.

Sir, I salute you.

# FOREWORD

I was walking behind a HMMV on the north side of An Nasiriyah, two days after the battle started. The HMMV had a Corporal standing in the turret. His hands were stuck back into the armholes of his flak jacket. He was cold and tired. I distinctly remember the stare in his eyes, staring a thousand miles away. He was done mentally but there was no doubt in my mind he was fully aware of what was going on. Looking, waiting for that one sign, that one mark that would give the enemy away to where they were. He stood there not flinching or blinking at the wind and sand, undisturbed by what was being said or what was going on around him. On his TOW missile there was some writing that he had inscribed with a rock. It said, "I am my brother's keeper..." He truly was.

If you're looking for a literary masterpiece, you have picked up the wrong book. Joyce and the others are on a different bookshelf. I was just a grunt, an Infantryman in the Marine Corps. I never graduated high school, never went to college, and the only way I ever learned anything was when I had the hell beat out of me. Those that beat the hell out of me didn't care about my grammar, only if I could assemble a claymore or disassemble my M-16 blindfolded. They did not care if I could convey my thoughts to words; they were more interested that I kept my mouth shut and did what I was told to do. I kept notes as things happened, and on my return to the world via ship, I wrote down my thoughts. But as you read you will see that sometimes writing what happened was not the foremost of my thoughts or desires. So if you care to, read on.

I was with the 1st Battalion, 2nd Marine Regiment, which was part of the Second Marine Expeditionary Brigade, known as Task Force Tarawa. During this time, I served with Weapons and Bravo Company. I really don't expect you to know any of the places and times I mention or the people I talk about. What I wrote about could have been played out in any war or any battle. However, it is the battle of my brothers that I write about and the war we fought.

# Acknowledgments

I would like to thank Caisson Press for the opportunity of publishing my story. It took a lot of time and effort and I appreciate their patience in helping me make my journal into something readable. I would like to thank my editors, Kate Walsh and Lisa Mabli. Reading my story and helping me translate it from "grunt" lingo, where only a few could understand, to where everyone could understand it, is much appreciated.

This is where I am supposed to start thanking every one for everything but instead this is where I say I am sorry. Sorry to my father for worrying when I was gone fighting both wars or in harms way in some fucked up country that America did not care enough about to even put on the news. But you knew, and that was good enough for me.

Sorry to my brother Marines when I failed you. I am sorry, I couldn't take all the pain for you and remove all the fear, as hard as I tried, that wasn't good enough. I am sorry I wasn't around to talk to you when you got back from the war and this country told you that you were wrong. Most of all, I am sorry I could not bring all of you home alive.

We saw the best of each other, the worst of each other, and still stood next to each other. I thank God for the privilege of knowing and serving with you. Till our next port that lies over the horizon,


Semper Fi,
GySgt Doran

# TABLE OF CONTENTS

# The Beginning
## Chapter one

When I was growing up in Texas my dad would take my brother and me out hunting. I enjoyed spending time outdoors, but I especially enjoyed having my father's approval. He would tell my brother and me we were good shots, but I alone received the compliment of not being hesitant to shoot something. I didn't know whether I was a good shot or not, but I knew I wasn't hesitant. A lot of the hunting was done on ranch land that he and his friends worked on during the summer for hunting rights in the winter. I usually just ended up shooting a lot of air, but my dad would always tell me I was close and that I was getting better. The first time I did hit anything though, I was ten years old, alone, and it was a rabbit.

It was hauling ass up a hill into a bunch of thick bushes with vines and tangle foot. Just before it made it into the thicket, I pulled the trigger. The rabbit went tumbling head over heels, wounded. I walked up to it and realized I had hurt a living creature. I was scared that I was going to get in trouble. I threw some branches over it and started to walk away. Then I thought if someone found the wounded rabbit, I would get in even deeper trouble for trying to hide what I had done. I walked back, put the second barrel of the shotgun to its head, and pulled the trigger.

I carried the rabbit back to my dad, who was down by a lake. He said he heard the second shot and guessed it was me taking the rabbit out of its pain. He started telling me how good it was going to taste and that everyone would enjoy the meal. Then he showed me how to skin and cook the rabbit. I never felt guilty about killing again.

My mother and father divorced when I was five and his side of the family, being typical Irish/Italian Catholics, all chipped-in to raise my brother and me. It was a great life until my dad remarried. When that happened my brother and I were uprooted from our school. Our friends and our family became a distant mirage. By the time he divorced his second wife, I was thirteen and was ready to leave. I was in trouble at school and my grades were dropping. My home life sucked and I wanted as far from Dallas as I could get. I wanted a place I could start over and stand on my own -- a place where no one would question my honor or integrity, where no one could doubt that I could be a man. So I decided to join the American version of the French Foreign Legion, the Marine Corps.

At thirteen, I walked down to the recruiting office to join the Marines. The Marine on duty kind of laughed but took my information, showed me a movie, gave me some pamphlets, and told me to come back when I was seventeen.

Since I was going to join the Corps, and I felt that I was on my own, my grades got worse. I was expelled from school for skipping classes, but mostly for fighting. I started drinking and not coming home at night. At sixteen I ran away from home for about a year or so. I had failed my first attempt at tenth grade and was about ready to try a second time when two of my friends dropped out of school and joined the Army. I went down to the recruiting office and enlisted in the Marine Corps. My father was dead set against it and refused to sign the enlistment papers. Recruiters even came over and talked to my dad, and still he refused. Finally the Senior Marine, Master Sgt Lee, called my dad up and gave him a reality check. He told my father that given my history, I probably wouldn't finish high school, go to college, or work in corporate America. My dad signed the papers and three months later I was at MCRD (Marine Corps Recruit Depot, San Diego, California).

On 19 October 1983, I flew into San Diego with twenty or so other guys. There were several Drill Instructors at the airport to greet us. They herded us outside to a white bus that had all the windows spray-painted black. They made us stand there with our noses touching the side of the bus, staring at the white paint. As more of us arrived they ran out of nose room on the bus and the newer guys had to stand behind us with their noses on the back of our heads. One of the Drill Instructors called it "assholes to belly buttons." I couldn't see who was behind me but with all the yelling and shouting going on I thought the numbers were growing fast. It got quiet for a minute or two and I thought the Drill Instructors had gone back inside to greet more recruits. I was too scared to look behind me, so I just kept my nose to the bus. This humiliating treatment was taking away our pride and any hatred we might have had toward each other. It placed us all on the same level: rock bottom.

I was listening to sounds around me and I heard a couple of females walking by in high-heeled shoes. As the steps got closer, I heard one of the girls say that "we shouldn't be standing like that while we were in public" and then she giggled. I was pissed off to no end. A voice from behind me said, "don't worry, she's fucking ugly." All of us kids standing there were searching to be men. Not men like we reached puberty or in the legal sense; we wanted to be challenged and tested, to prove to ourselves that we had what it took to be men in the honorable and disciplined way. And as all men, we wanted the approval of beautiful and caring women. When someone said she was ugly and she had degraded us with her uncaring words, she became a lesser being, and was not worthy. I wasn't pissed off anymore.

Boot Camp stories are all the same. They are either like mine, "I got my ass kicked by the Drill Instructor," or they are a lie and it's "I kicked the Drill Instructor's ass." Ass kicking or not, I did learn two very important things at MCRD: it is never someone else's fault when we fail, and we are not allowed to fail. Those two things, those small standards, are not hard to live up to. If you think it is a high standard, you are probably blaming all your shortcomings on someone else.

My family instilled a lot of good qualities in me, but the Marine Corps gave me a lifestyle and environment to apply them. The Drill Instructors I had were great leaders and when I finished Boot Camp I thought every Marine I met should have acted and looked just as they did. It took me a year or two to find out that you don't have to be a Drill Instructor to be a great leader -- you only have to be a great leader to be a great leader. So I was taught and trained by others as well.

My two greatest influences as a young Marine were SSgt Garvin and Sgt Hayworth. Both of them were veterans of Beirut, Lebanon. I met them during my second enlistment in the Marine Corps when I was stationed at Subic Bay in the Philippines. Hayworth was a Dragon Gunner (anti-tank gunner) by trade but he really knew his shit as a rifleman. He took me under his wing and taught me what I should know as far as patrolling, tracking, navigational tricks, tactics, and techniques with different weapon systems. Hayworth spent a lot of time with me and answered a lot of questions. More importantly, he explained why things were the way they were. A couple of years later Hayworth re-enlisted for EOD (Explosive Ordnance Disposal). This is a job for someone really smart who wants to do something really stupid. SSgt Garvin taught me by his example. He taught me how to foster loyalty in Marines, showed me how Marines wanted to be treated, and how to support junior leaders even when they were wrong. He made the rank of Cpl seem like it was one step below The Sergeant Major of the Marine Corps. He taught me that you don't train, you prepare for war every day, and taking care of your Marines was more than just leadership, it was our way of life. The Marine Corps was never referred to as a job, but a profession.

3

Because of Garvin and Hayworth's leadership, I left the Philippines a Meritorious Sergeant, capturing more Philippine intruders in jungle patrols than anyone else in the Company's history. I also met and married the first of my four wives.

Warrant Officer Hayworth ended up catching the bad side of a landmine while defusing it somewhere in Kosovo and was medically discharged from the Marine Corps. 1st Sgt Garvin, I heard, died of a heart attack while doing what he loved most: preparing Marines for war at MCRD Pairs Island, South Carolina.

After leaving the Philippines, I was ordered to 1st Battalion, 6th Marines, and my first duty station as a Sgt. This is where I met Sgt "Tuck" Tucker and SSgt "Chesty" Regal. Regal got his nickname because he was a body builder and he was huge. Tuck was just as big but more in a corn-fed way. Both of these Marines were veterans of Beirut. (Are you starting to see a trend here?) They were both knowledgeable and never backed down when they were right. EVERYONE went to these two men when they needed to know something. They had a theory that an infantry Marine should be able to live out of his pack for years on end. It turned out they were right.

Capt Gauthier was the Commanding Officer of our Company, Bravo Company. He didn't play games and didn't tolerate bullshit. He was the first Officer I met that didn't just "talk the talk" but "walked the walk." The Battalion Commander, LtCol T.S. Jones was the same way. No one said it to his face, but we all said the T.S. stood for Tough Shit, cause he was one tough Marine. The only one older than LtCol Jones in the Battalion was SgtMaj Druery. LtCol Jones not only would do what everyone else in the Battalion did physically, but mentally he was even sharper. LtCol Jones and Captain Gauthier were like SSgt Garvin -- they believed in the young Corporals and Sergeants, but more importantly, in their combat abilities. I was fortunate -- I served in the First Gulf War with these Marines. When sailing through the Indian Ocean on the way to Saudi Arabia on the USS Okinawa, LtCol Jones pulled all the NCOs (Non-Commissioned Officer, the rank of Corporal and Sergeant) together for a meeting. He opened his speech as he always did, "Gents, I ain't throwing you a smoke screen for a frontal assault." Everyone kind of laughed from his catch phrase but then he said, "You have to be able to out-perform, and kill, the Iraqi soldier who is leading his soldiers to kill you and your Marines. You must not only out-do him physically, you must out-do him mentally." When he said they were trying to kill us, we stopped our laughing. Our leadership was preparing us, telling us what they knew and what they thought.

Tucker would later receive a medal for bravery at the breach into Kuwait. The last time I saw Tuck he was a Master Sgt and Operations Chief for Weapons Company, 2/2. He was preparing with his Battalion to go back to Kuwait for our second go around. Regal was also awarded a medal for bravery as we crossed the minefield into Kuwait. A couple of years later he made Master Sergeant. After returning to the world from Kuwait, Chesty kept the rest of us sane. As the Marines we served with in the war left the Marine Corps or received orders to other duty stations, and other Marines took their places, he served as our protection from those who did not fight with us but had something to prove. Chesty left the Marines after twenty plus years and went back to Pennsylvania, so I heard. Captain Gauthier kept leading our Company at the breach, even after his Amtrak (Assault Amphibious Vehicle) hit a landmine right under where he was sitting. Several days later, along with several other Marines, we tried to patch up a guy up who was playing with a CBU (Cluster Bomb Unit). The Marine died three days later, but he wouldn't have made it three minutes if it hadn't been for the Captain. The last time I saw Captain Gauthier he was a Major. Later I heard from Tucker he was a LtCol and was awarded the Bronze Star for his actions at the breach into Kuwait.

LtCol Jones was a Reconnaissance Platoon Commander in Vietnam; lead a Battalion into Kuwait, and a Regiment into Haiti. I heard he was promoted to General. He should be Commandant of the Marine Corps. He knows more about war fighting, how to prepare for it, and what war is about more than any other Marine in the Marine Corps, officer or enlisted. I guess that scares some people, including Marines who like to be politically correct.

Like Tuck and Regal, I was awarded a medal for bravery at the breach into Kuwait. Then I got orders for $2^{nd}$ Reconnaissance Battalion. By the time I arrived at $2^{nd}$ Recon, was happily divorced and was in the process of marrying my second wife. (Just in case you're wondering, no, I won't learn my lesson. Some mistakes are so much fun you have to keep repeating them.) I attended the school for Reconnaissance Marines but really didn't grasp the tactical concept of what they were teaching. I was used to large numbers of Marines and less fire support being available. Recon teams had neither. Thank God for $1^{st}$ Sgt Forney -- he was the $1^{st}$

Sgt of our Company.  When I was having problems he decided to work with me.  He had spent most of his twenty years of the Marine Corps in Recon, and he knew it inside and out.  His leadership and the time he spent with me helped in every aspect of Recon.  Because of him, I graduated with honors from Sniper School.  I was one of very few Marines to successfully graduate French Commando School.  I also had four successful counter-drug operation patrols, and most importantly I succeeded with my team.

1st Sgt Forney picked up SgtMaj and was sent to the Air Wing.  Few people know this but the Marine Corps has its own planes and helicopters, and they are commanded, flown and fixed by Marines.  These Marines are God's gift at air stuff but suck donkey dick at basic "anything" Marine Corps.  I don't know who I felt more sorry for, SgtMaj Forney, for having to put up with Marines who did not know which end of the rifle the bullet came out of, or the Air Wing, having to learn which end of the rifle a bullet came out of.  Either way, I heard after that he had enough and retired.

While on a three-year stint on Recruiting Duty, I divorced my second wife and married my third.  We had our first daughter, Addie Katherine, who was named after my father's mother and my father's aunt.  They had to induce an early labor due to problems Addie was having with her intestines.  I thought it might have something to do with Gulf War Syndrome but later blew it off and credited it to being the way life is.  I went back to the FMF (Fleet Marine Force) after my three year recruiting tour.

I met a great bunch of guys in Alpha Company 1st Battalion, 2nd Marine Regiment: Lt Moxey, SSgt Buck, SSgt Clark and SSgt Hand.  In '97 we shipped out for the Mediterranean Ocean on a six-month cruise.  Usually this was a liberty cruise, but we got the word that we were leaving a week earlier than planned to go sit off the coast of Africa.  Apparently the whole West Coast decided to have a revolution, killing innocent civilians in the process and we were sent to rescue the civilians.  My Platoon Commander was Lt Moxey, from Montana, an Annapolis graduate who had a great sense of humor.  He was short and always said that he wanted to marry someone tall, cause if he married someone any shorter than him his family would just disappear.  He took things seriously but never let on if something bothered him.  I did learn a telltale sign about him though: when he did worry or was in deep thought, he would take his pen and twirl in and out of his fingers.

6

In Sierra Leone, Lt Moxey asked a Nigerian Army Sgt if he could get rid of the crowds gathering in front of the hotel where we were evacuating civilians. The Nigerian Sgt responded in an impeccable English accent, "this task you have assigned me will be accomplished in a manner that is proficient and to your satisfaction." The Sgt yelled something to his soldiers and they all pulled the charging handle on their AK-47s and ran towards the crowd. Of course this sent the crowd taking off to the four corners of the world. Lt Moxey looked at me, smiled, and said, "Do you think they've done this before?"

There were three other SSgts in Alpha Company, and even though each of them had great points, a guy who looked like me, or as he would say, I looked like him, became a strong influence. SSgt Clark and I had a lot of the same experiences and had developed the same leadership styles. He confirmed that what I thought was right, was in fact right.

As luck would have it, I had a run-in with a Battalion Commander just as he was leaving the unit. While at an Army base doing some training, I had been assigned to run a live fire shoot for a mortar range. I told everyone that there was no way in hell I should be running a mortar range. I had no experience with mortars and needed to bird dog some one before I did. While on the firing range there was a dud mortar. I called EOD, as I was supposed to. I got investigated and relieved. He wanted to make an example out of me and he did. He was really fucking with me hard and doing everything to make my life miserable. I have to say, though, he was doing a great job -- I was relieved of my Platoon, then he held a meeting with all the Senior Enlisted and Officers to defend his actions against me, then had me count chairs in an auditorium, and he wrote in my fitness report that I was a better union leader than a Marine leader. Oh happy days!

A month later we got a new Battalion Commander named LtCol Beekman. I learned something from him that the Marine Corps should make Standard Operational Procedure: it is called a second chance. He talked with the Battalion Gunner, Gunner Abbott, and decided to send me to Advanced Mortar Leader Course (AMLC) and Advanced Machinegun Leaders Course (AMGLC), to see if I would be willing to step up to the plate if I was given the knowledge. I graduated Honor Grad from both schools. LtCol Beekman gave me the opportunity to learn, an opportunity to overcome my failures, the opportunity to succeed, and most importantly he gave me the opportunity to teach others. I can honestly say that when he gave me my second chance to learn from my mistakes, he saved lives in Iraq.

Lt Moxey got orders to Force Recon and accepted them, even though everyone told him it would end his career as an Officer. He married a lady who had been an Officer in the Navy and was shorter than him. I guess he figured out that his family tree wouldn't disappear. Force Recon didn't ruin his career; instead he went back to Annapolis and educated young cadets to be Officers. SSgt Clark picked up Gunny and was sent to be an evaluator at Special Operations Training Group, better known as School Of Tough Guys. LtCol Beekman retired and Gunny Clark told me over a beer that he was working for a bank down in Charlotte, South Carolina. Wherever he is now he is doing well and who ever is working for him is probably enjoying it. In fact I am so sure of it, "I'll bet you a Coke."

My third wife and I had my second daughter, Jennifer Grace. She was named after my dad's cousin, Aunt Jenny; and the Grace was after my mother's grandmother. As a child, just learning to walk, her right eye was always squinted. It turned out to be a small but uneventful tumor causing the problem. I was sure, more than ever, that I had a problem with Gulf War Syndrome. I decided to go to the Doc at the hospital on base and see what was up. I went through some testing and they said I was fine, but my daughters are still fucked up.

For a short time I trained Marines at the School of Infantry (SOI) at Camp Lejeune. At first I was cursed -- I was assigned to a unit that trained Privates who were not going to be infantrymen but still had to be trained in basic infantry tactics. Then my luck changed. I was sent to Infantry Platoon Sergeants Course and trained Sgts and Staff Sergeants in advanced infantry skills.

There was another Gunny there, GySgt Mackey, an awesome guy who really knew his stuff. Mackey, back in the early 80s as a young Marine, was shot in the leg in a firefight in Beirut, Lebanon, at a place that was referred to as Sniper Alley. He spent a couple of days on ship healing, and was sent back into Lebanon with bandages and crutches. He received an award for bravery as well as a Purple Heart.

A couple of years later, when the US went into Panama, the Army awarded a young soldier the Purple Heart for dehydration. Mackey, with five other Marines, held a ceremony with the Division Commander

(General Grey, who would later become the Commandant of the Marine Corps) and turned in their Purple Hearts as a protest. Neither Mackey nor the other Marines ever wore their Purple Hearts again. That is fortitude.

Anyway, with Mackey, and the variety of classes we taught, life couldn't have been better. After a year or so, I was promoted in billet to be the Senior Instructor at the Advanced Mortar Leader Course. I had the some of the best mortar men in Division working for me there. Even though the subject was always the same, the students and the instructor's personalities made AMLC a blast. Before I left the School of Infantry, I divorced my third wife. And it would be several years later before I married my fourth.

Deployments, training operations, real world operations, military schools, additional duties, and just plain old-fashioned field training all led to my divorces. I remember the different reasons why I married each of my four wives, every great quality, but there was only one reason why I divorced them. I left the Philippines and went straight to Kuwait; after Kuwait I went straight into Counter-Drug Operations. A couple of years later I pulled two operations in Africa. Like a lot of Marines I served with, we were constantly on the go. And what we were doing was not exactly every-day stuff. It wasn't that I wanted to be alone, but I couldn't stand still. I felt like I had to be on the run, like I had committed Holy sins and while temporarily forgiven, if I slowed down my forgiveness would be revoked by society, those that sent me off to these other places.

One Marine that I learned from continuously, not only from when I was at one unit in particular but throughout my later years as a Marine, was 1st Sgt George Erb. He was one Marine that bluntly told me how things were; he never sugarcoated anything. He was the kind of Marine that would chew anyone's ass from one side of the earth to the other and then sit down and have a beer with them like nothing ever happened. He was one that truly cared about his Marines and never shirked his duty. As I write this he is doing time in Iraq. He could have retired like the 1st Sgt he was ordered to replace, who didn't want to go. He could have stayed in Texas with his new bride and been close to his children, but the bugle called and he left without any half-stepping.

The Marines I mentioned before aren't the only ones who influenced or raised me. I can think of a Battalion of names, great leaders that I learned from. But unfortunately, or to my benefit, depending on how you look at it, I learned from bad masters and from them I learned what not to do as well.

So my father, his side of the family, and the Marine Corps raised me. Marines, who instructed me, beat me, pushed me further, and made times I would never want to relive the best times of my life. I was raised and taught to serve others, and that is what I strived for. Leadership is servitude. If you don't believe me, ask Jesus.

The day before I graduated Boot Camp, the Battalion Sergeant Major, SgtMaj D. R. Barr said, "We have taught you just enough to get your ass kicked." There was a lot of wisdom in that simple sentence on and off the battlefield. Of course, being a new and young Marine, I doubted his pearls of wisdom. Twenty years later, after having carried more dead and wounded Marines than I have good-looking girls on my arm, I realize he was right. We get so wrapped up in what was done yesterday (Okinawa, Saipan, Bealleau Wood, Inchon, Chosin, Khe Sahn) we forget what we have to do today (Iraq, France, Libya and Iran). Don't misunderstand me, holding on to a strong and honorable past will give us reason to fight for the same future. My point is, a lot of unprepared countries died for a future that they could not hold. The Marine Corps is holding.

In late November of 2002, at the age of thirty-seven and two months into my fourth marriage, I was already in divorce court. I checked back into my old Battalion, but a different Company. I was the Javelin Platoon Commander for Weapons Company, $1^{st}$ Battalion, $2^{nd}$ Marine Regiment, $2^{nd}$ Marine Division. I was really pumped about this new assignment. I was to be given six of the Marine Corps' new FAVs (Fast Attack Vehicles). I spent long days and weekends with my Platoon writing SOPs, training, and preparing for our float to the Mediterranean in six months. The mission of Javelin's Platoon was to engage Tanks from a shoulder launched weapon system. The system worked off thermal imaging and could either have the missile fly into the side or top of the tank, depending on how the gunner thought the tank was most vulnerable. They were talking about giving me some machine gunners to put on the FAVs, which would have made my Platoon larger and given us a lot more continuous firepower. The Javelin gunners could shoot machine guns but they couldn't shoot machine guns, drive the FAVs, be an assistant gunner to the Javelin gunner, and shoot the Javelin at the same time.

10

The biggest problem I had with the Platoon was discipline. The Platoon had been treated like a stepchild for so long without any <u>direct</u> senior leadership that they had gone civilian on the Marine Corps. I cut that shit out, reveille at 0530, immediately followed by PT (no matter what the weather), inspections of uniforms, haircuts and rooms, and more importantly having them take training more seriously. In a matter of weeks, Javelin Platoon was a tight, kick-ass bunch of motherfuckers. Don't misunderstand me, I didn't make them tough, or turn them into Marines. I just treated them like SSgt Garvin treated me when I was young. They were held to a standard. That's all any Marine wants: to be treated like a Marine and to see that their leaders are doing what they are doing. If you take a wild pack of wolves and let them loose in the forest, and the alpha male of the pack is always by the fire, never digging in, sleeping late, not pulling a symbolic amount of watch, not doing a challenging PT session, or just plain not doing what everyone else is doing, the pack will go its own direction. The Arabs have a saying, "I fear a flock of sheep led by a lion, more than a pride of lions led by a sheep."

The Platoon had two strong Corporals: Cpl Wakefield and Cpl Worthington. These two were eager and wanted the best for the Platoon but lacked direction as far as how to get it done. So off of those two I got things moving. Of course the Platoon had its leadership challenges also -- Private First Class Thornton and Lance Corporal Vierra. Don't misunderstand, just cause someone's a leadership challenge didn't mean I hated or wanted to get rid of them. They were still my brothers, and as their "older brother" it was my job to teach and train them.

Overall, things were going well in the Platoon when we checked out for Christmas leave in 2002. I wasn't getting everything I wanted, but I was getting most of what the Platoon needed. Morale, discipline, knowledge, and PT (physical fitness) were getting to where I wanted them. But things were about to change. Rumors were flying around the Battalion like it was cool, but I didn't pay any attention to what was being said. Well, I did pay enough attention to start packing my house up and putting it in a trailer.

Right before we left on leave, we lost our FAVs, which fucking sucked. It meant we weren't going to the Mediterranean, at least not the way we had planned. But it made me think that my paranoid precaution of packing my house was not a waste of time. I signed my Platoon's leave papers, drove home, parked my motorcycle in my living room, got in my truck with trailer in tow, and drove to Dallas.

It took a couple of days to get to Dallas but overall I didn't have any problems. When I arrived, I gathered my belongings that were scattered throughout my Dad's house and loaded them in the trailer. My dad found a storage unit large enough and cheap enough to just park my trailer inside the unit – no need to unpack. Somewhere inside I knew that if the rumors were true, and if I didn't come back, the trailer would not leave this storage unit for several years. Dad would just pay the monthly fee instead of having to sort out my things.

After I got back from the First Gulf War in '92, I had gone to a traditional Christmas Eve party thrown by a man named Pat, who was the father of one of my Dad's close friends. He had been a Marine fighter pilot in the battle of Okinawa and I had just returned from the First Gulf War. We talked and drank whiskey together for most of the night. I was drunk enough to give him my Marine tie clip and he was sober enough to keep it. Even though I enjoyed talking to Pat, our conversation did not last all night. I was walking around the house talking to other people and that was when I noticed a blonde haired girl there. I only saw her for a moment before she left, but I remembered her.

In 2002, ten years later, I went to that same traditional Christmas Eve party. Pat had passed away and his son Randy had continued the tradition. I saw that blonde girl again. Her name was Kelly and it turned out that she was Pat's granddaughter. We talked about her travels and my time in the Marine Corps. Right off the bat we hit it off. She later described the way we met as "just crazy." We were so different from each other in everything we thought, did, and believed. But we just clicked. Since our families were friends, I asked her father if I could date her, and he said that it would be fine with him. Our first date was a non-date on the 27$^{th}$ of December, and I saw her every day till I left. The last I saw her it was two in the morning on the 3$^{rd}$ of January. I did not know if I would ever see her again. I just wanted to lie in bed with her and never have the sunrise, but even if I had had the chance I wouldn't have stayed. I had to be with my brothers, till it was over.

# Setting Sail
## Chapter 2

**3 January 2003**

I reported back off Christmas leave with the rest of my Battalion, expecting to get the official word that we were leaving for Kuwait. Rumors had been flying around before leave even started that we would be going to Kuwait for a possible attack on Iraq. The Battalion Commander, LtCol Grabowski, had kept telling us that as far as he knew we weren't going, and that he had not been told anything. He wanted the Companies to keep on course with our logistical planning and the training schedules in preparation for our annual visit to Fort AP Hill, Virginia, in late January and February.

I had heard while on leave that leave would be called short and that we would be leaving for Kuwait the first week of January. It never happened but when I checked in off leave I heard from other Marines that Regiment was packing up to leave for Kuwait.

Around noon we got the word we were shipping out. Actually, the official word was that we were just getting on ship and "might" go and sit there in the middle of the Mediterranean Sea. The kicker to all of this was, we were leaving in about a week. I got the same scenario that we were leaving in one week when I was with 1/2 and leaving for Africa.

An hour later, after the word came down that we were probably going to sit in the middle of the Med, we got more word to go and draw our desert gear from CTEP (Division Supply). Why in the hell were we going to draw desert gear if we were going to be surrounded by water? Not just the individual Marines had to draw gear -- the Company was being issued a ton of gear also. This job usually would have been left up to Master Sgt Hendricks, but he was filling in the Company's 1st Sgt billet, so it was left up to me.

I was dual-hatting two jobs: the Weapons Company Operations Chief (Ops Chief) and the CAAT (Combined Anti-Armor Team) Platoon Sergeant. Since we had lost the FAVs, the normal employment procedure for Javelins was going to be used. And frankly, being a static Javelin Platoon Commander is like being a burro at the Kentucky Derby and I didn't want the Ops Chief job of kicking boxes and counting water cans. So by the grace of God and Capt Rohr, the Commanding Officer of Weapons Company, I was made CAAT Plt Sgt just before we went on leave. That was what I wanted: to lead Marines. Like I said, till then I was dual hatting two jobs.

Our original Company First Sgt, 1st Sgt Bixby, wasn't going because he was having eye surgery done and he did not know if he was going to catch up to us later on. Both of his retinas were detaching from his eyeballs. To read anything he would have to hold the paper as far away as he could, turn the paper parallel to the ground, and tilt his head to read it. Then he would mumble something about having to read like that because he was so tired. 1st Sgt Bixby was an awesome 1st Sgt. Everyone respected what he said and how he said it. Some mornings, he and I would be the only ones in the office -- around 0530 or so -- and we would talk about our daughters, other people we knew (like the previous First Sgt of Weapons Company, 1st Sgt Erb), or just bitch about life in general. These conversations would last as long as a cup of coffee. His daughters were fourteen and three. The two of them would drive him so crazy all he could do was smile. The stories he came up with would have a punch line that would end up being the joke of the day.

Bixby had quit smoking, so during the day when I knew he was stressing I would go out the back hatch, light up a cigarette, and exhale in a way that the smoke would carry into his office. This would usually get his nicotine fit going and stress him more, and he would go off on the clerks who did the typing in the office. Fuck, I am funny. Evil, but funny.

I was hoping that when we hit land, if we hit land, I would be just the Platoon Sergeant for CAAT, and Hendricks would dual-hat as the Ops Chief and First Sgt. As CAAT Plt Sgt I could run the countryside. The Platoon Commander for CAAT was Lt Letendre. He was a realist, a levelheaded person who would listen to what anyone had to say. He was not the kind of officer who said something just to hear himself talk. When he said something and had made a decision, it was usually right on the mark. If he wasn't sure, he would ask questions and take advice. He wasn't stuck on the fact that he was an officer; he was living on the fact that he was a leader.

There were two other SNCOs (Staff Non-Commissioned Officers) in CAAT besides me. SSgt Troy "Caveman" Schielein was one of them and we quickly became good friends. We both had Harleys and did a lot of riding together. And of course the rides were always accompanied by a beer or two. The other Gunny in the Platoon was GySgt Hanson.

14

Gunny Hanson was a bald, quiet man who could run forever. He had picked up GySgt with eleven years in the Marine Corps, which at the time was unheard of -- it usually took sixteen to seventeen years. He was the Platoon Sergeant but when I came along he did not have a problem stepping down as one of the Section Leaders. The Marines in the Platoon were awesome.

Most of the day, Hendricks was trying to get accountability of the Company's Marines as they came off leave and take care of any personal problems the Marines might have for the deployment. I was running around with Cpl Day trying to get everything locked on and squared away with all the extra gear we were to get from supply. Cpl Day worked directly for me, as the Company Police Sgt. He was a tall, well-built young man with blonde hair and blue eyes. He was raised on a farm and you could tell because it was the subject of everything he talked about. Day busted his ass in his job and did a lot in getting everything ready for us to leave. The thing I really did like about him right off the bat was his need to have everything planned out and the gear always staged in an orderly manner. His skills in leadership were what you would expect from a good Corporal. He was overly demanding and did not play favorites. His one weakness, and the Marines knew it, was women. If a Marine was doing something and wanted a break, all he had to do was talk about women to Day and everything halted.

Late in the afternoon Hendricks told me I was leaving on advanced party to Norfolk, Virginia, on the sixth, and all this gear from CTEP had to be signed for and passed out. So not only did I have to get all the gear issued as I had planned to do by the sixth, I also had to have all the pack-out lists made and make sure no one left anything behind.

As things were moving along, I would try to keep everyone on the same sheet of music as far as what went where, what was being done, and what needed to be done. The Platoon Sgts were driving me fucking crazy. When I would be somewhere locking something on, a Lance Corporal from the S-3 or the S-4 would come in with some word from higher and tell one of the Platoon Sgts. The Plt Sgt would keep the information to himself but act on it, leaving the other three Platoon Sergeants in the dark. Despite this snag, we issued out a lot of our gear and everything got on line.

We had been so busy during the day I didn't have a chance to talk to CAAT Platoon. They knew I was to be the Platoon Sgt but they still didn't know who I was and what I expected. I had seen them jacking around in formation on the way back from the armory and decided this night would be as good night as any to set the operational tempo of the Platoon. Besides, the sooner the better to let the fuckers know where I was coming from and what was going on -- at least let them know what was going on in my mind. I told Hanson to have them form up on the second deck conference room across the hall from our Company Office. Hendricks heard I was having this "talk" and wanted to sit in the back of the room to hear what I was going to say them. He knew they had been fucking the simple shit up and he wanted to see how (not if) I was going to put them in line.

Lt Letendre started the formation off by saying his part about me taking over as Platoon Sgt and how things were going to work out and such. When he was done, I stepped up and thanked the Lt and asked if I could have "some quality time with the boys." He smiled and left the room. I chewed them out on some things I had seen and did not like. I brought up some of the problems that 1$^{st}$ Sgt Bixby filled me in on and what I had heard from him really pissed me off. I cussed, threatened, and tore their asses in two, to be honest, on some things that I saw that I could have given a rat's ass about. But it was wrong, so I corrected them on it anyway. After that, I never had a problem with any one of them. They heard me and now knew where I was coming from. They dug it, so we meshed.

Hanson came to me after the meeting that night when I was smoking a cigarette on the back ladder well. He told me that he did not think the Marines were used to such "cordial talk" and started to laugh.

### 4 January 2003
Around 0400 I had a working party, Day and a RTO (Radio Transmitter Operator) from CAAT Platoon, meet me at the Communications (Comm.) Shop. If I had known how useless the radio operator was going to be, I would have gotten a whore from Court Street instead. At least then I could have seen the fucking I was about to get. He wasn't sure what radio equipment went with what radio and did not know for sure what batteries were needed by different radios. It was a cluster fuck. It took most of the day to square it away.

As we were getting radios passed out I heard that some of the other Companies had been issued some of the radios that I was supposed to get. Murphy (as in Murphy's law) is not only a loser but an asshole. The shortage first came straight at the 81mm Mortar Platoon. The Line Companies (Alpha, Bravo and Charlie) were supposed to supply our 81 Forward Observers with radios but they weren't doing it. They were arguing that they had their Table of Equipment (T/E) and it did not include the radios for the 81 FOs. The T/E they had did include it when Battalion issued the gear out, but they just wanted us to use our own radios for that purpose. I wasn't really sure what the 81's Plt Sgt (GySgt Leggett) did, but I thought he must have worked out a crack deal with the Line Companies. I was told that he told the Line Companies to go pound sand. If they wanted 81's support on the battlefield they would have to supply the FOs with the radios. If that was the case, I didn't care -- as long as the problem was taken care of.

CAAT Platoon's radios were a different story. The Battalion had rarely gone to the field as a whole, so when CAAT went to the field they were used to getting radios in each vehicle. The Comm. Shop had been giving them whatever they needed or had. Now that everyone was going to "the field," they weren't getting as many radios as they were used to. This time, not only were they not getting a radio for each HMMV like they were used to, the radio mounts that some of the HMMVs had were being taken out and given to H&S (Headquarters and Support) Platoon's Motor-T Section (Motor Transport). CAAT had a fit with this. While I agreed with CAAT that they probably needed the radios more than Motor-T, I thought they should have been training with what they would get in battle, not with what they had available in training.

CAAT is a weird animal. It is basically fifteen or so vehicles (it varies cause there is no set doctrine) and half are machine guns (M2 .50 caliber and MK19 Automatic Grenade Launchers) and the other half are TOWs (Tube-launched Optically Sighted Wire guided missiles) used for killing tanks. So the idea is basically that the machine guns suppress the target, i.e. a tank, and the TOW kills it. Looks real good on paper, but the same theory applies to toilet paper.

Our Weapons Company had a Scout and Target Acquisition (STA) Platoon attached to it -- Snipers. This was unusual for a Weapons Company because Snipers were usually part of H&S Company. The Comm. Shop did not know they had been moved over, so H&S was getting some of the communication equipment that the Snipers were supposed to get. SSgt Tueichi, the Platoon Sergeant, was writing out a list of radio equipment he thought his Snipers needed. Tueichi was a Samoan. He was well built but his muscle wasn't bulk -- it was defined.

17

He kept his hair cut high and tight. He never joked around and even though he wasn't perceived as unfriendly, he kept to himself. He was always professional and even-tempered. When he said he had this problem with Comm, he said it matter-of-factly but you could tell he knew the seriousness of it. I went to the communications shop four times trying to figure out where our radios were. Finally, I got hold of MSgt Williams, who told me what was going on and said we would unfuck it on ship. Sounded fine to me. MSgt Williams was a stocky, bald Marine that was laid back and had a lot of patience, but you could tell that to get on the wrong side of him would have been a bad thing.

It was late in the evening when I met up with MSgt Williams for this simple solution. Day had done everything else I had tasked him with while I was gone, so I called him on the phone and had him sort out the radios like I needed him to. The Platoons all got what they needed, would get what they needed, or would have to suck it up. I started the walk back to the Company Office.

By the time I got back to the office everyone was gone except Lt Clayton, the 81 Mortar Platoon Commander, and Lt "Barney" Barnhart, the Company XO, who were both finishing up some paperwork and starting up a case of beer. These two guys were great. Lt Clayton was a little bit older than the average Lt. He had a Doctorate in Physics, a family, and a love of his guns. We started talking about why they had joined the Marines. After Lt Clayton gave his response, I had to ask him why he didn't go enlisted. He said there was no way he could have asked his wife to go from the pay he was making as a rocket scientist to a thousand bucks a month as a private; the drop to Lieutenant pay was bad enough. I heard once that he and a couple of other officers were arguing about the capabilities of a missile system. He stopped the argument with the first few words out of his mouth: "When we first designed that missile..."

Lt Barnhart was from Guam, had a brother in the Army, a wife and daughter, and was always in a great mood. Always smiling, always glad to see you, always being himself, never a front. I had heard once that during CAX (Combined Arms Exercise) he had gone off on a Captain so viciously that no one thought with his good-humored nature and laid back attitude it was even possible. The Captain he chewed out was an Air Controller who was calling in Cobras without clearance. Barnhart, doing everyone's job at once, saw the Cobras in an unauthorized holding area and told the Captain to pull them back. He didn't and started the

Cobras on a run in across the target that was getting shelled by artillery. Barnhart jerked the hook out of the Captain's hand, called the Cobras back in the nick of time, finished out the mission, and then turned to the Captain to set him straight on procedure.

The three of us, Lt Clayton, Lt Barnhart, and I started to drink more and throw the bullshit. I had talked to these guys before we went on leave but not in a way that let us know where we were coming from. Lt Barnhart started talking about how Officers in general did not know weapon systems like Senior Enlisted Marines did. I told him Officers did not need to know how to work the systems, just properly employ them on the scale they were fighting on, and the only reason that Senior Enlisted knew their weapons so well was just from being around them for twenty years. If you stand in a boxing ring long enough, you'll get hit. I also said that if you really want to learn about a weapon, ask a Corporal. A good Corporal would pride himself on his weapon no matter what the system was. The two Lts and I killed some more beer, which meant they had to get home to their wives, and I wanted to catch 1st Sgt Parker over in Bravo Company before he left.

Parker and I were in 2nd Reconnaissance Battalion as Sgts about ten years prior to meeting up again at 1/2 (1st Battalion, 2nd Marines). During the time we had not seen each other, we had both gone on Recruiting Duty and he had been a Ranger Instructor at the Florida Camp. I had moved out of my house prior to Christmas leave and I had been staying at his home till we left for Iraq. He also let me store some of my gear and my motorcycle at his home till we got back from Iraq or Kuwait or wherever the fuck we were going.

Parker had a brown pick up truck that he had fixed everything on at least once -- it was old, beat up, and most importantly, it was paid for. It was the kind of truck you would expect the old war horse Marine out of a movie to have. His first priority was his family and then himself and he enjoyed every minute of his life being that way. He, like Schielein and I, had a Harley. I had a good buzz from drinking with the Lts and he had a few with his Officers (Capt Newland, Lt Daniels, Lt Beere) and some of his SNCOs (GySgt Carrico, SSgt Jones) in his Company Office. I sat in on them and had one more beer with them. Parker had to run something upstairs and everyone else went home. That left me, a Captain from H&S, and Lt Fanning drinking and talking. We were having a pretty good time till one of them asked me if I had seen anyone get shot in the First Gulf War. I told them that the worst I saw was some Marine step

19

on a land mine and told them the scenario and what Capt Gauthier had done. They got real sober, and that ended the drinking and the conversation. It bothered me that they acted that way. Parker came down a little while later and by then I was standing with some Marines next to a burn barrel. They were burning any classified material that could not be taken with us or be left lying about when we left -- simple things like rosters with names, socials, addresses and such. Parker finished up inside his office and came out to get me. We got in his truck and headed to his house.

I told him about the conversation I had with the Lt and Capt, and asked him why they would act that way. He said it was because "Marines don't die." Fucking "Parker Wisdom." The Marine Corps is so pumped up on itself about how we don't die, we just kill. When we actually hear a story about a Marine dying, it throws us off center. The two Officers were thrown off center. The truck took us over to his house where his wife, Dawn, cooked up my last homemade meal. I spent most of the time saying good-bye to my motorcycle in his garage and my new girlfriend on the phone. Drank some more and hit the rack.

### 5 January 2003
The next morning we got up earlier than we wanted to, but probably a little later than we should have. Dawn had made us some lifer juice (coffee) and put some more in a to-go cup for us and we headed out to work. Today should have been an easy day. Most of the gear had been handed out to the Platoons and all that remained were a few stragglers who still had to get the gear that everyone else had already received. Day and I went over to the Company storage area with a working party of about ten bodies and cleaned the cage out as best we could. Then we headed over to NBC (Nuclear, Biological and Chemical) to get our gear with the rest of the Company.

The Platoon Sergeants had the barracks pretty much squared away but it would be a few more days before they actually moved out of them. The barracks were starting to show the signs of a departing unit. Dumpsters were starting to overflow with porno magazines, used irons, and ironing boards.

Most of the offices in Battalion were vacated of all the extra gear and had a good cleaning started. Except, of course, our Company Office. Fucking SNCOs and Officers sometimes lose perspective on what they need and don't need to do. I looked at the Company Office and lost it.

Some of the Marines knew me and some of them didn't. The ones that knew me knew that I could get evil; the ones that didn't, only knew what they had heard about the prospect of me getting evil. I stood at the back hatch of the office and yelled that everyone needed to get the fuck out, and that I had seen whorehouses that were better organized than our office was. I wanted everything and everybody out now. The CO (Commanding Officer), Captain Rohr, stuck his head out of the hatch to his office, and with no facial expression at all, looked around and went back to his desk. Within five minutes I got what I wanted. All the extra gear that needed to get out was gone and no one was hanging out in the office that did not need to be there. Lts Clayton and Barnhart were holding back laughter at their desks.

I really had not had a chance to talk to the CO yet. His wife had just had a baby daughter and he was on leave for a while. He still of course came in to do some necessary work and then left again. But if what everyone said was true, this was going to be an awesome Company.

SSgt Schielein took off later that afternoon to finish packing up his house in town. I got off work late that evening and walked up to the 7-day store on base for some beer and food. When I got back to the Company Office, I was ready to eat, drink and crash. The bus taking us to Norfolk was leaving early the next morning, so I planned on crashing out on the floor at the office. Before I could crack my first beer open, Schielein gave me a call. He asked if I wanted to go out drinking, and I told him no. Then the bastard started making more promises than a blind date on prom night. He promised he would "have me home early," gave me some shit about this possibly being our last night ever to drink, and told me he would pick me up in 20 minutes. We went to a laundromat first so I could do some last minute cleaning. That may not sound appealing but just try a laundromat outside Camp Lejeune. My favorite was Suds and Duds, which had a washroom on one side and a bar that played hard rock through its speakers on the other. By the time my clothes came out of the dryer you could have poured both of us into the washer. I called my girlfriend in Dallas from Schielein's cell phone, we went to a couple of other bars, and I crashed at his house. While I lay on the floor waiting to fall asleep I talked to Kelly again.

## 6 January 2003

I remember sitting outside that sorry motherfucker's house waiting for a taxi, thinking I was glad this would be the last time I would ever drink. I was hung the fuck over and that bastard was still crashed the fuck out.

(Schielein if you are reading this, fuck you.) The taxi pulled up and I was able to get to work with just enough time to get me and all my gear out of the office and down to where the buses were going to show up.

The buses showed up late enough for my hangover to wear off. We had a formation of everyone heading to Norfolk for the advanced party and we were short a couple of bodies from Supply Platoon. I initially thought that some cowards had decided to skip out on this little adventure we were planning. Turned out the two guys that were missing had never been told that they were advanced party and that this was the day they would be leaving. They finally showed up. One of the Marines, a Private First Class (PFC), found out in enough time to have his wife bring his gear in from home and see her one last time before he left. I don't know why we do that to our Marines and not keep them informed. The PFC's wife had this dumbfounded look on her face. I seriously believed she could not fathom what was going on, that her 18-year-old husband was going off to war. Another Marine Corporal's wife understood exactly what was happening. She was crying her eyes out, and you could tell it was killing the Corporal to leave her. Another Sergeant had angrily but firmly told his wife to leave. She had been out all night with her friends drinking, leaving him home alone with her child from another marriage. He had already taken the child next door and called a taxi when she came staggering in. She started making a scene at the buses, telling him that she loved him and was going to miss him. When he told her to leave she got angry and started cussing him out. He shook his head and walked away. The buses closed their doors and we left.

We pulled into Norfolk early that afternoon. To be honest, at first it felt good to go to sea again. After lugging my sea bag, pack, and all my war gear on ship and into my berthing area, I soon got over that "good feeling" and was ready to just fly over. All the SNCOs, Gunnys, and Staff Sergeants found one berthing area we could all rack in. There were about 21 racks and about seven of us. The only person I knew on the ride up was SSgt Goodyear, a Section Leader from 81's Platoon, who was one of my students when I instructed over at Advanced Mortar Leaders Course. He was younger, had pulled duty for three years guarding American Embassies, and was dating some girl in Italy or China. Later on ship he had gotten hold of some word that some of the other SNCOs and Officers were going to the club on base. So much for the last time drinking.

22

A couple of us unloaded off ship and funded an expedition to the Marine Bar on base via a taxi or two. The bar was known as the Mar Bar and was run by the Marines on the base there. The bartender's name was Mary, and Mary knew how to keep the glasses full. Five of us (me, Goodyear, GySgt Barry, SSgt Jordan and a Captain) ended up sitting at a table playing poker, drinking, and telling lies all night. At one point I called my dad and girlfriend. As I was talking to my girl, Kelly, my beer evaporated and I had to get a new one. I did not want to leave the phone hanging there so I called Jordan over to talk to her while I got a beer. When I got the phone back from Jordan, I finished talking to Kelly. She said she was amazed at what a gentleman Jordan was. I remember thinking "hell honey, if you think so." I knew what she meant though that Jordan would never act like an idiot to another Marine's girl. She told me for the first time she loved me and that she was going to wait for me no matter what I decided. She said that she was stubborn, that both her grandmothers had done it for her grandfathers during the Second World War, and some other things that made me believe her. I remember telling her "what ifs" of what might happen to me and she said she didn't care. We agreed that we would write and see how things turned out. Later that night, three sheets to the wind, my pockets a little lighter from the poker and tequila, we found our way back to the USS Ponce and hit the rack.

## 7 January 2003

The next morning we all went to chow and decided that we would not go out that night. So we all got together and did our numbers and figured out the racks we needed and the berthing areas we would take. We decided that there was no space to have a dedicated armory room, so we would store our weapons and other serialized gear in our own areas and have a guard continuously on them. The Captain assigned Officer berthing and we SNCOs assigned our brother SNCOs the spaces that they would live in for the next month. Sgt Stephens did most of the work though. He tallied all the numbers to the racks in certain berthing areas and tried to keep unit integrity as much as possible. The area where we had settled at first was going to be for Gunnys only, but some of the Gunnys got racks up in the Officers Berthing area. I had seen the Officers billeting when I first got on ship and it wasn't much better than what some of the junior enlisted Marines had. Giving some of the Senior Enlisted racks to sleep in up with the Officers berthing area gave us more racks than we needed in the Gunny's berthing area. I was then able to worm all of the SSgts from Weapons Company a rack in my own area.

That way when they came aboard, I would not have to run all over the ship to pass word to them.

We all felt better about our hangovers by the time the afternoon came around so the same group from last night plus some others Marines headed out one more time for the Mar Bar and Mary, and started up another poker game. The game was "between the sheets" and the stakes started getting a little heavier than we all knew they should have been. Goodyear, in a fit of bravery, lost a hundred dollars on some shaky cards. With no hesitation he pulled out his wallet and paid what was owed. Now, SSgt Jordan was a gentleman in every sense of the word. The pot was around two hundred dollars and he was dealt a two and a king. Instead of betting the pot of two hundred dollars, he bet thirty. He wanted to give the people who lost their money a chance to win it back -- which, in time, Goodyear did. That was Jordan. He was six foot plus a few inches, a good two hundred and twenty pounds, bald, had a rugged face that was always clean-shaven, and even though he was not a body builder, his weight was muscle. He always had a good temperament but only once did I ever see him truly smile.

The Captain that was with us started some karaoke up and we all ended up singing together, but only after Jordan sang solo. Lets just say watching Jordan sing, was, uhmmm, entertaining?

**8 January 2003**
The ship pulled out of port with all hands accounted for and headed south to the port at Morehead City, North Carolina. The USS Ponce, USS Gunston Hall, and the USS Saipan were the three ships taking the 1$^{st}$ Battalion, 2$^{nd}$ Marines over to the other side of the pond.

There was this one Navy Senior Chief on the ship who was the stereotypical Sailor: rather tall, overweight, tattoos up both sides of his arms of naked women, clouds, tropical islands and birds. He had cussing down to an art form and a mustache that almost qualified as a brillo pad. I wish I could remember his name, but even if I did I might not mention it for his own good. He would at times run the cook out of the galley of the Chief's Mess and make up some chow for all of the Senior Enlisted, Sailor and Marine alike. He was a good enough man, though, and knew what was going on when no one else did.

**10 January 2003**

It took us a couple of days to get from Norfolk to Morehead City, NC. The ship pulled into port and dropped its back hatch onto the port. All the Marines that were getting on ship, except the Amtraks, were waiting there for us. I could tell by looking down from the flight deck of the Ponce onto the pier where my Company was. The vehicles started driving into the back of the ship as Marines started moving sea bags and packs up the plank to the flight deck. Gunny Leggett and Lt Barnhart were the first up.

I told the Lt where his quarters were and off he went to find them and to get the other Officers where they needed to be. I took Leggett down to where our berthing area was and asked him to get the other SNCOs there in about ten minutes, and then I would take everyone around and show them where their Marines were to be quartered. MSgt Hendricks made it up topside and I showed him where all the 1$^{st}$ Sgts were living. Hendricks was a great guy. He was with Parker and me at 2$^{nd}$ Recon Battalion, and then he was my boss in Dallas when we were on Recruiting Duty together. He was my boss again at Infantry Platoon Sergeant Course for a short while and now again while we were at 1$^{st}$ Battalion 2$^{nd}$ Marines. While he was storing his gear away, we caught up on what was going on with the Company, and then I headed down to show the Platoon Sergeants where their Marines were living. Goodyear and I had all the areas labeled to show which Platoon went where, so there was little confusion. By the time the Platoon Sergeants found out where they had to take their Marines, the Company had all their gear up to the flight deck and was ready to store it down below. The passageways were crowded with Sailors, Marines, weapons, and gear being brought aboard and trying to be put in their proper places. I hit the rack for a while till things settled down.

I woke up about an hour later and went to find Lt Barnhart. He was getting weapons counts from the Platoon Commanders. The first count came up as I sat down next to him at a table in the enlisted man's mess. 81s, then CAAT, and then STA Platoon brought up their weapons and serialized gear count. The count was wrong. They went back and did the count again. It was wrong again. This honestly kept up for a couple of hours. I would have had the whole Company out on the flight deck holding up each individual piece of equipment and doing it by the numbers, but there was not enough room on the ship. The count was off by rifles, then bayonets, and then something else.

Capt Rohr was keeping his cool, but you could tell he wanted the situation taken care of quickly, and more importantly, correctly. Ever since I was a little kid my father and grandfather would recite the poem "If" by Rudyard Kipling that says, in part, "if you can talk with crowds and keep your virtue or walk with kings nor lose the common touch." I never got the full gist or meaning of that line till I met Capt Rohr. He was a man well over six feet tall, educated, firmly spoken, and had a job that I did not envy. He was responsible for all the fire support that our Battalion received or had in its possession.

After seeing the counts come in, again, fucked up, I figured out what the problem was and told the Platoon Sergeants to do the count themselves and not to rely on the small unit leaders. Leggett, Tueichi and Schielein were already doing this. They all went away and came back. Everyone had their numbers the same as last time except for Hanson. So Barnhart had the Lts go with the SNCOs this time and do it again, even though we knew where the fuck-up was coming from. This time the numbers, for the first time, added up right. This little fiasco set the pace for the rest of the time on float. We did no-bullshit weapon counts every morning, noon and night for the rest of the time on ship. The Platoon Sergeants and Section Leaders eventually knew by heart every piece of gear they had by serial number. Schielein kind of got a kick out of doing it; either it must have reminded him of his Drill Instructor days or he really liked leading those he was responsible for. I think the latter.

### 11 January 2003
This day is new to us. What we don't feel yet is that this "everyday" is about to be our same routine for the next month or so. We floated down the North Carolina Coast to Onslow County Beach, where we would pick up the last of our compliment to the ship, the Amtrakers. They swam up to the ship and loaded on. This whole process took less than a couple of hours. So in our minds we were ready to go, and needed to leave so we would not miss the war. Fuck, we were stupid. The reality of it was that while there might have been only three ships carrying 1/2 and its attachments, there was a whole Regiment going over and a total of nine ships had to load up. This kept us within eyeshot of the shore for a couple of days and drove us crazy, because once you are on ship; you're fucking stuck there. I mean, *we* loaded up quickly, what was taking everyone else so fucking long? Why not load their slow asses up first so we could be enjoying liberty, women, and drink?

26

Chow hours went in rotations. First it was Weapons Company, then Alpha, Charlie, and H&S with attachments. You might have had to get up early for chow as Weapons Company, but you usually got the best food. By the time H&S came through the line there was little to nothing left in quantity and only slop for quality. At first, some of the other Companies would jump in line during our time, so we had to have SNCOs monitor the chow line. This might sound cruel but after a week of the good life, rotations would change and you would be on the end. It seemed to me that the Marines that had non-fighting jobs (pogues) in the Marine Corps had the hardest time adapting to ship life, especially the younger ones. I knew a SgtMaj Rupp who once said that he thought you were not a real Marine till you did a 6-month float on ship. I could see what he meant, being around these young Marines.

The SSgts had to get their chow out of the same line the NCO and enlisted Marines did, but they had their own eating area on ship, which was kind of cool. The GySgts, MSgts, 1st Sgts, SgtMaj, and MGySgt got to eat in the Chief's Mess. Just like the officers, we had our own galley where the food was cooked, we served our own portions, and we sat to eat in our own area. This again may sound like a raw deal for the average Marine or sailor but it had its purpose. First, out of all the sailors and Marines that ate in the Chief's mess, only one GySgt had never been on ship before and spent his time in the trenches. We all had lived the life of long lines, quick eating to free up table space, and separating our trash before we turned in our silverware and tray to the scullery. Second, the Chief's mess was more than an eating area. They actually ran the ship from there. No long, boring meetings and no word was passed that did not apply to everyone. They would eat, talk about what they needed from each other to get stuff done, and sometimes argue and cuss at each other till they were blue in the face. But when you saw them in front of the sailors you would have never known a harsh word was said. I never ate in the Officers mess, but I would hear the Lts bitching about how they had to follow protocol on everything from the moment they entered the room to the moment they left. They compared it to one of the Mess Night traditions we have in the Marine Corps, but without the fun. A Mess Night is basically a formal dinner that turns into a drunk fest.

**14 January 2003**

We sailed south and then headed east. It took a couple of weeks to reach the rock of Gibraltar because a hurricane had slowed us down while crossing the Atlantic. A lot happened in that time. Hendricks and I decided to post guards down with the vehicles along with a watch in the berthing areas. The berthing area held all the personal weapons and individually signed-for armory equipment. In the vehicles we stored individual packs, radios, and the crew-served weapons. I did not get the other Companies to help with the watch because I didn't want another Marine from another Company responsible for our gear. Besides, if they wanted their vehicles watched, let them post a guard. Eventually one of the vehicles from H&S had something stolen out of it. Hendricks and I were sitting at the Chief's Mess when the H&S Company Gunny came bitching to us about how our Marines were not doing their job watching the vehicles. When he said that, we both looked at each other and started laughing. The other Companies started posting their own guards on their vehicles after that.

**January-February 2003**

Every day is the same.

I started moving more into my role as CAAT Plt Sgt. I would have the Marines do assembly and disassembly of the all their personal and crew-served weapon systems with full light, blind folded, and with Night Vision Gear (NVG) on. One of my Marines would actually close his eyes when wearing the NVGs because the headset was bulky and hard for him to look through. I made the machine gunners learn how to assemble and disassemble all the wiring and control boxes to the Anti-Tank Missile, and made the TOW gunners (who fire the Anti-Tank Missile) do all the things machine gunners had to do. Since we had little room for movement and none for maneuver, the Marines got a lot of practice changing out the weapons systems while in the turret of the HMMV.

Then there were the written tests that I had come up with. I would write them up and then Schielein, somehow, would pull some strings and get enough copies for the Platoon. Each week the test would repeat itself and have additional questions on it. So while the Marines were learning new things they were repeating what they already had been taught. The subjects covered simple things such as characteristics of their weapons, first aid, and navigation, as well as more complex things such as coordinating artillery, mortars, and air support on a limited target, the Arabic language, and road signs. At first the Marines were a little hesitant but it gave the Cpls and Sgts a chance to step up and teach their Marines. It did more than that though -- I think it gave the younger Marines a belief and reason to follow their NCOs. But it also did the opposite to the NCOs that didn't step up to the plate and lead.

We started off having a meeting every morning and afternoon that included Capt Rohr, Lt Barnhart, MSgt Hendricks, Plt Cmdrs, Plt Sgts, and me. Toward the end of our little trip there was just one meeting after evening chow and the Platoon Sgts didn't have to come. Hendricks would gather them up and pass the word to them afterwards; it was just simpler that way.

We were starting to get near the north side of the Suez Canal and we were having one of our meetings when the question of issuing ammunition came up: when, where, and of course how much. Lt Clayton and I got into an-depth conversation about how much High Explosive, White/Red Phosphorous, and Illumination rounds he would need for different missions. The Capt just kind of sat there listening like he always did, and the MSgt was smiling like he saw something funny. I paid them no mind and just reckoned they were enjoying the conversation as much as the Lt and I. Toward the end of the conversation, Lt Clayton and Lt Barnhart liked my recommendations for 81's ammo requirements. The MSgt, just smiling, knew I wanted to fully turn the Op's Chief job over to him so I could just concentrate on CAAT Plt. The MSgt and I walked out of the meeting and down the ladder to pass word to the Platoon Sergeants. He told me what was on his mind: "Doran, you're going to talk yourself right out of a job." I knew what he meant; it's kind of like someone telling you to stay out of trouble, but as soon as they say that, you're jinxed.

The Captain of the ship gave us a phone to use, just for us Marines. It was in an office that the GySgt and Lt from Administration used. Each Company got the phone in rotation, so you might have used it once or twice a week at ten minutes per Marine. The phone was open from 2200 to 0500. First you would sign in a logbook showing who you were and where you were calling. Then you dialed a number that would connect you to Camp Lejeune, and from there you'd call family that was in the area or call long distance using a phone card. While you were talking to whomever you called, an NCO would be sitting there listening, making sure that you were not talking about information that was classified. If you started to slip, the NCO would stop you. If you continued to slip, you lost your phone privileges.

The same procedure was used with the five computers in the library. Each Platoon had an account and off that account everyone could e-mail home. When a family member would write back they would put the Marine's name in the subject line so everyone would know whose e-mail it was. I never heard of anyone on my ship going into someone else's mail. Of course, there was an NCO standing over the computers doing the same thing that the NCO by the phone was doing. I am sure this method of security and control over what was said worked to some extent. Just as we pulled through the Suez Canal, a Lance Corporal on another ship wrote his wife about the location of the ships and our off-load date in Kuwait. When asked why he did that, he replied that he was not going to keep a secret from his wife. Because of his selfish behavior and lack of devotion to duty, everyone in the battalion lost their e-mail privileges. Fuckface, if I ever find out who the fuck you are!

There were also phones that everyone could use and they were open pretty much all day. The catch was that it cost a dollar per minute to use. I used this phone the most to call Kelly. You could only buy a phone card in 20-dollar increments (20 minutes). I would play poker down in the berthing area till I won enough to buy a phone card to call her. But most of my time was spent writing letters. I wrote letters all the time to whoever I thought would write back. I knew that to receive mail, you had to write mail. I hate that feeling when mail call comes and there is none for you. Fuck that. Goodyear was an apostle of my belief also: if you want mail, you've got to write mail.

I will never forget one night around 2300 or so, maybe later, I was lying in my rack writing Kelly. The small berthing area was dark except for the light above my rack that gave a small amount of light for reading and such. Everyone else was sleeping. I heard the hatch open and shut and then the curtains to my rack ripped open. It was Jordan, about as excited as a kid at Christmas. There was no "hey, how you doing" or "what you up to." He went straight into talking. He said he had just gotten off the phone with his son. All he could say was that his son was the smartest and best kid around. He talked about how his son had said that if he falls off the ship, he should swim real low so the sharks won't get him. Big J said his reasoning was that his son had only seen sharks on the top of the water, and when Jordan was at Paris Island as a Drill Instructor, he would take his son to the pool, put him on his back, and swim under the water with him. Then he started going on about how his son was telling him how to be careful around the "bad guys." Somewhere in all this I

30

saw a man whose only true joy was his son. That was the only time I ever saw Jordan truly smile.

Our first mail call came while we were in the Mediterranean. Man we needed it too. I got letters from Louise (my dad's girlfriend) and Kelly. I opened Louise's letter first. Then I carried Kellys around with me unopened. I am a mail hound. Mail is the best thing since canned beer and bottled whiskey, and from a girl that says she loves you there is no comparison. I took the letter with me when I went to work out and to the shower afterwards. Then the letter came to dinner with me and to a movie down in the berthing area. About five hours after I first received the letter I went into the ritual that would precede opening all of the letters that Kelly would write while I was on ship. It was late and everyone was hitting the rack, and then it was time to open it. I went back to the Chief's Mess, got a cup of coffee, sat down at a table, drank some of my coffee, and ripped into the letter. I could not take it any more. The letter was written on paper that was rough and white and had small flowers and leaves impressed in it. She wrote in cursive and her writing was just as I imagined. She talked of waiting for me, how crazy this all seemed, her friends, her family, and how much she loved me. I must have read that letter a thousand times, but the part that I liked the most was that she was waiting for me.

While we played poker on ship, we would watch movies. If you ever want to be a movie critic some day, join the Navy. Every ship I have ever been on has cable television running through it. And every ship has at least two channels dedicated to movies. Usually there is a place where they have a log of all the movies they have, and you can request the movie with a time slot for when you want to watch it. Someone requested the movie *Jerry McGuire* with Tom Cruise for a week straight. We knew every line by heart. The line that caught on was not "show me the money" but "who's your mother fucker" and the reply would obviously be, "I'm your mother fucker." Schielein, Pompos, Berry, and Jordan ran it into the ground. My favorite movie on ship was *Road Trip* -- you have to admit that Tom Greene is one whacked-out fucker. I would get up before anyone else in the morning and start watching it on the VCR. After everyone went to breakfast and came back, it would have been taken out and we would be watching something useless, like the news. The news would just piss me off. Fucking French. You know, I appreciate what their ancestors did in helping us get our liberty, and the Statue of Liberty is an awesome lady. The way I saw it, when they needed our help in WW I and II, fine, we kind of owed them. But when a great man like Colin Powell is talking to you on the phone 15 minutes before his daughter's most important day and you say you will do something, and then you don't. Go to hell.

Every Tuesday and Thursday Father Hoedl had RCIA (classes for heathens who want to be Christians) for us Marines who wanted to be Catholic. There were two guys from my Company there: Doc Sabilla, who just needed to finish up his confirmation, and PFC Thornton. Thornton was like me -- he had to do the whole shooting match. There were a couple of others from Charlie Company that I had seen go to classes, but they were not regulars. When I saw them on ship I would give them a hard time about not showing up, more fatherly than serious. Religion was and is a good thing. I know that is not politically correct, but like I give a fuck about your thoughts anyway. Those who don't believe in God have not been shot at or have led such a sheltered life that they don't have a need to believe. Anyway it would suck being Johnny-come-lately at the altar. Get it while the getting was good was my theory.

Every night on ship the Navy Chaplain and Marine Chaplain, Father Hoedl, would trade giving the nightly prayer. 2155 sharp every night they would come over the ship's 1-MC and give some words of encouragement or a blessing. The Navy supplied the Marine Corps with the Religious Leaders for their units. Father Hoedl was in the Navy but was as tough as any of the Marines in the unit. He would usually pray something about peace but if we had to fight let us do it well, that God had blessed our unit with Marines who had seen combat, and that he hoped that all would be safe through the night. He made us feel like we were ready, like we were doing something honorable. The Navy Chaplin would, no shit, pray about the fucking donuts, that the Navy Chiefs wouldn't be too hard on the young Sailors "who are doing their best," and when we die like all the warriors of history past, that it wouldn't hurt too much. Fuck me running. We Marines would give the Chiefs so much shit for this. Every time they said they were going to have a Sailor's ass for something, we would smile and tell them not to be hard on the young man, "he is doing his best."

The chow hall had been slowly going to fuck. The Sailors and Marines were lining up in two different lines and eating out of the same serving line. Some squid fucker (a fat Marine pig cook let it happen) decided to run the Sailors through one serving line and the Marines through another. Charlie Company was being served last out of the Marine Companies on

32

ship. It was just their turn to be last. As they were going through the chow line the sailors were serving them one piece of ham. In the other serving line where the sailors were, they were getting the full course meal. Jordan and Pompos saw that and told all the Marines to stop. Told them not to move through the line and not to walk away. One of the cooks told them to take the food and leave. Pompos told him to shut the fuck up before he went to the other side of the serving line and kicked his ass. The Navy cook started complaining about how he couldn't be talked to like that. Pompos was a tall, well-built Marine with the same haircut as Jordan -- bald. Pompos reached over the serving line, which is a good distance itself, grabbed the cook by the collar and explained to him the reality of the situation. When the cook started crying, Pompos let go of him in disgust. Jordan went and got 1ˢᵗ Sgt Henao.

Henao was a stocky Marine with a little patch of hair in the front. He was from Columbia and had a thick accent. Sometimes when he started chewing ass you couldn't understand what he was saying. He was the only one allowed to fuck with his Marines in Charlie Company. Don't misunderstand -- he truly cared about his Marines, but God help the motherfucker that laid a finger on anyone of them. Jordan told his First Sgt what was going on. Henao went through the chain of command, which was the SgtMaj. The SgtMaj looked at Henao and asked him what he wanted him to do about it. I thought 1ˢᵗ Sgt Henao's head was going to explode and the fragments would put a hole in the ship. Henao went up to the Battalion Commander, Lt Col Grabowski, who was eating in the officer's mess. The First Sgt asked the Battalion Commander how his breakfast was. The Battalion Commander, not being a stupid man and knowing something was wrong, told the First Sgt that it was fine and asked what was wrong. Henao told him that his Marines were only eating a slice of ham for breakfast. Not five minutes later the Captain of the ship was on the 1-MC, which broadcasts throughout the ship, that those cooks better feed those Marines with a proper meal right now. They did get fed properly right after that announcement. We never really had a problem after that. I admit that being a cook is probably the toughest and most unappreciated job to have in the military. But it has to be done right or everyone suffers. I don't know if an army fights from its stomach but I know morale starts and ends there.

Everyone was talking about the Suez. The only thing I knew about the Suez was that it was in Egypt and a friend of mine, Doc Howard, told me he sailed through it a couple of times and kept referring to it as the "ditch." Doc Howard was a retired sailor that had been a corpsman with the Marines in Vietnam and for most of the rest of his twenty-plus years of service. Skuttlebutt had it that if the terrorists could blow up a ship in the canal, then not only would they kill some Americans, but all of us would have to go around the south of Africa to get where we were going. All I could think of was some dumb fucking terrorist believing that he would stop our attack by shutting off the canal. It would have made the already long trip longer, and us that much more pissed off in the fight.

As we floated in the Med, waiting our turn to go through the Suez, you could see ships in every direction waiting for their turn to get through the ditch. It reminded me of a line breaking down and everyone trying to get a ticket to a rock concert. We started our sail-through about the same time the galley started serving morning chow. After I ate I went up topside to look around. I ran into Capt Rohr and Master Sgt Hendricks. We talked awhile but Captain Rohr had to go to a meeting so it left Hendricks and me alone. Hendricks pointed out some Mosques here and there and commented on some buildings and I did the same. Then he said something which I understood as soon as he said it: "it's like we never left."

Lt Romero, the STA Platoon Commander, had been tasked with providing security during the ride through the ditch. He and Tueichi were pulling some serious hours in meetings with the Navy side of the house. I think this is what Lt Romero lived for -- real-world missions. They needed little from me and Tueichi had pretty much done all the coordination himself as far as what he needed. He did what I asked, and let me know what he had drawn and from where so that if someone asked me about it I could give them the right answer.

Weapon systems were a different story. Lt Romero was short, with dark tanned skin and black hair. He was smart but in trying to take care of his Marines he lost sight of the big picture. He was not the only one who did this. It is a common disease among Marine leaders. Weapons Company had six SAWs (M249 Squad Automatic Weapon that fires 1000 rounds a minute) and before we left they had been given to CAAT Platoon. Lt Letendre had come up to me and told me that Lt Romero was talking to Captain Rohr about getting the SAWs to STA. He had two points; one was that the only reason the Company had the weapons at all was because when STA was transferred to Weapons from H&S, the SAW was part of the Table of Equipment transfer. Secondly, even though each Sniper team had an M-16 with them, a SAW could put more suppressive fire into a possible threat. I thought this was a good point, but it didn't make it right.

Some guys in STA thought, that because they were Snipers, the rules did not apply to them, such as haircuts, proper wear of the uniform, a clean barracks, or formations. They thought that because they excel in field skills, their daily garrison routine could go to fuck. I knew Lt Romero and Tueichi were not like this, nor were the prior Plt Sgts (Boutin, Parisi, Clark) that way. In my opinion this STA Platoon was above par, in and out of the field. Anyway, I went to Lt Romero about his plan of moving the weapons from CAAT to his Platoon. I told him his teams had never taken the SAW to the field, so why should they be given it when we hit the ground. He said something about seeing a picture of SEALs with SAW with shortened barrels. I said that the missions a SEAL team has and what his Snipers will have are totally different. He changed tactics and moved on to why Weapons Company had the SAWs in the first place. I said again if he was tasked with a mission where a SAW was needed, we would take a SAW from a CAAT Team and give it to his Sniper Team. I was a Sniper just as he had been, so it was kind of hard for him to make a weak point and have it stick as it would have been with someone who didn't know Sniper tactics. The argument continued for a while and then I ended it by saying that the TOW vehicles had no protection except for the Machinegun vehicle, and the TOWs did not have enough individual firepower to provide individual security for itself at close quarters. I told him the only reason I was talking to him anyway was out of courtesy and respect. I wanted him to know that I was going to Captain Rohr and Lt Barnhart with different thoughts than his, and I wanted to give him fair warning. Captain Rohr decided the SAWs should stay with CAAT. Lt Romero didn't argue, fight or complain. He said okay and continued to march. Too many times people take things personally when it is professional. Lt Romero was a professional.

After a while on ship you know everyone's business, some bad and some good. We had a steel beach picnic on the flight deck of the ship, and I found out from SSgt Pompos that his Platoon Commander rode Harleys and his wife had sent him some biker mags. You got your different types of biker rags out there. I liked the kind that had people partying and having a good time but also passed some good scoop on how to work on your bike. The other type of magazine had pictures of motorcycles that would never be ridden, with girls posing on them who did not know that it was a motorcycle they were sitting on. I went and found Lt Seeley out on the flight deck bullshitting with someone about something. I told him who I was and that I had some biker magazines, and thought maybe he had some in trade. He smiled, said he did and would. He left his conversation and we went to each of our individual berthing areas and met again to trade the magazines. I felt like a little kid trading comic books. He told me about his motorcycles, the three of them and I got envious. I decided then that I would finish my bike out, and when I did, I would build a rat bike. This gave me something to think about and plan. Something to keep me mentally occupied.

Weapons Company had two large areas on ship, CAAT and 81s, and two smaller ones for STA and Javelins. I enjoyed walking through the areas. I learned a lot of what was going on in the Platoons, which I needed to do since I was CAAT Plt Sgt and Ops Chief.

Turned out Hendricks was right, I talked myself out of a job while I had talked about ammunition a few days earlier with Lt Clayton and Lt Barnhart. As we turned out of the Suez and entered the Gulf, Master Sgt Hendricks pulled me aside before lunch and said that the Captain had made a decision: I was to be the Ops Chief and the Ops Chief only. Hanson would take back over as the CAAT Plt Sgt. I was so fucking pissed. Hendricks and I were old friends and knew each other's secrets like it was cool and usually when I went off he just laughed. But he knew I wasn't going off cause I was mad over something silly, I was mad cause I wanted to lead Marines. That's all I wanted to do. I went to Lt Barnhart and asked him what was going on. He said that was the way the Captain wanted it. I asked him why and he said he didn't know. He and I went back to Hendricks and I told him I wanted to speak to the CO. He said fine, and off the three of us went.

Capt Rohr was in his berthing area when we knocked on his hatch. He answered the door and the Master Sgt and Lt went in while I waited outside. I was called in and was told by Capt Rohr that I was going to be Ops Chief. He thought I would do the best for that job and he didn't think the war would be a cakewalk like everyone thought. You had to know Capt Rohr. He never yelled or cursed. I never saw him not stop to listen to what you had to say, and really listen. He NEVER talked to hear himself talk; what was said was always said for a reason. The way he said what he said, I knew there was no give. I left out of his berthing area thinking I had fucked up somehow and this was my punishment. If I knew then what I know now, I wouldn't have argued. He knew I would object but he was a warrior who not only fought but also thought.

I went down to the berthing area and Jordan was the only one in there. He was standing up over our poker table reading a newspaper. I thought I would try a new line of bullshit on him and act like I was excited about being Op's Chief for the war and the fact that Hanson was going to lead CAAT. Without even lifting his eyes off the paper, he calmly said, "there is no greater honor than leading Marines in combat."

# Been Here Before
## Chapter 3

**5 March 2003**

We woke up early, as we always did when something big was going on --- and off-loading was no different. I went to chow before anyone else, as usual, and then went back to my berthing area to tell the Plt Sgts I was ready to inspect the berthing areas. Surprisingly, what I thought was going to be a cluster fuck went rather smoothly. All the areas were squared away. What was not a surprise, though, was that the Navy said we had to do things over. Typical bullshit. They had inspected the areas the day before and had given us the "good to go" except for a few minor things. The things they found wrong could not be fixed until the Marines had left the ship. Usually the Navy and some jackass Marine will threaten not to let us leave the ship until the area is fixed. This threat usually works when you are pulling into a liberty port or you're about to fly off ship back to the world, but not when you're about to invade a country. I knew getting us off ship had higher priority than a clean bulkhead.

We all loaded up down in the well deck and waited for the landing craft to give us a ride to shore. The Company lined up in a column of twos, except for the CAAT Platoon and a few 81s. They were going to ride off in their HMMVs. The Amtraks went ashore first, one by one dropping off the edge of the ship in to the ocean. And like ducks on acid they made their way home to land. The landing craft came next and picked up the rest of us in Weapons and H&S Company. MSgt Hendricks and I counted the Marines as they started to load up onto the boat. Our biggest fear was not leaving a Marine behind, but leaving a piece of gear. It was an awesome ride. For once we could smell fresh air not mixed in with the oil that just lay like a blanket over the Ponce.

When we hit shore there were some Marines with red tabs on their trousers and on the center bands of their covers. The only thing these Marines with red patches did during their whole time in the Marine Corps was load and unload gear and Marines -- anything from the back of a truck to a C-130 that was still flying. They wanted us to move to an LZ (Landing Zone) as soon as we unloaded. I wanted to get all the Marines in formation but we had to form up as we walked to the LZ. Apparently we were in a hurry. No problem for me, I was up front. We were walking with all our gear, flak, helmets, LBVs (Load Bearing Vest, a vest that carries rifle magazines and other gear), packs, sea bags, and weapons. A Marine with so much gear on his back can't hold his head up and needs to know whose feet he is following so he won't end up in the wrong place. We walked maybe 750 meters or so when we got to the LZ. The NCOs were still trying to square away their units when I was called out with the advanced party to leave on the first helicopter to base camp.

Our base camp was originally known as Camp Arnold. Arnold was a Master Gunnery Sergeant at the Regimental S-3 and worked as the Operations Chief. I had known him when he was a Gunny several years before. There were four things I remembered about him: he could run like a rabbit for miles on end, he would be in the office working from reveille until the bars closed, he was never wrong, and he enjoyed training Marines.

I loaded up with Major Tuggle, GySgt Blackwell, and a few others on the first bird out. The ride was pretty uneventful except a few of the really young Marines were getting a kick out of the view. Most of us had already seen the view about ten years earlier.

There was one area I was interested in seeing from the sky. I knew, though, that I would not recognize it if I saw it. When I was last in that area it had still been a war zone. We had been in the hundred-hour push north to the outskirts of Kuwait City. We had set up defenses outside the city just so we could watch the other Arab forces -- who had been trailing behind us the whole time -- go in. There was a road that crossed in front of us about a click away. As the other Arab countries drove by, they would stop and put on a fake firefight show for the camera crews. The media was eating it up as each new unit drove through. I think it took all that Capt Gauthier had inside him to keep from telling us to light them up and give them fuckers a real firefight.

We landed outside Camp Arnold, which was now called Camp Shoup, got our gear loaded up into a 7-ton, and walked over to our Battalion area. The Camp was set up like a triangle. There were to be three battalions and each battalion had a side. Our area, of course, was on the far side from where our helicopters landed. All the tents were either set up or just about set up. They were huge, white, long tents, decorated on the inside with a second cloth that was yellow and with a decorative lining around the top edge. The tents that the Marines would sleep in and that the Companies would use as offices were the same design, except that there were wood floors in the ones that would be used as offices or sleeping quarters for the Senior Enlisted and Officers.

I walked around and was told what area was to be mine, how many Marines were to be in a tent, and where the heads were located. I was also told where the chow hall was going to be, but it would be a week or two before it was up and running. The bivouac area for our Marines was on one side of the Battalion area and our Company office was the last tent on the other end of the Battalion compound. I didn't mind at first, but I had forgotten my experiences with sandstorms in this part of the world. Our Company office had to share a tent with a bunch of reporters and the Battalion Priest. I counted out the tents in a way that kept as much integrity as possible with the Platoons.

I had just finished touring the area when I saw Captain Rohr. He strolled up with a smile on his face and asked where the Officers and Senior Enlisted were sleeping. I told him that I knew where the other Companies were sleeping: on the wood floors in their Company Offices. But I thought we should sleep in the tent area where the Marines were sleeping, which was in the sand. He asked why? Not "why" like "I am stupid, explain it to me," but "why" like "I want to hear the reason." I told him, "If our Marines are sleeping in the sand, we should be sleeping in the sand." He smiled, shook his head, and said, "The sand it is then." He was the first Marine in our Company to set up in the sand and, of course, with no bitches and no complaints.

I gathered the Platoon Sgts together and passed the word I had, and said I wanted a formation before it got dark so I could pass some word that I was going to get later to the whole Company.

At formation I explained the camp rules, where the different Companies and Battalions were set up, chow, security, sanitation, and other miscellaneous items. I remembered this one Marine I served with before, Master Sgt Sizemore. He always knew what was going on, even when no one else did. For once I knew what it was like to be him. I finished passing the word and said there would be a formation in the morning at 0600. After moans and whaling that sounded like they came from the bowels of hell, I turned the Company over to the Platoon Sgts.

**6 March 2003**
We had formation at 0600 and on my way to where the Company was formed up I checked the tents for cleanliness. The Platoon Sgts reported

all present, I called at-ease, and I had the Plt Sgts come up to where I was. They told me any problems they had; I assigned work details, and passed the word that I had received. They would go back to formation and I would call for an "inspection arms." As the weapons were held at the port, the NCOs would go through and check the weapons. The NCOs then checked each others. After they were finished with the individual inspections, I finished out the command and sent them back to their tents to eat breakfast. Breakfast was an MRE for the first week or two until the chow hall opened up. But till then, while we were eating MREs, there was no eating in the tents. All we needed was for the rats to go in after the chow buried in the tents, and then have the snakes coming in after the rats.

Nothing was happening. Every day was turning into the same. Training was continuous, but the camp allowed little room to maneuver. Every day was like being on ship, except we were on land in the middle of the desert. There was something about time. For one thing, there was a lot of it. For another, it could be your friend or your enemy or both at the same time. When there was nothing to do your mind locked onto things. We were bored, which was bad, but we were alive, which was good. But if death was waiting for you, did it matter if you were alive? Your time was coming and there was nothing you could do to stop it. Whether it was our time or not, one thing time did give us was time to think. I didn't like thinking about the past, only the future.

The poem that my grandfather used to make me read, "If" by Rudyard Kipling, in one part in particular goes, "if you can meet with triumph and disaster and treat those two imposters just the same..." My past was full of triumph and disasters, and the only way I knew to treat them the same was to deny their existence. By denying the good with the bad, my life was tolerable and then also useless, and if it was useless, my death would be inconsequential.

I thought a lot about my grandparents on both sides of my family, my Dad, Kelly, my daughters, and my son. I thought about the friends that I had as a teenager who no longer wrote me or returned my calls when I was on leave. I thought about the home that I had made for myself in Camp Lejeune, NC. I thought about my bills and what I money I was saving and what would be done with my life insurance policy. I thought about all of this, and it reminded me that I could die and that all the sand would pass over me and it would not matter. All my children had good stepfathers, all my bills would soon be paid off, and I owed no one anything.  My brother had married and the prospect of him having children, by his account, looked good.  The family name would be carried on.  Kelly told me several times that she would wait for me, but that wasn't for sure.  She could find another boyfriend and I would be a memory as quickly as I had met her.  Everything I owned was in a storage facility in Texas.  My father just had to pay the monthly bill and what I owned would never have to be sorted through.  There was no house or apartment where anything had to be moved or thrown away.  Then Time, being the motherfucker he is, let me think about some more things, and I thought maybe it was my time to die.  If I was to die, I wanted it to be with these Marines that I had around me.  Let me die with my brothers and all would be good.

Doc came up to me bitching about Day.  I expected this -- they had kept far enough apart on ship -- but now that they were in the same vehicle, things were changing.  Day was being a Cpl and Doc didn't like it.  They were like two children bitching about who got more ice cream.  But fuck if it wasn't funny.  Like I said Cpl Day was a country boy, and so was Doc Sabilla, but he was a country boy from Central America.  Doc was married, Catholic, and proud of both his countries: the United States and the Dominican Republic.  His accent was so thick that at times I couldn't understand him, but I never asked him to repeat himself in front of Day.  These two were best friends who were also mortal enemies.  If Day heard me ask Doc to repeat himself because I didn't understand him, he would have ragged on him till no end.  No, Day was not evil; Doc would have done the same thing if he had the chance.  They worked close together on a lot of things.  They had to -- they were in the same vehicle with me and I wouldn't put up with their childish shit.  Even though I did get a kick out of it sometimes.

Doc spent a lot of time teaching me Spanish.  I thought I would need it since I would be going back to Dallas to work in real estate and construction.  He was patient about it, but admittedly his choice of words had nothing to do with working on construction sites.

### 9 March 2003
The only reason I remember this date was mail call.  I received my first packages and there were two of them.  One was from my brother and the other was from my girl, Kelly.  My brother's package had an MP-3 player in it with a couple of music cartridges.  My Dad had told my brother to get the player but Kelly had picked the music.  It was heavy

rock and some songs off a CD called "Celtic Women of the World." The second package contained dental floss and two bottles of "Listerine."

The bottles were made for Listerine but they held something much better. I ran around the tent barefoot, listening to Irish music, sharing my newfound fortune with anyone. No one refused my offer. Between Listerine gargling, I smoked a cigar that someone had given me a couple of nights before. There was not enough in the bottle to do any real damage. When Kelly had put the lid back on the bottle, it had lost its seal and most of it had leaked out. The package was soaked. I didn't complain; I was happy for what I got. I am still happy for what I got. I rolled my clothes up into a ball on top of my pack. I lay on the ground and got into my sleeping bag. I went to sleep listening to Rob Zombie. Life was good.

**10 March 2003**
This morning should have hurt, but it didn't.

**13 March 2003**
During our time at Camp Shoup, the Battalion Commander authorized a few runs back to an Army Base to get needed supplies or luxuries from their base exchange. As the Company Gunny, I got to go, and Day as my Police Sgt got to go with me. We loaded up our vehicle, got a radio check, and with the Company Gunnies from the other Companies and the Battalion XO, we headed out.

We got to the base after about an hour's drive. The scenery sucked on the way there and when we got there, things didn't get much better. But the exchange did have a lot to offer. Day and I picked up sodas and chips for the Marines, some of that canned air that you clean computers with for the TOW wiring systems, cartons of cigarettes and dip for the Platoons (they could divide it as they needed to), and a few personal items for the Officers and Senior Enlisted -- which was nothing more than pipe tobacco for Lt Clayton and Near Beer.

After my shopping spree, Day and I pushed our carts down to where our HMMV was and loaded it all up. Just as we finished loading up, an Army Staff Sgt with pressed utilities and shined boots walked up to us and asked us who was in charge. I said I was, and I could tell my good mood was about to leave. He said that the carts that we were using didn't belong at the HMMV but back at the PX. He then told me that someone had shut down the PX privileges till all the carts had been returned. He then let me know how bad life was already, and that losing the Base Exchange was, well, "unbearable." I asked him where he was going and made a point of the fact that I outranked him. He said he was going to get a haircut. I told him that he probably wouldn't mind taking the carts back for us then, since he was headed that way anyway. He said no he wouldn't. I laughed to myself and told him that because he was so unprofessional in the way he approached me, and that I had rights, I wasn't gong to return the carts. He and the Soldier he was with took the carts back down to the PX. When he got far enough away, we all cracked up laughing at what had just happened. Look, I am not trying to rag on the Army -- they are good at what they do. I am ragging on the fact that this guy had no clue as to what "hard" was. What was even funnier was the fact that I acted like I had rights.

Another time, Parker and I had gone down to this base together and tried to get some fresh fruit for our Marines. The chow hall's chief cook wouldn't give it to us. He said it had something to do with cost. He asked why I wasn't getting chow from my own chow hall. I told him we didn't have one yet. He said that it was not his fault the Marine Corps wasn't taking care of its men. I could have leveled him out for that. Instead I reminded him that the Marine Corps had given the Army its chow in the First Gulf War off supply ships that the Army had earlier called stupid. I told him he had thrown away more fruit in one trashcan than I was asking for. He started telling me how he had been hand picked for the job and blah, blah, blah. I just let him go on. I knew I wasn't going to get the fruit unless I stole it, but his office was fully air-conditioned and I did enjoy that. When he was done, I told him "fuck you very much" and left. He started yelling something, but I figured if he wanted a piece of my ass, he would follow me and then it would have been worth the brig time.

When I got back later that night with the Near Beer, I split it up between all of us, and we sat down and drank it like it was the real thing. We couldn't get a buzz off it, but the fact that it tasted like something from home really lifted our spirits. It made us feel like we weren't so far away.

**14 March 2003**
We had to go out and practice for the Quartering Party. As the Battalion Quartering Party, our job was to direct the different Companies and attachments of the Battalion to specific areas so that when we launched into an attack it would be organized. We drove out to an area like it was

the area we were going to and drove around like we knew what we were doing. It was truly a waste of time. But on the brighter side, it was time out of the camp.

I talked to Lt Martin for a little while and coordinated with him about where the 81s would go into his position. We talked a bit and figured things out. No sooner had we finished talking than the Battalion XO, Major Tuggle, told us we were headed back to Camp Shoup.

**17 March 2003**
I talked again to Father Hoedl about becoming Catholic. He had no e-mail capability and mail was damn near nonexistent. He had tried to see the Catholic Bishop in Kuwait City but due to the terrorist threat, the Battalion Commander had put restrictions on who could go outside the gate. He knew the war was fast approaching and asked me when I thought I was leaving for the advanced Quartering Party. I told him the nineteenth or twentieth. He said tomorrow I could do confession and then the next day I could do a "make sure" baptism, be confirmed, and take part in the Eucharist. He said I needed to find a Godfather. So I asked Lt Barnhart.

After Lt Barnhart got through laughing at the fact that he would be a Godfather to someone ten-plus years older than him, he looked at me seriously and said he would be proud to. Then he asked me what day I was born; I told him and asked why. He said, so he could tell his wife and she would be sure to send me ten dollars on my next birthday. He started laughing again.

**18 March 2003**
Ammo was passed out. I had never seen so much shit in my life. CAAT vehicles were stuffed to the brim. 81s didn't have enough room for the mortar men and ammo so I ended up carrying a lot of their ammo in my trailer. Javelin gunners had done a shoot a couple of days prior and when they saw all the Javelin missiles they were getting, their morale shot through the roof.

My confession was scheduled for later that night so I asked Father Hoedl where and when we should do it. He said now was a good time, so we went into the corner of his half of the tent, which he was sharing with a lot of reporters, and away I went. He gave me my penance. It was all I thought it would be. It felt good to tell someone my problems and sins and then be told that God loves me and all is forgiven. I know the

Protestants tell each other that all the time but it really felt good talking to Father Hoedl about it. He was not a stereotypical Priest. He was six-foot plus, a good 210 pounds with a strong face to match, very down to earth, and very understanding of what you had to say. He was and is a good man.

**19 March 2003**
I thought we were leaving today for the border to prepare for our launch into Iraq. The Captain got everyone together to let them know what was going on. The Marines in the Company were ready to go, but you could tell there was an air of apprehension. Not apprehension about the unknowns of combat or death, but apprehension about being able to do their jobs or not.

I rounded up Lt Barnhart, MSgt Hendricks (to take pictures for me), Doc Sabilla, and PFC Thompson for my "make sure" Baptism and Confirmation. It went off great. After I was through, Thompson was confirmed. A lot of people stopped by and would watch awhile, and then they kept on walking. One of them was 1$^{st}$ Sgt Thompson from Alpha Company. He ran into me later that day and said he was glad to see what he saw. There are two kinds of people in the Marine Corps when it comes to religion. The first type I despise. They use God as a crutch. They can't work because they have church or they can't pull duty because they have a fundraiser to go to, so someone has to pull their load. Call a meeting at a topless bar, though, and they show up early. Then you have the kind like First Sgt T. Name a war and First Sgt T has been there. He had the ribbons to prove it. He was the most decorated Marine in the Battalion. He looked, acted, and lived the life of a Marine and could chew out a Marine by simply looking at him. 1$^{st}$ Sgt T was a truly religious man, but he was a man and all that it implies.

I had had the Mystery Machine, my HMMV, loaded for about two days already. I smiled every time someone called our vehicle the Mystery Machine. It reminded me of my daughters and I enjoyed thinking of them. I kept getting word that the Quartering Party was going to move north to prepare to set the battalion up for the crossing into Iraq. Cpl Day had the Mystery Machine loaded just right. He had taken a lot of time and pride in organizing the HMMV and trailer so that any piece of gear could be taken off quickly and without a lot of hassle. He knew where everything was on the vehicle and how much of it we had. I was keeping a roster of what we had just so I would have one, but Day was so organized I didn't need one.

As we got closer to the day we would invade, the more I started to have issues as Operations Chief. Lt Barnhart and I were sitting on some sandbags outside our tent. I was writing Kelly and he was just enjoying the sun when one of the Lts from Bravo Company came over to talk to him. Lt Barnhart was known for his ability to call in some serious fire support and, more importantly, his ability to orchestrate it. The Lt started talking about his new way of conducting 60mm fire support. I stopped writing Kelly because I just had to listen to this guy talk. I couldn't believe what he was saying. Barnhart tried really hard to tactfully tell him that he shouldn't be doing things that way, but the other Lt kept on arguing. Finally I had to jump in. I told him he couldn't do what he wanted to do, that the battlefield was fluid and not rigid like the sand box he made it seem to be. I also pointed out that the way he was doing things kept the individual Squad Leaders from calling for fire. He didn't want to listen and soon left. Lt Barnhart started talking and I told him what I knew about fire support and coordinating procedures. He asked me a few questions and an hour later I was the Air Support Liaison for Bravo Command. I finally had a job, or so I thought.

I went over to 1st Sgt Parker to talk to him about what I had heard his Lt say about running the mortar section. I knew that if Captain Newland knew about the conversation, he wouldn't have approved. Parker listened but he said that he wasn't too familiar with the mortars and asked if I would talk to Captain Newland with him. I said fine.

Later that night I was looking for 1st Sgt Parker about some motorcycle magazines and happened to run into him while he was having some quality time with Captain Newland. I started to turn around and walk away when Parker called me over and told me to tell the Captain what I had heard. I started off by telling the Captain who I was, my mortar experience, and how I used to be Weapons Platoon Commander for Charlie Company many moons ago. He kind of nodded his head like he didn't give a fuck about my resume but he did give a fuck about what I had to say. I told him what I had heard his Lt say, what I had said to him, and his response. I then went into how long it takes to get mortar fire and how much longer it would take the way the Lt wanted to do it judging from my experience from the last war here in Kuwait and such. When I was done, the Captain asked me a few more questions and said thanks. I left and waited for Parker to get through so I could get some biker magazines from him. When he finally did come out, I got the magazines and left.

Word came down that the Quartering Party wouldn't be leaving till tomorrow. Morale was about eye level with the Titanic. Apprehension turned to anger; it was like we were supposed to be executed but the switch kept blowing a fuse.

**20 March 2003**
We got up early, and as we had every day, we had a Company formation and a weapons check for safety, and the Company was dismissed for chow. Usually when we did this in the morning, I was the senior man doing it. I didn't want any Officers around in case something went wrong because they would be liable, and it also taught the Marines what they were responsible for as they picked up rank. We were the only Company that got up early like that. Capt Rohr said some of the other officers in the Company were ragging on him good-naturedly about it, but he said he was glad we were doing it. But today, Capt Rohr, Lt Barnhart and MSgt Hendricks were at the formation so we all ended up going to chow together. On the way back, I headed over to the Company office tent and I ran into Cpl Day.

He said he had heard some word that we might be leaving that morning. I checked in with Master GySgt Malone and asked him what was up. He said he hadn't heard anything as of yet. I told him what I heard and from who. He laughed, as he does at everything, and said, "well you know that Lance Corporal hotline -- low people sitting in high places." There was a lot of truth in that. If you don't believe me ask a secretary what they have heard is going on. I checked in with Capt Rohr to tell him what I got for news, but before I could he told me that it was true that the advanced party was going today, and the main body might be moving up also.

I got Day and Doc up and started moving the final details into place. Day was on top of things and eager to go. I remember thinking, "why would a man be in such a rush to go get killed?" I guessed it was for the same reason that I had been eager at his age: to prove myself.

Around lunchtime, the whole Regiment's advanced party was lined up to head north. It was like being in a car show. Everyone had their HMMVs tricked out really cool. Some Corporal over in 2nd Battalion, 8th Marines had out-done himself. He had radios recharging in a case he had built, he had see-through cages so you could see what was in them, and it was well organized. I told him if he needed a job he could come work for

48

me. He laughed and said, "I'll ask my Gunny." I felt a little evil so I went back over to my HMMV, where Day was sitting in the driver's seat, and told him to come look at what I had found. Day went over and looked at the HMMV as I described all the little things that made it awesome. I left Day behind as he asked the driver questions about his fine piece of machinery.

I ran into the Gunny that was riding in the vehicle Day was looking at. Turned out we knew each other from when I was an instructor at Infantry Platoon Sergeant's Course. He was enjoying life and had some stuff to do so I walked around with him and went over to the Company Gunny of H&S 2/8. He was carrying a shotgun like me, so I asked him if he had any ammo. Lt Clayton and I had pulled teeth to get what we had but he hadn't been so lucky. Turns out one of his Marines had an M16 that did not work and the armory had failed to fix it, so he gave the kid his own M16. This left him either with a broken M16 or a shotgun with no rounds. I gave him three boxes of mine, which was about 15 rounds. He thanked me and then said, "If we would just treat these Marines like they were our own children, we would not have the problems we do." That Gunny was up for 1st Sgt. I never saw him again, but I am sure that if my kid ever joined and had him for a First Sgt, he would be fine.

We were all called to the center of this car show and a Major from Regiment gave us a long speech on how we were to move out and where we were going, and after much debate on how we would handle a broken vehicle, we left for the border. As we were driving out of Camp Shoup I could see Captain Rohr talking to the Marines one last time. I couldn't hear what he was saying but I knew what was being said. I had heard that same speech several times before. The ride up did not take long and with the doors off the HMMV it was not as hot as I thought it would be.

We arrived at the location where our Assembly Area was going to be, but it was a different area than we had previously staked out. Regiment stopped the convoy. Our Captain in charge took us to my Company's specific area and showed us where he wanted his "gate." Now it might sound stupid to put an imaginary gate in the middle of nowhere, but if it works, it's not stupid. The idea was that as the units came up in increments from Camp Shoup, guides would take them to their assigned areas from this one central point. The guides -- us -- put out markers so we could find the right area for the right unit. It took us three or four hours to do this. Just when we finished, an Army Captain in a HMMV pulled up.

He had all his NBC gear on and his mask and he started yelling that there was a gas attack. I thought our Captain would have some knee jerk reaction to how the Army Captain was behaving, but he didn't. He told the guy thanks and told me and a few other Marines with vehicles to gather everyone up and bring them to the "gate." We did as we were told. When we got back with the Advanced Party, he had us all move to a little protected area of ground where no one would get hit if there was any shrapnel flying around. While we were going to pick everyone up in the Advanced Party, he had called Battalion and the Regimental Advanced Party to see if there was an actual Biological or Chemical threat. We all put our gas masks on for a while and kind of hung out in this group of sand dunes. I slept for a while and when Doc woke me up we were taking off our gas masks and moving back out. The Captain in charge did an awesome job in getting everything done and even took suggestions on a plan he already had worked out. We received word that our unit was moving up and we were to get ready for them to arrive.

I drove down to a link-up point that was one of three checkpoints and waited for them. The plugger (a device that picks up satellites and tells you your position on a map) that I had gotten from the Comm Shop was making big bucks in getting me around, but I was following everything up with a compass and a map anyway. As we drove down I could see a lot of other quartering parties already forming their units up or waiting for them. We picked up the first batch of Marines that needed to be put into the Assembly Area and drove them through the gate. By the time we went to pick up a second batch to bring them in, it was starting to get dark and more units were moving in. The route we usually used had other units on it. It was taking longer than expected and I am guessing either the whole 2$^{nd}$ MEB's (Marine Expeditionary Brigade) timeline was off, or people moved in before they were supposed to. Somehow, one of our groups had gotten separated in the darkness and did not know exactly where they were. Another group had lost comm. I don't know for sure but I think Basra was being attacked at the time. I was starting to leave to go find the lost group when word came down for us to go into MOPP 4, the highest state of readiness for a chemical or biological attack.

We were still carrying some of the gear from the Lts we had picked up earlier that day, so we drove back and dropped their packs off first. They were spazzing out, but I would too if everyone else was dressed like Michael J. Fox in *Back to the Future* while I had as much NBC gear on as Jed Clampet going squirrel hunting. What kind of made me laugh at this whole thing was one of the Lts was one that I had already had a run-in with. When we had gone out a week before to practice setting up the quartering party, I had stopped by Lt Martin's position to ask if he was going to set up camouflage netting. Before he could answer, another Lt started laughing and saying "hell no." Lt Martin looked at him and then looked at me and said, "Gunny, we aren't setting up a tent tonight." Then he turned to the laughing Lt and said, "we are setting it up tomorrow morning at first light." It was that lazy Lt who was now the frantic Lt who didn't have a MOPP suit. Lt Martin could rub people the wrong way but he was <u>never</u> lazy, he did what was right, and he was <u>always</u> doing the best he could.

As we started to head out about to find the lost group and the group with no communication, five or six Patriot missiles shot through the air. I said it wasn't a good sign, and Doc Sabilla asked why. I told him that there had to be something up there for them to shoot Patriot missiles at, and the question was, what was up there. It was really dark and so many units had moved into place now that we could not even travel the same route we had before. Since Day could not see with his gas mask on, I sat on the hood with some night vision devices to be sure we would not run over anyone or get stuck. As we were driving down, word came down to unmask, so we did and kept on going. I got back into the HMMV and we started to move out. I asked Day if he could see or if he wanted the night vision goggles. Day swore he could see fine. I asked him if he wanted me to wear them and tell him what I saw, and he said no, he could do this, and we weren't going to get stuck.

So after a while we were sitting on this sand dune, stuck, three wheels off the deck. We broke out the shovels and started to dig. As we were digging, more Patriot missiles flew through the air and the skyline to our south started to light up. We dug faster. At one point Day and Doc almost had us out but the senior guy there (me) had a bright idea and made things worse. The three of us were back to digging. The whole time we were trying to get unstuck, the lost convoy kept on asking us how much longer till we arrive. For about a half-hour I gave them the same answer: "five minutes." Nothing takes five minutes.

We finally moved out and found the lost convoy. To be honest, I don't know how we did it. There were units everywhere. Then we got comm with a unit we didn't have comm with before. I told the lost convoy to stay where they were and that I would be back in a minute. We drove over to where the other convoy was and it was Lt Letendre and some

CAAT vehicles waiting on some tanks. We drove back to where the lost convoy was and the Battalion XO was there. He said he was going to take them back and that I was to bring the other group in. Day drove us over to where Lt Letendre was and we waited for the tanks to show up. The Marines seemed to be in great spirits and were ready to go. I went to crash out for a while when the tanks pulled up. We got organized and headed to the Assembly Area.

The sand road we initially used was jammed with vehicles and I didn't want to get stuck in their lot, and who knew where they were going anyway. So we headed a little farther north and tried to get to the gate. We ended up driving through a couple of other units' Assembly Areas and we had to find ways around sand dunes and ditches, but we got there. When we did, there was another part of our unit pulling in. I left Lt Letendre and the tanks and headed to the COC to report to Capt Rohr that we were all up. Day drove the vehicle to the Log Train (Logistics Train, the part of the Battalion that carries supplies). Day and Doc would be driving the Mystery Machine with this group of Marines. After I reported to Capt Rohr I ran into Lt Barnhart, and we talked a bit but both of us fell asleep in some sand ditch in the process.

Even though the plan held for us to cross the breach the next day, I knew there would not be any change. We were too close to the border.

# The Devil Laughed and The Angels Cried
## Chapter 4

**21 March 2003**

I got up around 0300 and found Day and Doc Sabilla. Day was already with it. He had found out where our vehicle was going to be in the logistics convoy, and when it was his turn to fall in line he would be ready to move.

I pulled my air maps and pens out of the back of my pack, which was hanging on the side of the Mystery Machine. By now it was getting light and I went back to Lt Barnhart. As planned, I was to be the Forward Air Controller for Bravo Command. Until that point I had never been in a Command Track. He showed me where I was to sit and the radios I was to use. Always thought that there would be lots of room, at least more than what the Grunts got. With the Battalion XO, Bravo Fire Support Commander, Arty Liaison, Radio Chief, Logistics Chief, Air Officer, S-3 Liaison and the two walls full of radios, there was little room for anything. All I could think of was that if we got hit, we were fucked. Then to make things a little more claustrophobic, the top of the track was kept shut. So the first thing I did was a radio check, and Murphy's law must have been on the other end because none of my three radios worked. The radio chief in our track got them to work but the clincher was that I had only two working handsets. So in order to talk on one of the radios I would either have to get the Logistics guy to do it, or unplug my handset from one radio and put it on the one I needed -- then repeat the process if I wanted to use the one I had just unplugged.

I found Capt Rohr and asked him if he had any good fucking rumor. He said that some Marines were in Basra and the Iraqis were giving them a hard time. I asked the usual questions, like what kind of hard time, and he gave me what he thought he knew for sure, but he never would speculate. Capt Rohr was good about that. He never dealt in rumors like I did. If Capt Rohr said something, it had merit to it. It might not happen cause of some unexpected circumstances, but it was not speculation that he passed on. When he was talking about Basra and what was going on there, he seemed disturbed. Not like he was scared or anything, but as I look back he was disturbed that everyone thought the Iraqis would just roll over and give up. I think he knew different; no, I know he knew different.

I went back to my track and was sitting on top enjoying the view when one of my Sgts from the Javelin Platoon came over. He said he needed a Javelin round, batteries, and some chow. I held my tongue till I climbed off the track. If I could have gotten away with killing him I think I would have. I chewed his ass for waiting to the last minute to tell me that he needed supplies. For the last week I had gone over everything he would need, and had given him everything plus some. He said he never got issued chow, which was bullshit. The little cocksucker had eaten the chows he liked and had thrown the rest away. He had let his men do the same and then realized he did not have any chow left. As far as the extra ammo and batteries, he was second-guessing himself on what he would need, so I gave him what he asked for and sent him on his way.

We rolled out about ten minutes later and went through the breach. Wish I could remember it but I was in this sardine can looking at three radios that could not decide if they would work or not. My Godfather was behind me plotting shit on the map board. This board was used for plotting positions of units so that when we would coordinate artillery and mortar fire with air support, the air support being either fixed or rotary wing, the rounds would not run into them. It is called the "big sky, little bullet" theory. We had this thing called a Blue Force Tracker that the Army had given us to use. It would plot your position on a screen along with where everyone else was. You could not use it for de-conflicting indirect fire and air support, but it was great for what it did. Of course, what we had been using before the Army gave us this thing cost more and basically sucked donkey dick. But who said sucking a donkey's dick was cheap?

About midway through the first day of the war, I'd had it. Fucking communications wasn't working; there wasn't enough room to work the boards, my shotgun kept falling over and getting stuck in the seat next to me, which honestly kept freaking me out. When communication did work, I couldn't get a hold of Alpha Command for a report of what air support we did have on station. Later, at one of our checkpoints, I found out that we did not have any air support and were not scheduled to get any. Great, cool, lovely, fun, fan-fucking-tastic. I am sure you can imagine working on something and the whole time it was for nothing.

Time to move on. I asked Lt Barnhart if he really needed me there. He started laughing at my frustration and said no, and told me to go do Operations Chief stuff. If you ever get the chance to meet Lt "Barney"

Barnhart, don't miss it. The world could be falling apart and he would be laughing like the devil himself.

I found the Mystery Machine, and to be honest I was glad to be back with Day and Doc. Doc had been teaching me Spanish and Day could tell a good story, which is a whole lot better than that sardine can I was in.

I did not like riding with the Logistics Train but it was better than that Amtrak. Besides, I think even though Capt Rohr could have halfway used me in the FSCC and re-supply of the platoons was already figured out, he would have rather had me traveling with the logistic train. I don't know how to say this, but it was like he knew I had to be in the Ops Chief vehicle. I had enough supplies in the HMMV that I could re-supply every vehicle in Weapons Company with fuel, water, and chow for 24 hours. I could also re-supply about 75% of the ammo that the machineguns, TOWs, 81mm mortar and any Javelin from any of the line Companies needed.

During our stops, Day would drive us up to the 81 Mortar Platoon or up to one of the CAAT Sections and we would re-supply them. I liked re-supplying 81s because GySgt Leggett knew exactly what he needed, down to the last drop of water. SSgt Schielein did not always know what he needed, but when I would pull up he would have his Marines moving so fast to re-supply, it really did not matter. GySgt Hanson hung out with the other CAAT Section and with him it was hit or miss on the re-supply. Usually he was traveling back as security with the logistics vehicle so he would re-supply himself, but there were times he would need communications fixed or a weapon was down and needed to be taken to the armory.

Time I got back with Doc and Day and away from the sardine can of non-working radios, it was getting dark so our Battalion started to set up for the night. Defenses were set up, fire plans established, security set out, and units made sure they had overlapping fields of fire -- and then nothing happened. It was like sleeping in Kuwait but we were in Iraq. I plugged our position in on our map, and crashed out on the hood of the HMMV.

## 22 March 2003
The next morning we got up, early, and headed north. The sand was a lot finer the further north we went. It would get into everything and literally

covered us like a fine mist. At first it was kind of funny but after, I don't know, three minutes, we were sick of it. The sand was starting to fill up the air vacuum can to the filters on the HMMVs. This caused the HMMVs to start to struggle through the sand. Motor-T came by the different units and cleaned out the filters and did some other preventive maintenance on the vehicles. We wouldn't have made it as far as we did without Gunny Tyre running Motor-T.

That morning the only people driving by us were either friendly or they just acted like we were nothing special. Mostly we ran across sheep or camel herders and we did have a lot of guns, so that might have explained the lax attitude. Later in the afternoon we stopped for a break. To our left front was a small shepherd's tent. Someone started yelling to get on line facing the tent. All the logistical vehicles went from being spread out and facing outboard to getting on line and facing this tent. I told Day to do the same. I broke out my binoculars and started looking at the tent area and tried to figure out what we were about to kill. All I saw was an old man smoking his hash pipe, some children walking with their mothers, and a loud, small dog that was either barking at us or chasing its tail. I asked someone what we were going to shoot, and someone yelled "the tent." I thought to myself, I have to get away from these logistics fuckers before they get me killed.

We moved out and later on that evening we set up by a highway cloverleaf. It was a pretty good set-up. The Line Companies set up far enough away from each other that they wouldn't shoot each other, and the Logistics Train set-up was in the middle. It was probably the best set-up so far, I thought. We did our re-supply of 81s as usual and I asked Lt Clayton if I could ride with them tomorrow. Gunny Leggett said it would be great cause it would be easier for him to re-supply. I then re-supplied GySgt Hanson by the Logistics Train. He had some gear that needed fixing but nothing pressing.

I sat around and bullshitted with him for a while. One of the Sgts in his section had some candy from Mexico. It was like a lollipop but it was sort of green and had a white sugar coating over it. As soon as you got past the sugar coating, it was awful. Everybody got a laugh out of it but me. I had some chow with them, an MRE, and then moved out. We re-supplied Schielein up by the cloverleaf to our east. They were spread out in a circle. So we drove up behind the vehicles on the inside of the circle and dropped off the water and fuel jugs and MREs if they needed it. I would always make Schielein's vehicle last so I could talk for a while about Harleys, women, riding the both of them, and the bars we were going to go to when we got back. I could always find someone to talk to about Harleys but it would usually end up being a one-way conversation, with me doing all the talking. With Schielein I could rest my jaw and make my ears work. About this time it was getting dark and he was ordered to move out on a route reconnaissance mission. His Section was to find a way for the Battalion to get across some obstacles so we could get up on the hardball (the highway) and head up to An Nasiriyah. As he was about to take off, we saw some lights heading up from the south. As the first set of lights got closer, we could see more lights behind them, and then more lights. It was an Army convoy moving supplies north to the Army's Third Infantry Division. That convoy did not end and I don't mean that figuratively. I left Schielein there with his Marines, staring at the never-ending supply line, and went to re-supply Lt Letendre with the other CAAT Section.

Getting to them was a bitch. We had to drive over a berm of sand and I thought the vehicle would get stuck or flip, and then we couldn't find the fuckers. When we did find them, getting them their supplies was a cluster fuck. But I knew that tomorrow we were supposed to go into that city everyone had been talking about, and I did not want anyone to be without any supplies at all, even if they thought they could wait. We headed back, after about two hours of re-supplying them, to the Battalion CP. Over by the CP was Lt Clayton, and just to make sure I asked him again if we could travel with him tomorrow. Since the logistics fiasco of wanting to shoot an old man who smokes hash, I really wanted to travel somewhere else. Besides, he was traveling closer to the front. He said "yea, no problem."

We went to crash out at the FSCC where Capt Rohr and Lt Barnhart were. The Army convoy was still heading by us like one long snake. Later on that night, I was woken up for watch and the convoy was still going with no beginning and no end. I did not know we had that many vehicles. I still can't fathom the logistical nightmare it was to get all of that over there. I was used to seeing the Marine Corps with our Logistics thrown on our back and making do with what we had. I woke up Doc for watch and hit the rack. I remember thinking as I fell a sleep, "This war is going to be easy."

**23 March 2003**
We got up early, which was routine by now, and headed north. Schielein, who was leading CAAT, was the lead-screening element to

our front, followed by tanks and the rest of the Companies following in trace, with the 81's Platoon in the middle of them. Then there were the logistic vehicles. We joined into the endless line of the Army's supply convoy, headed north on the highway.

We started to come out of the sand and get on the hardball when Day ran over a metal stake that used to be a guardrail. It took out our front tire and the flooring from underneath my feet. For a second I thought it took off my foot. We drove about a half-mile on that flat tire till we decided to pull over. I got on the radio and called up for Motor-T to come help us. Doc immediately started giving Day shit. I told Day he was going to miss his only chance for war because he had given us a flat. Day started to do everything he could to get ready for the mechanics to fix the vehicle as the rest of the Battalion drove on by.

It did not take long before GySgt Tyre showed up with the Beverly Hillbilly's Mobile. Picture a long pick-up truck that is really high off the ground and just a little wider. Now put in a box that is half the size of the trailer but twice as high, and throw some spare tires on it. Then on the back of the toolbox, put every tool known to man. Tyre jumped out of the front of the vehicle and said he was sorry for taking so long, but he had to fix a flat on another vehicle. I kind of chuckled cause I didn't think AAA had a time record like he did. By now Day had the vehicle jacked up and the tire off. Tyre threw on another tire and pulled out an air wrench. I said to Tyre that the Marine Corps was getting their money out of that air wrench he said "no, they aren't." All the tools in the back of the truck were his own, which he had brought along. I guessed as much by looking at all the stickers of women and tool manufacturers on the side of the toolboxes. Day and Doc got the vehicle back together and we took off. We were a good distance behind 81s and the logical thing would have been to latch back on with the logistics vehicles, but fuck that. It was still dark out so we hauled ass forward.

For some reason the Battalion kept stopping, so we made up some time that way. But we really made up some time because Day was driving like a madman passing the Amtraks. This in itself was kind of an adrenaline rush. It was like driving past a bunch of 18-wheelers with no rear view mirrors that had twelve-year-old drivers with no sense of what a yellow line in the road was for. The drivers were Amtrakers, which are Marines with a desire to destroy shit and with the vehicle to do it in. It was still dark when we caught up to the 81s. The sun started to come up and everything was now going normal. As we were briefed, we stopped short of An Nasiriyah so the tanks and other vehicles could refuel. I called up Schielein and asked him how he was doing on fuel. It was the night before when I last refueled him and he said he was doing fine. About that time about fifteen Army trucks drove by.

We got word that some Army convoy made a wrong turn and went into town, and when they tried to turn around they jammed each other up. As this was happening the Iraqis put up a roadblock and faked surrender. The Army vehicles got ambushed. Just as some of them made it out of town and were still receiving fire, our tanks (GySgt Howard from Kentucky) and SSgt Schielein's CAAT Section pulled in. The rest of the Battalion was still south of the city but there were scattered buildings along the road up. CAAT started receiving fire from the left and the right along this road. They were in the thick of it.

I remember hearing a lot of rounds being exchanged up north from our position. Schielein requested a call for fire from the 81 mortars through the FSCC. The 81s broke out the mortars and ammo and started laying the aiming stakes in. Day and Doc started helping them. I walked over to Lt Clayton as he was receiving the call for fire from the Battalion FSCC. For some reason there was a problem with the direction to the target. The target they were shooting at, which was to the east, was completely different from where I heard the TOWs and machine guns shooting from, which was to the north. I didn't want to stop the fire mission because something could have been going on that I didn't know about. Schielein was on the radio asking if the mortar rounds landing next to him were theirs or ours. No one was sure. I told Doc and Day to get in the Mystery Machine and that we were going forward. Doc had this look on his face that said, "if you say so, but you know, that is where all the firing is and we are being pretty helpful right here."

We got to the COC, which stands for the Center of Command, but at times it stands for the Center of Confusion. I tried to get Capt Rohr's attention but he was too busy. Gunner Dunfee asked me what I needed. Both of us moved to the top of this mound, and I showed him in what direction, and at what, the mortars were firing. He went back to the COC and got on the radio and told them to cease-fire.

About this time a majority of the fire to the front had ceased and we were moving again. The tanks had not been refueled yet, which I remembered was the Battalion Commander's big logistical thing in Kuwait. CAAT and the tanks kept pushing north, and US Army Soldiers that we were driving by said there were more of the enemy to the north. The tanks still didn't have time to refuel. A few minutes later, an 81's Section rushed past us. We jumped in behind them and moved forward. I saw Gunny Leggett and he was setting his people up on the east side of the road with the gun line running north to south. I drove about 100 meters more to the north where there was an open field with a small house. There was expended brass from machine guns; an empty TOW missile tube on the road, and to the north a little farther was a burned patch on the ground that looked like it had been made by a small explosion. I figured it was from an RPG that had been shot at them.

I went back to Gunny Leggett and told him about the place a little further north and that he could run his gun line perpendicular to the city. He said "awesome" and moved north. We went with him and scoped out the far northern area to make sure that the area was safe before the 81 Section just started piling in. One of the rifle platoons pulled in behind them and cleared the houses on both sides of the road. While this was going on, the rest of the 81's Platoon pulled in, and in a matter of minutes they were ready to fire. And fire they did -- the CAAT and Tanks were hitting a lot of T-55 tanks that were dug in along the road to the city. The area to the north was becoming thicker with structured buildings because of the city and the area was quickly turning into heavy vegetation since we were rapidly approaching the Euphrates River.

CAAT reached a couple of the injured Army Soldiers. Three were wounded and five had no injuries at all. I drove back to the COC cause that was where the ambulance (1st Sgt Thompson from Alpha Company) that had the wounded was going. I thought Doc might have been able to help them out and it would not have hurt for them to see the reality of what was going on. When the Amtrak pulled up, Doc got to work with the other Navy Corpsman. Two of the wounded were walking and one was in a litter.

Just a few seconds later, Schielein pulled up with a couple of his CAAT vehicles. It was good to see him. He had just rescued the Soldiers. He was pumped up but not losing his cool. We sat on the hood of my HMMV as he waited for another mission order from the COC and we bullshitted a little. All his Marines were talking like the battle was over. The CAAT Plt Commander, Lt Letendre, was now up front. I thought he had tried to go forward earlier in the battle but probably like a lot of guys he did not want to be impatient with what was going on -- which was probably the wisest of choices. But he did try. Earlier, when the ambush first started, he had told an SNCO with CAAT that Schielein was in trouble and that they should go help him. The SNCO said that Letendre could go if he wanted to, but that he was staying with the logistics train in the rear.

Schielein told me what had happened and what he had done, and then he looked me straight in the eye and asked me how he did. I told him he did fine, just like I knew he would. He smiled and was back in the war. There was movement off to our west and he was waiting for orders to track it down. For years the Army has cheapened their award system while the Marine Corps has been too much the opposite. When someone goes into battle and after all is said and done, they **need** to be told they did well. And if there were mistakes made, the warrior should be told that those things happen -- "its war." Medals tell us we did well and that all is right with the world.

I started to take a picture of the Corpsman working on the wounded and after I took the picture I felt as though I had invaded their privacy. How anyone can take a picture of something like that and feel okay about it is beyond me. Day was giving the Marines from CAAT a re-supply on some ammo as all this was going on. About that time Schielein received his marching orders and he was off. I gave him my binoculars, as I didn't think I would need them as much as he would.

I picked up and moved north along the highway. Some of the Soldiers who were not wounded were on the other side of the road by a vehicle. They were next to their vehicle and it was shot to shit. The mortars were not where I had left them in the open field. They had moved forward, closer to the city. They had chosen a trash yard. I would say "junkyard," but there was no junk -- just trash. I would say, "Trash pile" but it was not a pile -- it was a couple of acres. The flies were everywhere. I swear you could see them reproduce and appear in a matter of seconds. As we pulled in, I overheard Gunny Leggett yelling at the platoon, "Quit your bitching! Your living conditions have improved over the Ponce!" That pulled up quite a laugh from the Platoon. I realized that we were getting closer to the city, so we headed back south to the log train to get more ammo for CAAT and more fuel for the Company.

On the way south I ran into the same seven Army guys I had seen on the way north. Someone had brought them south to some degree of safety. They stopped me and asked about their buddies. I told them what I had heard: that we were trying to work our way north to get them, and that we had three at our Battalion Aid Station being worked on. The Soldiers looked like they had had the fuck beat out of them. One of the Soldiers said that they had gotten lazy. He said that when the Iraqis started to surrender, no one knew what to do.

We got to the refueling point, which is south past the COC, and they wouldn't give me fuel. The refueler said there was not enough fuel even for the tanks, and he couldn't give us any. In fact, he said he might have to move north they were so low, but at that point the tanks were being pulled out of the fight to refuel. The ammo guys, though, were giving me all the ammo and chow I could handle. Whatever I asked for, I got it. No questions, no paperwork, no request forms. I swear to God if the Marine Corps was always like this I would have stayed in forever, but then we would go broke because we are some thieving bastards at times.

While we were loading ammo, I stopped and told my guys to hurry up, that something bad had just happened. I did not know what, I just knew that something bad had happened, but that everything was okay in a big picture kind of way. We just had to get going and head north. As we are leaving the logistics point, some Marines stopped us and asked if we would help them clear a house on the side of the road. I told Doc Sabilla and one of their Marines with a SAW to cover us from the vehicle while Day, the other four Marines, and I went to search the house. There was nothing there but a scared old man and a fucked up old donkey. To figure out which of the two was in better shape would have been a contest in itself. We headed north again.

We went past the 81's position at the trash yard and they were not there. They must have had to move north. So again we were playing catch up. As we approached the city, Iraqi citizens were standing outside their mud houses. They were not smiling, not waving, children were hugging the legs of their parents and they looked at us as though they were watching dead men still alive.

As we were driving north we saw the ambushed Army vehicles on the road. The vehicles that had made it out of the city were shot to shit, tires flat, some were on fire, bullet holes decorated the sides like lights on a Christmas tree. They littered the highway like someone had been throwing stones of chance along a line. I needed fuel for my Company, so I raped their vehicles of the gas in their exterior fuel tanks. We grabbed ammo and parts that might be used later on. Day found a Fanta Orange soda and some Oreo cookies. There was a TV with a VCR, movies, candy, regular food, cots to sleep on -- these fuckers were living the life of Riley. There were rifles still in the vehicles. HMMVs have latches that hold personal weapons in place when you are traveling. The weapons were still in these holders. Some weapons weren't in the holder but the ejection port covers were closed -- the weapons had not been fired. They had the good life and they paid for it with their lives. I took some personal binoculars from one of the vehicles because I had given mine to Schielein and I thought we could use them later on. We took nothing else personal, but in retrospect we should have destroyed everything so the Iraqis could not get it.

I thought Day was starting to get nervous but he was controlling it. Doc had adopted an attitude of, "if I die, fuck it, my soul belongs to God." I felt like I was picking up from where I left off in the First Gulf War, like the past couple of years had just been a break, a time-out. Once in a while, when we were gathering fuel and water from the Army vehicles, we would receive sniper fire, but Day and Doc did not seem to notice it so I played it off like it was not happening. The snipers weren't accurate; they were just a pain in the ass.

The Mystery Machine was full. I don't think we could have fit another jug of water or fuel in the vehicle or the trailer. The whole time we were doing this, we were on our own. I mean the logistical support area was to our south and the infantry was to our north. This whole time we were bouncing around the battlefield by ourselves. You're not supposed to go anywhere alone, but we had a job to do. We headed north, again, and to be honest we didn't know what was happening in the city. I was seeing all these Iraqi tanks burning along the side of the road. CAAT, Tanks, Cobra helicopters, and Javelins had done a job on those fuckers. Their shit was burning everywhere along the side of the road, in the tree lines, inside buildings, and along bends in the road.

We were about a kilometer from the Euphrates river bridge when I got a call over the radio. It kind of startled me because it was the first radio traffic we had gotten in a while. All I heard was my call sign, "Thunder Cloud 7, Thunder Cloud 7..." I got on the radio and asked who I was talking to. It was Capt Rohr. "This is Thunder Cloud 6, it's good to hear your voice." Then silence. I tried to get communications back up with him but it wasn't working. I couldn't get comm with anyone. Capt Rohr told me later that he had been calling me from the top of a tank because the two Command AAVs (Amtraks) were stuck in an obstacle and had to be abandoned. Then, as the AAVs got stuck in this trap, the communications went out and they couldn't talk with anyone.

We were about 500 meters south of the southern bridge going into the "Naz" when I saw a burning vehicle in the middle of the road. It looked like a ship with just its rib cage. It had been burning to hell. I was trying to figure out what kind of Iraqi vehicle it might be. Then I figured it out. I could feel my heart go to my throat and then my stomach. It was one of our Amtraks. I couldn't fucking believe it. I did not want to believe it. Day asked what kind of vehicle it was. I told him it was an Amtrak. He said it wasn't, and just stared at it. He did not want to believe what his eyes were telling him. Then Doc asked us what type of vehicle it was and Day told him it was an Amtrak. I guess he believed me then. It had belonged to SSgt Pompos and Lt Sealy's Platoon. It had broken down and had to be abandoned, and I guess after they left it some Iraqis threw an RPG at it thinking it was an easy target. Doc started praying something in Spanish.

As soon as we caught up to 81s just at the crest of the southern bridge, we started receiving AK-47, RPK machine gun and RPG fire. It was coming from both sides and in front of us, and it was no bullshit. About a hundred meters past the bridge, all the vehicles had jammed at a T-intersection, with the top of the T running north into Ambush Alley and heavy fire coming from the leg of the T coming from the east. The amount of fire we were receiving and the number of vehicles that were trying to get through put all of us in a cluster fuck and stopped us cold. There was the bridge behind us, a built-up area to our left, and an open garden to our right. To our front was Ambush Alley with buildings along both sides. To our right front was a three- or four-story building.

I knew the HMMV was a target so I jumped out and told Doc to do the same. There were no doors on the vehicle so getting out quickly was not a problem. But the HMMV in front of me had mortar men in it and they were not as lucky. There was not enough room for all of them to return fire, much less take cover. I yelled at them to get out of the vehicle, but as they started to get out, the vehicle moved forward. I told them to get the fuck out as soon as the HMMV stopped. I didn't think they could hear me over all the rounds hitting around us and the fire we were returning, but they shook their heads like they had gotten the idea. Lt Clayton was leading the platoon to the open field to our right, which was the only place to go cause sitting in the middle of the road where we were really sucked.

Our vehicle had not started to move yet but Day knew to follow 81s without me telling him to. I got out and ran to the back of the trailer, using that as cover. Doc was between the trailer and the HMMV itself. I looked off to our east down the leg of the T- road and I saw an Iraqi with tan pants and a black shirt holding something. I started unloading my shotgun into him. Someone, I think it was Doc, yelled "RPG!" I was still shooting, some Marines from 81s were pointing at our vehicle and yelling, and Doc was yelling "RPG!" as the round bounced off the tarp of our HMMV and exploded on the telephone pole behind us. As I was looking at Doc and reloading, dirt kicked up beside him. I looked back at the bridge, and I saw Iraqi soldiers running from one side of the road to the other. We were surrounded.

We were now moving with the rest of the HMMVs into the open garden to our right. But not fast, though. I was walking on the outside of the vehicle with Doc, both of us shooting and reloading. As the vehicles pulled off the main road and into the garden area, there was a sewage trench that ran along the southern side of the garden road that was on the north side of the garden. Marines from 81s and Alpha Company were all down in this trench taking and returning fire into a building that was now to our southwest, as well as from the bridge we had just crossed. Gunny Leggett and Lt Clayton were starting to get their Platoon to set up their mortars. I told Lt Clayton that he needed to pull the vehicles farther from the main road and deeper into the garden because when it came time to get out of there we would need to be able to move around and go.

We received some RPK machine gun fire from a small building to our west. Some Marines returned fire. They captured one Iraqi and the other one was dead. The dead Iraqi must have had the flu or something because he was missing the whole of his head and most of his chest. The Iraqi that surrendered was flex-cuffed hand and foot, gagged, and blindfolded. As I checked on him and started to walk away I tripped over his leg. I was afraid it may have looked more like a kick than a trip.

Day was taking charge and un-fucking the vehicles in the garden. Doc went with me to check out the area where the prisoner was taken. Some Marine took the bolt out of his AK-47 and the RPK and threw it in a pond to our north. We went back to the area where the 81s were set up. The prisoner was by the vehicles and had about three Marines standing over him. They had not yet started taking their frustration out on the Iraqi, but I knew it was coming. I took the binding off his feet, undid the tape on his mouth, and unwrapped the blindfold. I then told the Marines that the prisoner was mine. I felt there would be enough killing still to come, no use rushing things. I told Doc to take care of him and put him in the back of the Mystery Machine, which he did. That EPW (Enemy Prisoner of War) was a scared motherfucker. Guess I would have been too if I was in his shoes.

We were still receiving fire from all around us. Alpha Company was fighting hard to the west, building to building. In Alpha Company's area, about 125 meters from our mortar position, there was a Mosque that the Iraqis were fighting from and getting supplies out of. Alpha Company was fighting to get to the mosque but had hit an alley that they were having a hard time crossing. I didn't know where any other unit was, nor do I think any one else did. We just knew we had our hands full.

81's mortar men were firing their mortar at targets so close by that they could see exactly what they were shooting at through their sights. I saw a Marine from Alpha Company come out and point at targets. A squad leader from 81s turned his gun and direct laid on the target. Because of the closeness of the targets, they were using charge zero on the rounds. You could actually see the rounds come out of the mortar and chase each other in the sky and explode on the target. Sometimes after the ammo man would drop a round in the tube, he would either immediately lie flat on the ground or run to the sewage trench to take shelter from all the incoming fire they were receiving.

The road from where Iraqis had earlier been shooting RPGs at us now had a machine gun firing at us. I asked Lt Clayton if I could set up one mortar in the open to direct lay on our little problem. He said yes, so I took a mortar squad out to the open field and Sgt Griffin got his gun up. I ran back to tell Lt Clayton that if he or Grif heard or saw me shoot two shotgun rounds, it would be clear to fire the mortar. At the time, Alpha Company had some Marines in the line of fire and I did not want to have a short round take them out when I could simply move them back behind a wall.

I went down the garden road that the mortar line was set up on, crossed the main street, and walked over to Alpha Company. Two Marines were on the corner where I was headed, and as I walked up I ran into SSgt Cantu. He happened to be the Platoon Sergeant for the Platoon on the corner and he had been one of my students when I taught the Infantry Platoon Sergeant Course. He asked what I wanted and I told him that the

Marines on the corner needed to be pulled back, cause 81s were about to fire some mortars that way. He said it was okay to pull them back and he would go with me. The two of us moved down the road to move the Marines, and we pulled them back from the corner, as we did that, I must have flagged my weapon around the corner because a burst of machine gun fire poured onto the corner where we were standing. As I walked away I started to get pissed, so I turned around, went back to the corner, and unloaded on where I thought the enemy fire had come from. 81s saw the firing of my shotgun and took it as the signal to open up on the machinegun bunker.

I found some rubble next to the wall and sat down next to Cantu, who was smiling like a little schoolgirl. I knew he was about to laugh at me for getting pissed, so to change the subject I asked him if I could honestly ask him a question and he said, "sure." I asked him what he really thought of the Infantry Platoon Sergeant Course. He said he thought it was a drunk fest. I told him to fuck off, and headed back over to 81s while Cantu continued laughing.

I was walking down the line of mortar men on the garden road and in the lines were Marines from Alpha Company. As I walked by the Marines lying down in the shit trench, they would stop firing and look at me. I knew what they were thinking -- that I was crazy for walking around and not taking cover. I told them as I walked by, "Don't look at me, look at the enemy," "I am not the one shooting at you, they are over there," and "I know I am good looking, you can look at me all you want when we get on the other side of the city. Until then, kill them." You might think this was stupid but it made a lot of scared faces laugh. For a lot of Marines this was their first shooting match. I couldn't give them a pep talk like in the movies, with that magical lull in the fighting and the background music. It was my way of letting them know that all this chaos was normal.

I walked behind a mortar HMMV and there was a 50 cal. machine gun in the back. I may not be a smart man but I knew that it did not belong there, and wondered if CAAT had lost it. I was going to kill whoever lost their 50 cal. machine gun, if they weren't already dead. Gunny Leggett told me he had found it on top of one of the Army vehicles. He said it had not been fired, didn't even have ammo in it, and some sniper had been shooting at him when he took it down. He just didn't want some Hadji fuck to have it.

At this point the squad I had led out into the field was just pouring it on with their mortar. I never saw as many rounds flying out of a mortar as there were from that one squad that day. But after a few minutes they started receiving more than their fair share of small arms fire, and someone yelled out that Sgt Griffin was down. The mortar had literally been shot out of his hands. I ran out into the field to where the mortar squad had stopped firing and took cover behind a small berm that was not tall enough to grow peanuts on. I asked who the next senior guy was, and some Corporal said he was. I told him to stay with me and told everyone else to get the fuck out of there. The Corporal was lying next to the Sgt and I was covering the Sgt with my body. We were receiving so much fire I could actually taste the dirt the rounds were kicking up. I crawled my way over to the mortar and kicked it over, thinking that if the mortar was not up they would stop shooting at us long enough for us to get out of there. The Sgt said he thought he had been hit in the shoulder. I gave him a once-over, checking for wounds. As I was lying over his head I asked him if he knew the difference between being hurt and being wounded, and he said yes. I told him he was just hurt and we needed to get the fuck out of there. I asked him what part of the mortar he wanted to carry back to the trench and told him that I had the barrel cause I needed a reason for my old ass to run slow.

The Corporal disassembled the mortar as I went over the Sgt one last time to make sure he was okay. As we got ready to leave, Sgt Griffin said he had to button up his flak jacket because he had promised his wife he would not leave it open. The Corporal and I kind of just looked at each other, as in "you got to be shittin' me" which, considering our situation was kind of funny. We each grabbed a part of the mortar and started to get up and run out of there when a tank showed up out of nowhere. It started firing down the road where we had been taking so much fire. God, I had forgotten we even had tanks. The tank let lose on everything, fucking Goddamn everything, and everything let lose on the tank in return. After being on the scene just a few seconds, the tank was taking so much machine gun fire and RPG rounds we couldn't see it anymore -- it just disappeared under all the smoke and explosions. All we could hear was the tank pounding away with its main gun and machine guns. We were still in the prone position out in the open field when we started bouncing off the ground from the vibrations of the RPG rounds exploding on the tank and from the rounds the main gun was firing. Then, all at once, the tank and the Iraqis stopped shooting at each other. The tankers were dead -- no one could have survived that firefight. But then the tank slowly lurched forward and so did our morale.

68

A pay raise from Clinton could not have surprised me as much as that fucking piece of metal did. The three of us got up at the same time. The Corporal grabbed the bipod, the Sgt the base plate, and I grabbed the barrel as we hauled ass for safety.

As we got there, Lt Clayton was getting one part of the Platoon in some lower ground and getting two mortars up on a Mosque. Someone said that a squad had been pinned down by a group of Iraqis who were fighting out of the Mosque. The two mortars were set up on the edge of the garden road and main road, and they started firing. The first round landed near a med-evac site that Alpha had set up. The rest of the rounds were still dangerously close, but they started hitting the target with no other adjustments. The fire we were receiving started to die away. Those two mortars put over 150 rounds down into an area no bigger than 40 by 40 meters. Gunny Leggett was getting a Sgt to clear out and provide security on an LZ and told him to be ready to mark it for some casualties that needed to get med-evac'ed, ASAP. After they were med-evac'ed, SSgt Cantu came over to Lt Clayton and said that Alpha Company was leaving. Lt Clayton followed suit. We picked up and got the fuck out of there and headed north, through Ambush Alley.

By now Charlie Company had been on the north side of the far north bridge and had tried to get some med-evacs out by AAVs, but that wasn't working. They were getting direct fire from enemy artillery, mortar fire, and the Iraqis were also closing in on both their flanks. Rumor had it that the US Air Force had strafed their position, not once but several times. Alpha was now racing north to them. As we started to leave the garden, Day looked at me and asked if we could ride in the middle of the 81s Platoon convoy. I had to smile -- I knew exactly what he was thinking. Kind of like when you were a kid and the boogey man was after you. You did not want to be the first kid cause if the boogey man was in front you were a goner and the kid on the end, forget it, you were a goner for just being on the end. I told him no, that we had to be last cause I did not want to fuck up any of the SOPs they had on movement. Somehow we started in the middle of the convoy, but somehow or another we ended up in the back of the convoy. It was all that extra weight we were carrying because of the supplies we had raped from the Army convoy.

We headed north on Ambush Alley. We were receiving fire from our left and right. Gunny Leggett was in the vehicle in front of me, and his radio was literally shot up as it sat between him and the driver. At one point as I was reloading, I remembered a conversation that Capt Rohr had had with me about this alley. He said that in a meeting someone had called it Ambush Alley. I remember thinking, "What kind of John Wayne bullshit was that?" But whoever it was that named it had never been so right in their life. The rounds would either make a cracking or popping noise as they went over your head or a whistle as they flew by you.

As we were driving through town I saw an Amtrak blown to shit on the side of the road. The building behind it had a bunch of Marines shooting and a few waving their arms. Dead Iraqis lay on the ground like candy at a parade without any kids to pick the candy up. I figured with the number of Marines that I saw, plus the ones I didn't see who were conducting rear and flank security, the unit must have been about a Platoon or so. Doc yelled something but we couldn't hear him, so Day yelled "What?" Doc said, "We need to turn around." I told Day to turn around but he was already doing it.

We pulled up in front of the blown-up AAV, which was facing south, and some Marines from the building started yelling "RPG!" and pointing across the street. Having had as much experience with this as to my liking, I jumped out of the vehicle and moved some metal out of the way and Day pulled up between the Amtrak and the house. A couple of Marines came out and one said they needed something, but I couldn't hear over all the rifle fire so I asked him again what he said. He said he needed a battery, so Doc and Day dug through the gear in the back of the HMMV and pulled one out, and we gave it to them. It seemed like total chaos. I asked if he needed anything else, and he said, "No, we have a casualty collection point set up." Hearing that I again thought there must have been a little more than a Platoon there, and that they were holding security to cover all the vehicles moving north to the north bridge. We started to leave out and Day couldn't get the vehicle back out on the road. He kept jack-knifing the HMMV with the trailer. I moved some more metal out of the way and tried to get him to drive behind the Amtrak, but the vehicle would have gotten stuck doing so. He finally got the vehicle out on the road, and when he did, it took him a while to catch back up to the 81s convoy.

We took fire for the rest of the way out of town. Iraqis would pop out from windows and doors. They were in side streets, set up as bunkers, waiting for us to pass. Enemy soldiers fired from rooftops but as soon as we crossed the north bridge the firing started to cease. There were about three or four Amtraks that had been shot up and were burning on the side of the road. I remember seeing the vehicles burning and seeing shit

70

everywhere. I can't describe what I saw. When the vehicle was hit by an RPG, or whatever was shot at it, gear got strewn all over the place along with body and vehicle parts.

We followed 81's Platoon for about another kilometer past the blown Amtraks. We pulled in with Alpha Company on the right side of the road. Cpl Nichew got out of his vehicle to set up his mortar and an Iraqi popped out of a fighting hole. Nichew shot him dead. Nichew turned around and the man he had just killed shot back at him. The round grazed his neck. Nichew turned back around and with the help of a few other Marines; they made sure the Iraqi was dead this time.

We pulled into the circle that Battalion had set up and I got out of the vehicle. We were fucked up. Units were mixed together, Cpls and Sgts were taking charge of whoever was around them and trying to form a perimeter the best they could. SSgts and Lts were looking for their scattered Platoons, and Companies were trying to make some kind of plan for what to do next. There was still a firefight going on to the north from the T-intersection. Marines were being pulled left and right to help with the wounded and dead. Gear and Iraqi dead were strewn all over the battlefield. All the corpsmen were in one area trying to keep the wounded alive.

I saw GySgt Blackwell and I started to walk toward him. You had to know Blackwell. He was a short, barrel-chested Marine with a thick southern accent and always full of fight -- except for now. Blackwell looked like he had been awake for a week straight; tired was not the word. His vehicle was shot up with at least five bullet holes in the front window and two, maybe three tires were shot flat. As I walked over to him, I realized what he was doing: putting the dead in the back of his vehicle. There was one Marine lying on the ground with an American flag over him. Four Marines, all having the same blank, tired expression on their faces, walked over and picked the dead Marine up, one at each shoulder and foot. As they picked him up his body dragged the deck, his arms had locked out, and his right hand was bouncing off the ground. The flag just lay on him as they carried him and I could see blood on the white stripes and stars; dirt was on the corners and edges of the flag. They put him in the back of the HMMV, then took the flag and laid it over the next Marine and started the same process again. Watching this was killing me inside. I thought to myself, demanding from God, "NO MORE," but what started out as a demand turned quickly to a request. I felt so helpless.

I saw SSgt Pompos over to my left and in the best voice I could, I asked, "What's up brother?" He had this worried look on his face, like a parent that has lost his child at the amusement park, and said that he could not find his platoon. I looked at him and said, "I know where they are. I'll be back in a minute." I turned to Day and told him to start unloading the HMMV. He was already en route. 81's Platoon had some of the biggest Marines in the Battalion and I had them drop the trailer off the back of my HMMV.

I turned to a group of about eight Marines and shamefully said, "I need two SAW gunners who are ready to die." For a brief second, no one moved. Now when I say that, don't think for one fucking minute these guys were cowards. They were not. They were not just reading about this, they lived it, and the dead that were not more than twenty meters away from them were their buddies. The people they could hear crying in pain were their friends. Then one of the Marines started to lift his left foot off the ground, and only made a half step, but the dust had only just started to rise when he continued in a solid stride. And before he had that foot solidly on the ground, all the Marines behind him followed his lead. The Lance Corporals even started ordering the PFCs to give them their SAWs. By the time I got back to the HMMV, the trailer was off, my prisoner and the wooden box with all the extra gear was out of the back, and the two SAW gunners were jumping on board.

I started to tell Day to turn the vehicle around and Doc was on his way over from helping out the wounded. Lt Letendre came up to me and asked, "Can we go with you?" I said yes. He asked what the plan was. I said, "Drive fast, kill everything that gets in our way, and get our boys out of there." He smiled and said, "It might work." He asked if I wanted him to take lead, which would have been the smart thing, but I said I would take lead since I knew where we were going.

He headed over to his Marines to tell them the news. Lt Clayton started getting volunteers. He was telling the Marines that wanted to go back in that they couldn't be married or be fathers. I thought about Lt Letendre, he was both. I would do my best, I thought, to make sure he made it out of there.

Day pulled out of the Battalion area and up on to the road. Lt Letendre followed behind me with his four HMMVs, two with Anti-tank weapons and two with heavy machine guns. We were about two clicks north of the northern bridge of town when we started down that road. I remember it being so quiet, except for the sound of the rubber humming on the road. I felt like I had fallen backwards off a cliff. I knew there would be a sudden stop that would kill me, but for the time being I was enjoying the ride down. Doc was praying in Spanish and I was praying my "Hail Marys." When I got to the end of the prayer -- "now and at the hour of our death" -- I couldn't help but feel I was praying for all of us going in, and all of those who we were about to kill inside this town, again.

As soon as we hit the top of the bridge, it started all over. There were two anti-aircraft guns opening up on us from the left and right side of the bridge, so the SAW behind me returned the favor. He was firing so hard the vibration was rattling my teeth. Then when our 50 cals opened up behind me, the two enemy machine guns stopped firing. The SAW behind me was firing a thousand rounds a minute, and I could see the building windows to our right shatter as bullets were flung all around it. We were shooting at everything we saw move. Everything. I looked behind me at the HMMVs following us and I could see the barrels of M-16s pointed in every direction, with smoke being thrown out of the barrels. It seemed we were the only show in town and everyone wanted to come. I saw the Amtrak on the left side of the road where we had given the Marines a fresh battery the last time we were here. There were still dead Iraqis lying everywhere.

Day pulled in around the Amtrak close to the same place he had before, but this time he stayed on the street. The Lt and another one of his vehicles pulled up just south of us, and the two others stopped just north of the downed Amtrak. I got out of the vehicle and all I remember was thinking to myself "Don't lose it, Doran. You lose it, we all lose it, and everyone will get killed -- and it will be your fault." Everyone was yelling at each other and we weren't doing what we were supposed to do while covering areas. It was chaotic. I had gotten a cigarette from Lt Clayton before we left, and I had it hanging out of my mouth. I asked Day for a light but he didn't have one, so I bummed one off the SAW gunner and I lit my cigarette. I calmly walked around to the street. Lt Letendre and Day were looking at me like I was crazy, and some of the Marines were staring at me, but just seeing me stay calm made everyone start to act a little less sporadic and start to work more as a team.

Two Iraqis were at one corner of a house, and the Lt and I killed them. I wanted to get out of there fast but I knew if I ran or acted over-zealous the Marines would think something was wrong and start to flip out again.

I just opened an iron gate that joined up to a cement wall about 6 feet high, which surrounded the front yard of the house. I looked at my brothers who were inside and they looked at me as if I was a ghost. They thought they had been forgotten. I said, "Let's get the fuck out of here." Didn't have to repeat that order twice. The Lt started helping them grab their gear, and I went inside the house to make sure it was empty. There was a dead Iraqi in the back. Marines from the second floor were already on their way down. I asked if it was clear on the second deck. Some Marine said yes, but I went up to check it out anyway. It was. I went downstairs and into the back of the house and saw that one of the rooms was sandbagged up. The family that owned the house must have done it.

I started to leave and I walked out the front gate of the house. Some of the Marines that had been in the house were hunkered down in a line off the front end of the shot-up Amtrak. Small arms fire had them pinned down and they couldn't go forward. I did not know it at the time but some of them were down to their last ten rounds. I yelled at them to get the fuck on a HMMV. Someone asked which one. I told them any one, just get the fuck on one. As they started to load up I went to the back of the Amtrak to see if there were any wounded in there. Clothes, ammo, personal belongings, and body parts were everywhere. One Marine was headless and his back was split open like a loaf of bread, and I couldn't see the lower part of him.

I looked to my right briefly and I saw the front of a HMMV leaving, it was Day driving, heading right out of town. The CAAT vehicles to the north were leaving, too. Day, I guessed, thought I had given the order to move out. My first thought, though, was that he was leaving me. I saw another HMMV moving right behind my HMMV. I stopped that vehicle and jumped on the hood, and we made a run for the bridge. The Mystery Machine was starting to slow down. I saw Doc look at me and then yell at Day to keep moving. I was shooting my shotgun to the left, but switched to the right because the targets were closer and within range.

The 50 cal machine gun was barking away above me, shooting at some of the same people I was. I felt something hit my helmet then felt something warm on my neck. I thought I had been shot in the head but I was scared to touch the wound, thinking that if I knew how bad it was I would go into shock or start panicking. But then I thought, if I was having this conversation with myself then I was probably not shot. I reached up and pulled a piece of the machine gun's hot, spent brass from under the neck of my flak jacket. The hit had come from the turret swinging around so the gunner could engage other Iraqis. I started to laugh out loud as I was reloading. We left town a lot faster than we came in. We crossed back over the bridge and it started to get quiet again. The Lt and his other lead HMMV pulled into the southern part of the Battalion defense. The Mystery Machine, then Cpl "Big Will" Williams's vehicle, and then the last vehicle, with me on the hood, came into the northern part of the defense.

Things worked out well. We got the Marines out and none of us was killed doing it. Then someone came up and said we had left Poma behind. I said no, he was down on the south end with the Lt. Just as I said that, the Lt came up to me and told me that Poma was missing. He also said that he couldn't go back in because his machine gun was down and they were having trouble getting the other one up. I mumbled, "mother fuck" to myself. I told Day we were going back in, he nodded his head and looked back at the ground, Doc got in the back where he had been riding the whole time, smiling -- he was either ready to die or he was going crazy. I told the two SAW gunners, who had been smiling up until that time, not to get back in the vehicle cause they would not be going back in with us. No use in getting everyone killed -- I didn't think we were making it out this time. Doc and Day didn't think we would make it out either. Big Will walked up to me and said he and his other vehicle were going in with us. I said okay.

We headed back into town. It seemed quieter than the first time. The road sounded dull, Doc was praying in Spanish, and I was going over my "Hail Marys." Day was just staring out the front window. He asked me about how we were going to pull in to get Poma out. Fuck a plan --that was all we needed to fuck things up even better. I told him, "Mother fucker, can't you see I am Goddamn mother fucking praying over here?" Day started praying too.

We hit the top of the bridge again and all hell broke lose. The same two fucking anti-aircraft guns opened up on us to our left and our right. The 50 cal behind us silenced one of them, and that caused the other Iraqis to leave their anti-aircraft gun there and haul ass. My shotgun would not reach a soldier in a window on the second floor to our right. I grabbed Day's M-16 and unloaded a magazine at him. I saw some more people in another window and I unloaded a second magazine. We could see Poma from where we were. He was hunkered down behind the Amtrak. He was pinned, he couldn't move. Halfway to Poma the fire started to slow down, but as we started to get closer to him the enemy fire shifted from him to us. I guess they figured they had Poma sooner or later but weren't so sure about us.

We were spraying rounds everywhere. We pulled up in a small circle around the north side of the Amtrak. Poma had been part of the first rescue party and had gotten out of his vehicle to check a building for wounded Marines. He didn't make it back before his vehicle left. I did not realize that he had been left alone -- at the time I thought his whole vehicle had stayed behind.

I got out of the vehicle and went over to him and told him to get in his HMMV, which I told him was on the south side of the Amtrak. He left and came back and said it wasn't there. I told him to get in the back of mine then. I asked him if he had a hand grenade, and he said no. I really wanted to blow up the radio equipment in the back of that downed Amtrak. There was no way I could have climbed through the back of it because of all the equipment that was blown all over the place. The side of it was still hot from the RPG hit it took. I tried getting the dead Marine out of the Amtrak but I couldn't get to him. Some things are worse than dying. I got in my HMMV and Day started to drive off as Doc pulled Poma in. We headed back, firing every which way we could. As we started to reach the bridge we had the jump on the two machine guns that had greeted us on our way in. We got across the bridge without them firing on us.

We pulled into the Battalion defense and Poma went back to his Platoon. I went over to help Blackwell out with what I could, which was not much -- he had everything running the way he wanted it. There was not a Company Gunny's vehicle that did not have a bullet hole or blood from wounded Marines in it.

Doc Sabilla ran back over to the Aid Station and continued helping with the wounded. The Aid Station looked like it had been broken down into three groups: the wounded, the dying, and the dead. The dead lay in the clay sand, with torn ponchos covering them. One Marine was ghostly white. He had nothing but green shorts on and a large bandage over the lower part of his stomach. A Gunny from the AAVs was holding his hand and praying with him. There wasn't a corpsman working on him; maybe they thought he was not going to make it. I don't know what happened to him. I saw a Corpsman go over to a dead Marine and pull bandages off him, and place them on a Marine that was wounded and might live. There were no sterile gloves being used, no operating tables, not enough litters to keep the wounded off the ground, no bright lights to be sure of what they were doing. Just a bunch of Corpsman that actually cared about the Marines they were trying to save with what little they had.

The wooden box I had unloaded earlier was full of names, addresses, socials, weapons lists, maps and other crap. I had Day set the box on fire. I wanted it burned before the sun went down. I thought about the smoke giving away our position and looked around. Yea, like that would be a problem with all the burning Amtraks, helicopters, and shooting going on. The fuckers knew where we were.

A red smoke grenade popped out on the road. A group of helicopters came in and landed, the wounded and dead were dragged on board, and they flew off as quickly as they had come. We were alone again. 1$^{st}$ Sgt Thompson and I started talking. 81s might be ordered to move north and I wanted to go with them. I asked him if he would finish burning the stuff in the box. He said he would. 81s never ended up leaving then; no one did at the time.

By the time night came we had established a halfway decent perimeter for security. We were not organized enough to send out security patrols but we were organized enough to keep the enemy at bay. I had placed my prisoner in the back of my HMMV again, still bound. The whole time he would say something and then yell "bebe." I didn't know what he was talking about but he said this a lot when we picked him up in the garden. Fuck him, he was alive not everyone could say that.

We were tired but what had happened that day kept us up and our adrenaline running. I don't remember what time it was but it was dark when the word came down that we were going to move out. What the fuck! It was so dark you could not see your dick in your hand but they wanted us to move north. Then word came down they wanted us to go back into the city, then it changed to go back north. Day and I took the canvas off our HMMV and got in line on the road behind 81's Platoon.

It was stupid being on the road -- it sat higher than any other ground in the area. We were sitting ducks. Day asked again if we could get in the middle of the 81's Platoon. I said no, and made sure he didn't sneak us back into the middle this time.

We sat there looking through night vision equipment to our left and to our right. We would scrutinize every shadow, every rock, and of course every imagined movement. At one point I thought I spotted someone crouched besides a building and started to get Marines oriented in that direction. I was tired and I knew it so I got Gunny Leggett to double-check my work. It was a shadow he said. I took his word for it and stood everyone down but kept an eye on that fucking ghost for a good half hour.

Everyone knew it was foolish to be sitting on the road while waiting for the word to move out. If we were going to get shot up, we at least wanted to be on the move when it happened. I paced between Gunny Leggett's vehicle and mine. No one could keep still, but everyone had to stay in place near their vehicles or risk getting shot by another Marine.

The word finally came to move out. As we moved out, some Iraqi unit decided to move in. They never got close enough to do any damage -- tanks had spotted them first and had called in something. No one knew it was coming and I don't know if it was air or artillery, but whatever it was, if it scared them fucking Iraqis half as bad as it did us, then them fuckers were half-way to Baghdad before the ground stopped shaking. It landed close and gave enough light for me to see Doc's face. Someone said that it had hit a friendly Platoon. It hadn't, but it ended our night movement and we bedded back down for the rest of the night in the low ground off to the east side of the road. We set up security and hit the rack. Our lines were spread out thin.

Companies still could not account for where all their Marines were. Because of all the different med-evacs we had going out, leaders had just grabbed Marines inside the city to get them out of there and in some cases were still holding onto them. Our supplies were on the other side of An Nasiriyah and there was no way of getting to them. The only ammo, fuel, bandages, and rations we had was what had made it through town with us. Rumors were going around that someone saw the Iraqi soldiers executing our wounded Marines.

I kept a closer watch on my prisoner. I let him use my iso-mat to sleep on and gave him my poncho liner to use as a blanket. I leaned up against the rear HMMV tire and crossed my legs. I placed the barrel of my shotgun between my feet and covered the EPW, who was by my feet. We sat there and waited for the night attack that never came. None of us had to wake up the next morning because none of us went to sleep that night.

## 24 March 2003

Morning came and we were mentally fried to the bone. Bravo Company was tasked with taking the buildings to our north at the T-Intersection. I put my prisoner in the back of my vehicle, incase we got the word to move out quickly.

Up to this point I had written to my dad or Kelly every day. I didn't have the energy to write any more. I didn't think I would have the motivation to write for a while. What would I say? "Hey, we just got the shit shot out of us, we are separated from everyone else, and we're surrounded. Wish you were here!" I didn't have any last words to write to anyone, and even if I did, so what?

I had to go check on CAAT about a comm problem, so I told some guys from 81's Platoon to remove my prisoner from the vehicle and place him on a sleeping mat where he would be safer. As soon as they grabbed him out of the back of the HMMV he started crying and refusing to go. I guess he figured that if we were going to execute him he was going to get the last laugh and get blood all over the Mystery Machine. I walked over and helped him out of the vehicle. He dropped to his knees and tried to kiss my feet. Uhhh, no. I got him on his feet and placed him on the iso-mat. He started praying and talking that "bebe" shit again. I could understand his fear but some of the Marines were starting to feel sorry for him. They didn't want to harm him -- he had lost friends and had pained just as much as we had, but he didn't know that we thought that way. Don't misunderstand me, if that son-of-a-bitch had done something stupid no one would have hesitated to send him to the next world, several times over.

My prisoner got quiet, as always. I cut the binding on his wrists and tried to give him some water out of my canteen. He wouldn't drink it. I drank a little and tried again, and he drank. He wouldn't eat any food but I gave him some candy that my dad's girlfriend, Louise, had sent me in the mail. He ate a little. I smoked a cigarette and I could tell by the way he was watching it that he was having a nicotine attack. I laughed and gave him one. He smoked it down to the filter, and I gave him another one. He smoked the second one a little slower. He talked a little but I didn't understand what he was saying. I left him there under Doc's watch.

The mortar men had started to dig in deep. The area was trashed from mortar fibers, MREs, bandages, uniforms, gear, and vehicle parts. Charlie and Bravo Company pushed up to the north about 500 meters to a T-Intersection. Charlie was on the east and Bravo on the west. Captain Newland and 1st Sgt Parker from Bravo hooked their boys up. There was an old Iraqi Army Post on the southeast side of the intersection, which is where they were going to set up. They called in mortars and artillery and cleared out anything that was in there. After the fires stopped they moved into the buildings, which was a better set-up than being out in the open like the rest of us. It gave the Marines shelter from the sun and provided better cover from enemy fire.

Alpha Company moved to the south of our position and was facing back to the city. The COC had moved just south of the 81's position, which was great for me because it meant that Capt Rohr and Lt Barnhart would be close by to bullshit with and find out what was going on. CAAT was spread out all over God's creation. I never saw much of Hanson but Schielein and Lt Letendre were all over the place. The Logistics vehicles were still on the south side of An Nasiriyah and were not coming for a while.

As I started to go check on CAAT about their communications problem around 0800, Bravo Company spotted some movement about 1000 meters to our east. Schielein started to move his Section over with Bravo Company and took up a position along the wall inside their compound. A few minutes later a mortar barrage landed about 50 meters on the other side of the road from where we were sitting. When the Iraqis did this they gave their position away. Gunny Leggett took six M240 Machineguns and started firing on to their position. Lt Clayton worked up a fire mission and started laying in with Mortars. Lt Barnhart jumped on the hood of my HMMV and started looking for the fast movers that Capt Rohr had coming in for an air strike. I ate the peanut butter and crackers out of my MRE.

A minute later I could hear CAAT up north with Bravo Company letting lose with 50 cal and Mk 19 machine guns, with the occasional TOW round. CAAT Platoon on the whole was getting a reputation for shooting a lot of rounds unnecessarily. Not that they were shooting wildly, it's just that when they engaged someone, they engaged them without hesitation and at full throttle. Legalized murder, but that's what war is.

80

I didn't make the rules. I just know what they are.

If I had to go see CAAT, might as well do it while they were doing something interesting. Plus, I could confirm the reputation or not. Day and I jumped into the Mystery Machine and headed up the road to the compound to see CAAT. We parked our vehicle about 100 meters back from where they were firing because I didn't want the back-blast from the TOWs to fuck up our vehicle. The first vehicle I came to had Poma in it and he was firing away on the Iraqi mortar position. I jumped up on the vehicle and asked him casually what he was doing. He looked at me like I had a dick coming out of my forehead. He replied that he was killing "some Iraqis over there." I told him, "See? Not all Monday mornings are bad." He smiled and went back to shooting.

I found Schielein standing on the top of the HMMV with binoculars directing fire onto different buildings. Lt Letendre was reporting to higher about what was going on. Schielein had a smile on his face as he told me what was going on and that he was running low on MK19 ammo. I knew where there was some ammo but I didn't want to go.

Day and I headed back south and picked up Doc Sabilla, and we traveled past the COC -- but short of going past Alpha Company. Between the T-intersection and the north bridge, there was a bit of road that was not occupied by us. It was covered by fire but no one was really there. The area was where our Amtraks had been hit the day before. Day, Doc and I went into the Amtraks and pulled out the cans of MK19 ammo that didn't have major dents in them, thinking the ammo might still be useable. We picked up some t-shirts and rags off the ground to clean the blood and body parts off the cans as much as possible. I was ashamed of what we were doing. I didn't want to do it. This was the blood and body of my brothers. I felt that something more sacred should be done, like how we treat the Eucharist in Church. But there was no choice at that point.

We loaded the cans up into the HMMV and headed over to Schielein. I was fucking pissed. I knew we were low on ammo; fuck we were low on everything. I knew that Schielein was covering a lot of people's asses by moving around the battlefield like he did, unselfishly and without fear. But he was also firing rounds off at the maximum rate. I told him to cut the John Wayne crap out and conserve his ammo -- to only fire TOWs at vehicles, not at dirt houses. I finished off the ass chewing by telling him that his men had to clean the rest of the blood and body parts off those ammo cans, even though we had cleaned the cans well. He looked at me and said in a somber, relaxed voice, "No problem, pal." He knew what to say and how to say it. It was his way of telling me everything was all right.

We headed back over to the mortar position; they were still firing. Someone yelled that there was a white flag where the Iraqi position was, and then someone else yelled to keep firing. I heard that, and I ordered the firing to stop. Everyone looked at me like I was stupid, and I probably was. I am not without sin and my honor is as tattered as a battle flag, but on that day, on that battlefield, my unit was not going to lose its honor. They stopped firing.

Thirty minutes later, another barrage was fired at us from the position that had just surrendered. 81s returned fire and hit their ammo dump. There was a large explosion and we saw bodies running out of the trenches on fire. We let them burn. There was too much open ground to walk across in order to get to them, and besides, they had fired on us under a truce. Who says they wouldn't do it again.

The rest of the day was dog-eared with small firefights here and there. They would shoot at us and we would kill them -- payback was, and still is, a motherfucker. During one of these firefights, Sgt Rowe from Mortars was pumping rounds down-range at a building that had put one of the Companies under fire. One of our senior enlisted leaders walked up to him and told him he needed to stop firing his mortar and police-call the area. Without missing a beat in firing his mortar, Sgt Rowe said "no." The Marine walked off and sat in his HMMV.

The night came and security was better than the previous night, but everyone was uneasy. We got word that 400 Iraqis were heading south and would attack us tonight. I had my prisoner lying on my iso-mat, covered with my poncho liner again. He didn't try to talk much, which was good. I kept thinking about how I was going to handle him when we got attacked that night. I decided that if he acted quiet and just laid there, he would live. If he started acting up and endangering my brothers when the enemy came, I would kill him. We didn't sleep, waiting for the attack.

Late that night, with Bravo Company still in the compound to the north of our 81's position, some Battalion of the 1st Marine Division was going to come up through An Nasiriyah. Before they started out, they lit that fucker up with prep fires. I guess that Battalion had heard what happened to us in the town, and they had 1/10 throw artillery rounds down both sides of the street as they moved up while they pointed their guns out-board and shot at everything that was there and was not there. There was so much shit going off we thought there was another firefight going down. I heard later that not one round was shot at them. When they got over the north bridge to our side of town, they kept moving right up the middle of our position. They ceased fire before they got there though, thank God.

When they arrived at the T-intersection, the first vehicle of the unit moving through saw two Anti-Air Missile Marines moving around in the window of the third floor of the Iraqi compound. The Battalion fired at them with some 5.56 mm rounds. I saw and heard what happened back from the 81's position. Lt Barnhart came out and said they wanted us to go up there and med-evac some guy. We drove up the road and pulled into the driveway that went into the compound. Someone opened a gate for us and Day pulled to the side of a building and parked the vehicle.

The four of us went into the building to get this guy. It was dark as shit but I was paranoid of flashing a light because the convoy driving by might do the same thing again. We found the stairs and started running up; Doc kept hitting Day in the head with the stretcher. I could not help but laugh as I ran up with them. One of the Marines was on the 2 1/2-floor landing. He was not shot but he was in shock. Fuck him; he should not have been standing in the window. The second Marine was up on the third deck. 1$^{st}$ Sgt Parker had already kicked the corpsman off the wounded Marine and had taken over giving him first aid. He was also giving him an ass chewing for standing in the window, and was telling him he deserved to get shot for being stupid.

I started to help Parker. The bullet had gone through the Marine's shoulder and out his back. He started to whine about how it hurt and Parker told him to stop being such a little pussy and suck it the fuck up. This brought his whining to a low whimper. Parker asked the kid where he was from as he was sticking his finger in the hole in his back. The kid said some little fucking town, and Parker said he had been there and that it was all right. I asked him if it hurt and he said no it just stung a little bit. The Marine had been wearing a sappy plate, which is a piece of metal that slips in the middle of the flak jacket for extra protection, and the round had bounced off it. The Marine was lucky twice: first, it had not bounced off the plate into his head, and second, he was going home. I had not been wearing a sappy plate because it was heavy as shit and I hated the way it pulled on me to the front. After that I swore to myself I would get one.

Parker's hands and mine were covered in blood. The guy kept saying it hurt when Parker put a bandage or pressure on it to stop the bleeding. Parker told him again to shut up and quit his bitching. We got the kid up and I walked him down to the ambulance that was going to take him to BAS.

I started yelling at the corpsmen to open up the back. They said they couldn't put him back there because there wasn't any room. I asked why the fuck not -- this man was the only one wounded. One of the corpsman opened up the back to show me. All the litters and the walkway were full of the corpsmen's packs and shit. They had all their gear strewn all over the place. I cussed out the medical officer, telling him how fucked up it was that I had a shot Marine standing out in the cold in the middle of the night, and I couldn't put him in the back of the ambulance cause they had all their gear back there. He told me to wait a few minutes and he would fix it. I said fuck that, I would meet them at the BAS with the wounded Marine. I put the Marine in the back of another Amtrak and he was evac'ed to the BAS with the ambulance in trace. Parker was standing next to me now. I told him it was kind of ironic that he had known so much about that kid's hometown. Parker looked at me and said he had never been there, and then walked off into the night. Parker was quite the bullshitter.

Later, around midnight, the entertainment continued. We heard a high-pitched whining sound. It sounded familiar but I couldn't place it. It kept getting louder and louder. The whine it made was getting sharper. I got out of my poncho and walked to the road. Coming from the south was a small white headlight. It was a dispatch motorcycle and he was hauling ass. He was coming out of the Naz at a hundred miles an hour. He drove by me, throttle pegged, shoulders over the handlebars, head facing to the front, ass up in the air. I don't think he knew that other Marines surrounded him. I don't think he cared either; he just wanted to get as far from the city as he could. As soon as he passed me, his buddy came zooming along using the same techniques as he had. Even though we were waiting for an attack, I lay back down and started thinking of my motorcycle. I thought about how I had given Addie and Jennifer rides on the gas tank, and how good it was going to feel to cruise around Dallas with Kelly.

**25 March 2003**
The days started to wind into each other after a while. We were tired and everyone was just going through the motions of getting stuff done. MREs, which had always sucked, were not being eaten because people couldn't stomach the food any more. Those that did eat just ate a little. Marines would lie down for a while and rest without sleeping. No one was talking or joking around. We were beginning to show symptoms of combat fatigue. Life was about to get interesting.

Since MSgt Hendricks was with the Logistics vehicles on the other side of the town, I had been filling in as the Company 1$^{st}$ Sgt. One of my duties was to report to Capt Rohr and tell him how the Company was doing. This included morale, discipline, and the welfare of the Marines. It was pretty much the same thing every day; it all sucked ass, but even though it didn't change it gave him the warm fuzzy of what was going on. Since he was running the FSCC it really didn't leave him a lot of time to run around and see the Marines. He said that he wanted to kind of get away from the FSCC for a while, and he wanted to go with me when I re-supplied the platoons the next day. I was thinking it might be a bad idea because if he got shot, morale would fall like an Airborne Soldier without a parachute, and it couldn't get much lower than it was already. But seeing the Captain would be great for the Marines. Capt Rohr had always done what the Marines did, giving them instruction and leadership while allowing them to make mistakes. They respected him but they also really liked him. He didn't pal around with them or break any fraternization rules, but they considered him to be one of them. He told me to pick him up around 0800 -- that's when he would be getting off watch.

Bravo Company was tasked with going back into An Nasiriyah to look for the dead that had been left behind. For some reason the Battalion Commander wanted to go with them. I do know why -- those were his men. But still, if he got himself killed we were all fucked. Parker asked me if I wanted to go and I told him yes. I wasn't allowed to go, though. I thought about going anyway but I didn't want to make things worse than they already were.

Sgt Reiss was one of the Marines that Bravo Company found. I saw his body on the side of the road, covered by a green poncho. I could see the face of the Battalion Commander, LtCol Grabowski, and his face showed the strain of lack of sleep and the sadness of having one of his Marines die. I could see that even though he was a professional, he had taken the deaths of his Marines personally.

Reiss and I had known each other a couple of years before. At the time I first met him, he was a Private and I was his Platoon Commander. Sgt Reiss was a machine gunner by trade and in a Weapons Platoon, but when he picked up Cpl they sent him to Infantry Squad Leader School, where he did so well that when they needed a strong Sgt in a Rifle Platoon, they sent him. Reiss had the world by the tail. He was young, a Sgt, smart, physically fit, ambitious, ready to prove himself. He had a wife he loved and a child on the way. The only worry he had was whether he would be able to re-enlist in the Marine Corps. I honestly believed that we shared a sacred bond. I was Reiss' link to the way the Marine Corps was, and Reiss was my link to how the Marine Corps was going to be.

I couldn't approach Reiss lying there on the ground. I felt like he had followed me to hell and I had left him behind.

Iraqi civilians had found his body before the Iraqi military had had a chance to mutilate him. The civilians, not knowing if we were coming back for him, had cleaned him and given him a proper Muslim burial. They had placed his war gear over his grave as a tombstone. Not all the bodies that had been found were as well taken-care of as Reiss'. Two others were found mutilated under a bridge. EOD had been called out to make sure they were not booby-trapped.

I left early in the morning to re-supply CAAT. Our 81s were still set up in the same position. Lt Clayton and Gunny Leggett were thinking about moving the mortar position because they knew that by then the fucking Iraqis had to have their position identified, and it would only be a matter of time before they started shelling them. Other units were pushing through our position to go north. At one point a convoy stopped. It was an infantry battalion, and even though I didn't know what Battalion it was for sure, it was their 81mm Mortar Platoon. As the convoy stopped, the Marines in the convoy stood up and started applauding the 81's Platoon from 1/2. One of their Marines said that they had heard about the way that our 81s had fought and what they did. New York City, with all the confetti in the world, could not have said thank you or meant as much to our 81s as the Marines that were with us saying "good job." I pulled up as the convoy was leaving, and I could see a difference in the Platoon. It was a mellow sadness but with an air of victory that said "we did it, and we were not alone."

It was still morning, and as all this was going on, 2nd Platoon from Bravo Company was sent down to replace Alpha Company at the north bridge, and Alpha Company was given marching orders. They were to go to the road intersection where Charlie and Alpha were, and then go west to another road intersection. I wondered what the fuck we were doing. We had one Company all alone to our west with about 2 miles of open, unguarded road between them and us. The two Companies we did have together were covering a lot of ground. The Marines of Charlie Company didn't have any gear. They were sleeping in the rain and dust storms out in the open. So you know security was going to suck wherever they were. And we had one Platoon and some tanks facing the whole city of An Nasiriyah. The tank Plt Sgt was GySgt "Father Time" Howard. I had not met him yet, but the stories I heard said he wasn't fucking around.

We were spread so thin. But in retrospect, it made sense. It's as if we had turned on a kitchen light by doing what we did. We caused the fucking cockroaches to scatter. By spreading out, we had just turned on more lights. If the Iraqis tried to run north out of the city, using either of the two roads leading out, then they had to go through us. If they were going south, then 3/2 and 2/8 were there waiting for them.

I put my prisoner on the iso-mat again. His feet were torn up. He was found barefoot and he remained barefoot. I tried to pour water on his feet so Doc could check to see if they were as bad as they looked. He jerked back and started praying again. I prayed a lot too, but at that point I thought he was over-doing it. I mean, he was alive, wasn't he?

I ran into Capt Rohr in the afternoon. He was on watch for eight hours and then off for sixteen. He said he wanted to recon some things around the area the next day. We started to talk, and he told me we were fighting Fedayeen (Iranians who fought against Iran in the Iran-Iraq war), a brigade of republican guard, mercenaries from Jordan, Afghanistan, Saudi, and Syria, plus they had armed the civilians. That explained a lot. He also said that our counter-battery radar unit was picking up a lot of red rings. I had never heard of red rings. He said it meant that the Iraqi army was mortaring the civilians who were refusing to fight us. In other words, the town was revolting against the Army. Fucking bastards.

I was walking back to my HMMV to tell Day and Doc what I had heard from Captain Rohr when I saw Schielein waiting for me, halfway between the two points. I thought I would tell him what I heard, so I walked over to him. I started to talk, and he asked me if I had heard about Jordan. I said no. In a monotone voice he said Jordan was dead. He turned and slowly walked off.

I went over to find Parker at Bravo Company's position. He was standing at a building that served as a security building for the compound that his Company now occupied. There were rows of prisoners inside a concertinaed area. I went up to Parker and asked him if we could talk in the small building behind him. He said sure. I told him I couldn't take this shit anymore. He listened to me and didn't say a word. When I was done, he said we would be home some day.

At night, when the lights were out, the fucking Iraqi cockroaches came back out. They came in from the north and moved in between Charlie and Alpha Company, on that unprotected two-mile road front. A convoy was driving between the two Companies and got lit up with some heavy-duty machine guns from some buildings on the north side of the road.

That night, I had to report some word to Capt Rohr about our supply situation when in casual conversation he mentioned that Alpha Company, which was on the other end of that two-mile stretch of road, needed to be re-supplied. I volunteered. I knew where they were even though I had not been there. He said, "I don't know why I am even considering this." It was late into the night by then and he wanted me to go pick up the Company Commanders from Charlie and Alpha Companies for a meeting. I picked up the Company Commander from Charlie, Capt Wittman, and the subject of re-supplying Alpha Company came up. He said that he would go with us to make sure we knew where we were going. He also said we should expect heavy gunfire from the north. We then picked up Capt Newland from Bravo Company and went back to the COC. About midnight we got the word we were moving out with some supplies for Alpha. Just as we started to leave the mission got cancelled by the Battalion Commander. He said Alpha would have to stick it out for the night. So they stuck it out.

Before I had left to get ready to deliver supplies to Alpha Company, I had staged my trailer and HMMV with Day and Doc at the 81's Platoon position. When the mission didn't go, I walked back over to 81s to pass the word and hit the rack. When I got there, Day, Doc, HMMV, and trailer were all gone. I asked Gunny Leggett where everyone was and he said that Lt Clayton had borrowed them. Okay, I guess. About a half-hour later, Lt Clayton showed up with my trailer, loaded to the brim with Iraqi mortar and artillery rounds. I couldn't help but laugh and ask what the fuck. Someone had come by and told them that there had been some ammo found in an open field to our west. Our biggest fear was that the Iraqis would slip in behind us to a cached ammo and weapon point and attack us. He went to gather the ammo up before they could use it. It took balls to do what he did, but the number of rounds he gathered was crazy. I needed to empty the trailer but I didn't want to unload the rounds in our position, in case we got an indirect round into the pile. So I decided to go to drop them off in some low ground close by to our east.

Lt Clayton got on the hook and told higher to tell everyone that we would be moving outside friendly lines. We couldn't get the vehicle over the dune to the lower land, and when we drove over uneven ground the trailer would start to crack from all the weight of the rounds. So we had to hand-carry the rounds from the trailer to the low ground. Lt Clayton and Gunny Leggett gave me about thirty Marines to help. We put out security and started a human chain for unloading. It took hours, but we got some help from a friendly unit to our south. After about thirty minutes into unloading, a stream of tracers flew over our heads and we all hit the deck. I yelled for Day to get Lt Clayton to tell the friendly unit to our south to stop firing at us. After a few minutes the fire ceased, but it really sped things up a bit -- not only was there the possibility of being shot at from the enemy, but from friendlies too.

**26 March 2003**
Early that next morning, before the sun came up, Alpha Company got hit. Yea, the Battalion was turning on a lot of lights. Some Iraqi officers and senior enlisted had decided to get into their vehicles with civilians, and try to make a break for it through Alpha Company. The fuckers started firing and speeding up through the roadblocks, and the Marines let loose a wall of lead in every direction. It wasn't until daylight that the Marines could see what they had killed.

I picked up Capt Rohr at 0800 as planned and headed over to Alpha Company's position. As we pulled up, CAAT was digging graves with

Schielein. At first I thought they had really mowed them fuckers in half because the graves were so small, but as I walked up I saw the Marines crying. The Goddamn Iraqi motherfuckers had put children in the vehicles with them. Fucking children. The Marines would have rather died themselves than kill those children, but what was done was done. Schielein was mad; he was starting to lose it mentally because he had been on the edge so long. He wasn't so bad that the Marines knew it, but I could tell. We talked a while and he went back to burying bodies.

Finally, 81s displaced by Section to a new position. I liked hanging around them, but if they did not move away from the COC -- and they had to have been targeted by now -- I was going to have to move out on my own. The Lt and Gunny found an awesome place to move the Platoon to. It was across the street and right behind Charlie Company in some low ground with dunes around it.

Charlie Company was missing a lot of gear because of their fight in the city. Those Marines were sleeping on the ground without anything between them and the dirt, with no blankets to cover themselves, and with no water because they didn't have any canteens. The only thing they had a lot of was guts because they were sucking it up and not bitching. Lt Barnhart told me I needed to go back down to the Amtraks that had been hit and gather up any extra gear that could be found. I didn't want to do it but I knew it had to be done. If gathering and cleaning the ammo had about pushed me over the edge, I knew this would do it for sure. Doc and Day loaded into the Mystery Machine and we headed south.

The fucked-up Amtraks were north of Bravo Company's 2$^{nd}$ Platoon, and with them were four tanks so it was a safe area. As we were driving down, we were stopped by a Lt that I knew all too well. He said he was going with me and that he would be taking his own vehicle and Marines for security. He said he would do the coordination with the Tanks and 2$^{nd}$ Platoon. He also wanted a small security patrol sent out while we went through the Amtraks and he would lead the patrol. I didn't like this Lt so I kept Day and Doc as far away from him as I possibly could.

We pulled up to the first Amtrak and off-loaded. The Lt left to take care of coordination with the Tank Platoon with a Rifle Platoon from Alpha Company. There were about five of us pulling gear out of the Amtraks and gathering gear from around them. We were putting it all into a pile. The Lt came back and told me he had set two of our Marines, with claymores, down south of us about 50 meters for security. He also was going to lead a patrol, consisting of him and one other Marine, to the other side of a sewage creek. I told him that no one in Battalion had been issued claymores. He said he knew what a claymore looked like and left out on patrol. By now we had most of the gear in a pile. I started a small fire with some paper, lighter fluid, and matches that I had found in the gear. I told the Marines that everything not military was to be burned, and I stressed *everything*. I don't think the Marines understood why I had built that fire but I could see in Cpl Day's face that he did.

As the Marines were going through the MOLLIE packs, they found a lot of personal stuff: pictures of friends and family, letters and cards saying "we are proud of you son," walkmans, and books. All of it went into the fire. By one of the wheels on the track, I found two satanic bibles and a Holy Bible with a rosary. I threw the satanic shit into the fire and I kept the Bible and rosary. Once all the personal shit was burned, we went through the military gear and cut out the names that were on it. This gear had belonged to Marines who were now dead, and it was going to go to their brothers who needed the gear to survive. One of the Marines with us was asking me how he should cut off a name so it didn't ruin the gear. I looked at the gear and started to tell the Marine how to do it. I could see his eyes were getting red and watery. He didn't like doing this any more than I did.

There were dogs everywhere and I knew they had been feeding on small body parts that we had not found. We moved to a second Amtrak and started gathering what we could. By then we had enough gear, if not all of it, and the Lt was back off patrol. I told him we had enough and that we should head back. He said no, there was one more Amtrak to search. I told him that I had already been to that Amtrak the other day looking for ammo and everything was burned up. I didn't tell him that this was also where I had heard that Jordan died, and I didn't want to go over there. I could see from where I was that the Amtrak had burned to the ground, and it was obvious that nothing was there. He insisted that we check it out, so we went. We walked up to it and there was nothing in there or in the area around it.

We started to head back up the small hill to the road where our HMMVs were. On the way up, the Lt started yelling at the top of his lungs, "Lets go!" and pointing out to the field to our west. I asked what was going on because he had gotten everyone including Doc worked up, and for Doc to be worked up, that meant something. I saw two Marines in the bush next to the sewage creek. I ran out to get them and bring them in. They were the two Marines that the Lt had said he had set in as security. As I grabbed them I told them, "Lets go, something is going on." They picked up and followed me. Lt Stewart, the Platoon Commander from 2$^{nd}$ Platoon, ran up to us as we were running out and asked me what I was doing. I told him that I was pulling in my security. He said that it was his security -- it was LCpl Schell and Sitarek. The Lt ran up to me and I asked, "Hey Sir, is this the security you told me you set in?" He said that the two Marines belonged to 2$^{nd}$ Platoon. I asked him where the fuck our security was, which he had told me he set in. He said that he had made a mistake about that. I asked him about the claymores, and he said that he was wrong about that too -- there weren't any claymores, just empty ammo cans. Then I asked him what the fuck he was pointing and yelling at. He said he had seen some wild dogs and wanted to get everyone in before they got too close. I told him if he hadn't noticed there were more wild dogs than people here and that unlike the dogs, we were armed.

I apologized to Lt Stewart and walked up to the vehicles. At the HMMV was SSgt Jones. I didn't really know Jones but I did know that he was a brother to all Marines. He looked at me and asked if everything was okay. I told him to hold my shotgun, which he did. I took my helmet off and started to beat the living crap out of my vehicle with it. The Lt walked up like he had something to say. I gave him one look and he went away. The fucker had endangered us all. He was cocky and arrogant. Fuck him. We went back to the Battalion area. He and his vehicle went their way and the Mystery Machine and I went ours, to Charlie Company.

We pulled up to Charlie's Command Post where I thought Blackwell would be so that we could deliver the gear. I stopped the vehicle short and walked up, and I found Blackwell standing by the hood of his HMMV. I couldn't look him in the face. I told him that I had extra gear. He smiled and said thanks. He would definitely take it. Then I told him what my orders had been, and where I had gotten them. He paused and was very somber. We stood there for what seemed like a few minutes and he asked what some of the names were. I felt ashamed and I didn't want to talk. The names came out slowly. He shook his head every once in a while. The names ended, I couldn't remember any more. Blackwell called for a few Marines to unload our vehicle. I called Day over to pull up closer so no one would see what we were doing. The vehicle was unloaded and we left.

The chaplain ran into me later on in the day at the Battalion COC. I gave him the Bible and rosary. Lt Barnhart called me over and told me that they were gathering up prisoners to our south. So I went back to my HMMV to collect my EPW and turn him in. I felt like I was taking an old friend to a bus station so he could go home. We drove south and pulled off to the east side of the road where a bunch of EPWs were gathered up – they were being guarded and they were sitting on the ground. I walked up to a Marine who was a translator and handed over my prisoner. I asked him what "bebe" meant. He told me it meant "baby." I guess every time he thought we were going to execute him, which was every time we moved him, he would ask us not to execute him cause he had a child. When we left, he had a scared look in his face, like he did not want us to go.

I saw Lt Seeley for a brief moment. He was riding shotgun in a HMMV headed away from the Battalion COC and back to Charlie Company. I was walking across some open ground to see Capt Rohr and Lt Barnhart. I started to wave at him at the same time he started waving at me. His hand reached outside the window of the HMMV, his fingers spread out, giving the impression less of a wave than of an empty grasping. It looked as if he was reaching for something lost, and he hoped that he would find it in the palm of his hand. I grasped into the air searching for the same thing.

**27 March 2003**
The Mystery Machine was parked behind the 81 Mortar position, as always. Doc, Day, and I went through our daily routine. We would pack all our gear up, stand to, and then when it was daylight we would go back to sleep. My next reveille would be whenever I thought I had to get up because everyone else was up and I felt lazy. The three of us would shave (if it was a shave day), eat, and then Doc and I would start to make our coffee separately but end up doing it together because one of us couldn't get a fire going.

So around 0730, with all this done, I drove across the street to the COC and FSCC, which was in the first building of the Iraqi Army compound, and waited for Capt Rohr to get off his watch and turn it over to Lt Barnhart. The Captain looked tired as shit. We got in the HMMV and went to 81s first because they were the closest. He walked around the Platoon for a while and then we moved south to where Bravo Co 2nd Platoon was. We had a CAAT team down there. After we left there we found two more CAAT teams that were moving around the area. All this was in a pretty secure area.

Then we had to move west to Alpha Company. Our weapons went outboard and we were actually looking for shit while Day drove as fast as humanly possible. The Captain was digging it. He wasn't war-mongering it. He was just like the rest of us -- he enjoyed the camaraderie of living on the edge with his brothers. We got to Alpha and he looked a lot better, more awake. We moved up and down the line looking for Schielein. At first we couldn't find him, which was no big deal. When we did find him he and the Captain talked for a while. I bounced around from vehicle to vehicle talking to the other Marines.

We returned to the COC and the logistic vehicles from the other side of the city showed up with ammo. Along with the logistics vehicle came rumor. I loved rumor. Rumors were possibilities and the possibilities were endless. Rumors started again that a hospital in town was holding some Army POWs, and that one of them might be a female. Rumor also said some other things that we hoped were not true.

### 28 March 2003
This day was like the rest. I wondered a lot about what Kelly was doing. I wanted to talk to her, write her, just stand beside her, but I felt so far away, not in terms of distance, but just me. I...wanted to lie beside her and say nothing. I didn't want to tell her what was going on. We have killed so many people, and we should all be dead now. I did not know what to write to her or my dad.

Alpha Company, with Schielein, was shooting a lot of Iraqis over by the T-intersection off to our east. The bitch of it was that the Iraqi soldiers were doing the cockroach thing and still using civilians as protection.

Captain Rohr called me up and wanted me to take him over to the Intersection where CAAT was. So I picked him up at the Battalion COC, which was at the Iraqi military compound. While we were walking to the Mystery Machine we kind of looked around at our surroundings. We both commented how it looked like the battle scene in *Full Metal Jacket*.

There were a bunch of antennas sticking in the air north of the T-intersection that Alpha Company was at, and he wanted to see what was going on with them. We headed over. Day parked the Mystery Machine at the T-intersection, and the Captain went to tell the CO from Alpha Company where we would be and what we would be doing.

The only thing friendly in that area was a team of snipers in a house. There was a 100 by 100 meter area that had a vehicle compound on the northeast corner. Across the street from the compound, on the northwest side, there was a compound that had been used to train female terrorists. Alpha had cleared out the area already and had found a fuck load of weapons. They thought they found most of them but were not sure.

The Captain returned and we headed out. As we walked through the vehicle compound we saw some earthmovers and dump trucks. The Captain said it would be awesome if we could get them started and use them to help dig holes and move the obstacles around our area. I agreed, so the four of us kind of fucked around with the vehicles a little, gave up too quickly, and moved over to the antennas the Captain had seen. I yelled up to the snipers in the back of the building that we were moving forward of their position. They asked exactly where and I told them I didn't fucking know, just don't shoot me. The redheaded sniper laughed and we moved out. The only reason I did not go into the building was because those crazy cocksuckers probably had the whole building booby-trapped.

We went through what looked to be a small cooking compound with a garden just north of it, irrigation ditches and all. It was so peaceful. As we were looking around we heard a noise. It was some looters stealing some old food. More power to them. One of the guys approached Captain Rohr while I was standing back a ways. The other looters continued to pillage what they could and I didn't know where Doc and Day were. Life was getting interesting again, but not to our benefit. I watched while the Captain talked to this guy, and I waited for the guy to do something stupid so I would have a reason to kill him. I remember thinking back to a line in that movie *Major Payne* where he goes "it had been two whole weeks since I killed a man and I was starting to get the itch." The two of them got through talking and the looter left the area.

As soon as it was over, Day and Doc showed up. We shifted through some buildings and a few bomb shelters, if you could call them bomb shelters. I had seen better shelter at hand grenade ranges in South America. We finally came upon two vehicles that had the antennas running up to them. One was locked up and the other was open. I had knucklehead one and knucklehead two wait outside as the Captain and I went into the unlocked vehicle. Of course he did the officer thing and looked for intelligence information, and I did the enlisted thing and looked for a gift that Kelly might like. He found a shit load of documents and I found a gray beret with some emblem of an eagle on it. The Captain thought the intelligence officer would like the paperwork and I thought Kelly would like the beret. We both left the vehicle rather pleased with ourselves.

On the way back we stopped by the vehicle that was locked up and for the first time I saw Captain Rohr get "downtown." He pulled out his K-bar and sliced all the tires on the vehicle. I know he saw this shocked look on my face cause all he did was reply, "I'm just a Jersey boy at heart." Roger fucking that. We headed back to the Mystery Machine and I saw an anvil on a table. It reminded me of when I was a kid watching a man shoe horses at the ranch where I worked. I stopped and ran my hands over the anvil. I felt something on the other side. I looked, and part of the anvil -- not added on, but a forged part of it -- was a swastika. A fucking swastika! All I could think of was some psycho stupid fuck who didn't realize that World War II was over giving me thousands of dollars for it. I started to lift it for the two hundred meter trek back to the HMMV. Fuck it was heavy. I set it down and thought for a moment. Fuck the Third Reich and fuck that weirdo who would pay me a thousand dollars. That thing was heavy and I wasn't carrying it.

We arrived at the Mystery Machine, checked out with the CO from Alpha, and headed back home. I told She-bitch (Schielein) on the way out that I would be back later to re-supply him. He said he needed trash bags and MOPP gloves. I asked why. The gloves were for picking up the dead bodies, and the bags were for burying them in – and he had run out of both.

I came back later and re-supplied CAAT with ammo, food, water, fuel, trash bags and gloves. I wondered how long the gloves would last till they ran out.

### 29 March 2003
Today was my brother's birthday. I took an MRE and wrote "Happy Birthday" on one side and his address on the other. Nothing else to write, nothing else to think about, nothing else to do. But I didn't send it.

Captain Rohr was going crazy in the COC so I went by again to pick him up for another excursion into the wilderness. I had been sleeping with

81s and every morning was the same. I would wake up and shave, eat, and go back to sleep. We headed over a little earlier than usual and I ran into Lt Barnhart. We got into the back of his vehicle and had a smoke and a joke. We got on the subject of awards and talked a little about it. Schielein would be put up for the Silver Star -- apparently he was shooting a rifle in one hand and a pistol in another while directing the CAAT Section. Lt Letendre and Lt Clayton were both getting a Bronze Star. He said they were going for the stars on me. I didn't know what he meant, and left it at that.

By that time Captain Rohr was ready to go so we loaded up and headed out to Alpha Company. We pulled up and parked at the same point as yesterday and again Captain Rohr checked in with the Alpha Company CO, and again he would check out when we left. We started moving through the vehicle compound. The Captain said he wanted to find an earthmover or something we could dig holes with. We all kind of spread out over the area, jumping in and out of vehicles looking for something that might have a chance to do the job. The Captain said he should get Gunny Tyre over there so he could find something.

If anyone could get anything running it was Gunny Tyre; that old hick bastard could get a car to go a hundred miles without any gas. He was that kind of determined and dedicated man. He had already retired from the Marine Corps when our unit was called up to move out. They asked him if he wanted to go or not. He said yes. He said he wanted to take care of his boys, so he did. I have heard some Marines say, "Those are not your Marines, they are the Marine Corps." Uhhhh, bullshit. You make sure they are fed, covered, trained properly, you try to keep them morally straight, and they belong to you. And you then belong to them.

I found an earthmover that had a small green light turn on when I wiggled a switch. I yelled for everyone to come over and look. I started pulling off panels and shit trying to start the damn thing, like I knew what I was doing. Doc and Day got bored with watching me try to start the thing. I got pissed and shoved a screwdriver into the ignition. The Jersey boy was coming back into the Captain, cause he seemed to agree that breaking the ignition like that would fix it. And it did -- that bitch started right up. Day had a "what the fuck" look on his face and Doc looked like he had a new toy to play with. I screwed with the controls a little bit -- it was not hard to figure things out, it was all in English -- and got the thing moving. John Deere never looked better.

By the time I pulled out of the vehicle lot I had gotten it figured out. We pulled an American flag out of the Mystery Machine and the Captain tied it to the back of the earthmover. The Mystery was in front as we drove down the road back to our position. Captain Rohr was riding with me, which made me slow down a little. I was thinking that Mrs. Rohr would be mad at me if I got into an accident and got her husband hurt. Driving down the road with that thing was a morale booster. Some Marines stood up and watched and a Motor-T mechanic wanted to play with it, but when we pulled up into 81's position with it they just rolled with laughter. I don't know why it was so funny, it just was.

I started to dig a hole with the thing and while I was digging something started going click on it. I had busted it somehow. Don't know how, but I am a true Grunt so I managed somehow to do it. I drove it over to Motor-T and gave it to the mechanic who had wanted to play with it. He looked at it and told me he could fix it. I left it there on the side of the road and walked over to where Doc and Day were. One of the Mortar men said he could have told me I was going to break it. I asked him why he didn't. He said I looked like I was having so much fun he didn't want to stop me.

The Captain told me we were going back out tomorrow. He wanted to look at a bridge that was south of Alpha. Fucking bridges. But also that afternoon he wanted me to take some Intelligence and EOD Marines to the Iraqi communication site and show them where everything was. He also said that I was not to tell anyone that he was out there. He was afraid that if the Battalion Commander found out that he was running around in Hadji territory, the BC would take away his fun time.

That afternoon we picked up these guys and headed back over to Alpha. The Intelligence Captain that was with us seemed to want to do everything by the book. I did not mind going anywhere with Captain Rohr, cause it was Captain Rohr. But going outside friendly lines with these guys was a little different. I started to walk over and tell the Alpha CO we would be in the area up north. The Intelligence Captain stopped me and said that since he was the senior man he would do it. Fine with me, I would sit on my ass and let him walk the 200 meters. The EOD guys looked bored and the other Intel Marine looked excited, like he was about to get into the shit.

The Intel Captain came back and I pointed to where the antennas were. We started to move out on foot when he said he wanted to drive there. I told him the only way to get our vehicles in there would be to go north on the road for about 400 meters or so. And to do that, we would have to drive by an area that was not secure to our west. He said he didn't care, and we were to drive. I said I would walk down the road with my two guys and he could drive behind me on the road. He said I should be in my vehicle. I told him no, and that if he wanted to be stuck in a vehicle while being shot at, that it was his decision, but I wasn't doing it. The SSgt with EOD gave me one of his Sgts to walk with me up front. When I started walking with Day, Doc, and the Sergeant from EOD, the Captain got in his vehicle and was telling me that I was stupid. Yea, I might be stupid, but I was alive and planned on staying that way.

We walked down the east side of the road heading north. The Iraqi compound for training terrorists ended right at the point where we had to turn east. I set up security at the corner facing north and west. I saw some Iraqi men and women cross the street that we were looking down and then they ran into the compound. No problem. The Captain's vehicle and the EOD vehicle both pulled in behind us and headed east to the garden and the two vehicles with antennas. We started to follow them and then the group of Iraqis that had just run across the road came out of the building to our west. They had weapons. I yelled at the three Marines to kill them. The Marines looked at me like they did not understand. I took my shotgun, even though I was out of range, and fired at the Iraqis. The Marines then took their cue. Day dropped to one knee for better stability, the Sgt dropped his war gear off his shoulder to get a better stock weld with his weapon, Doc just aimed in the best he could, and we started killing the men and women that had weapons. They must not have seen us cause they did not start running across the street till I shot at them. When we were done, we turned back into the garden to finish what we had to do.

The Captain never asked what we were shooting at. I showed him the first vehicle. It was down a small path that was shaded by trees and high vegetation. It was the vehicle where I had found the beret for Kelly. The Intel guys rooted around for a while. The EOD guys blew it up. We moved down to the second vehicle, which was in a more open area. Off to the north about 500 meters was a small cluster of buildings on line. I put Day and Doc on that. EOD put some charges on the back hatch of the vehicle and blew it. Intel went inside and rooted around some more. Intel did not find anything, or if they did they did not tell me. We all headed back to our vehicles, which were parked in the garden. EOD stayed back and blew up the vehicle that Captain Rohr had sliced the tires on. We left the same as we came. The only difference was that the three other Marines and I were walking in the rear.

When we got back to Alpha Company, the Captain checked out with the CO and we left. Later, when I did my re-supply to CAAT, Alpha's CO asked me what was going on with the shooting earlier. I told him what had happened. He asked me why I did not debrief him on that earlier. I told him that I thought the Intel Captain would have done that -- I mean he was intelligence after all. The Captain laughed a little and said, "Well next time make sure YOU debrief me." I told him "Roger that." I fucked up and should have checked in with him. I had killed people and had ordered people killed and had never given a second thought about having to report it. I guess killing had become routine by then. It was just something we did.

### 30 March 2003
Again we all awoke and stood to. I was to pick up Captain Rohr that morning, again. I went over to the Battalion COC. I saw the Chaplin and asked Father Hoedl if I could have confession real quick. He said no problem. I gave him my confession. He gave me three Hail Marys as retribution. I must have had a dumb-founded look on my face, like, that's it? He said he had heard what I did, getting the Marines out of Ambush Alley and all I had to do was -- three Hail Marys. Master Sgt Hendricks walked up and saw me talking to the Father so he started to turn away, but I told him to hang on. The Father gave me the Eucharist and the three of us talked a while.

Father Hoedl was called away and Hendricks, who was the acting First Sgt, said they were sending Gunny Hanson to Charlie Company to be the Weapons Platoon Sgt because he was the junior GySgt. He would be taking SSgt Jordan's spot in Charlie. No one could take Jordan's place -- they might fill the billet but they would never be able to fill his shoes. Gunny Hanson had his work cut out for him. So I asked if they were going to make Schielein the Platoon Sgt for CAAT. He said no, they were thinking about making me the Plt Sgt for CAAT, since that's what I had been promised on ship. I thought it was cool but I did not know how the Platoon would take me. Not because I was taking Hanson's place, but because I did not know if their brotherhood would have room for me.

I went over to First Sgt Parker to see what he was up to. Parker and I would always talk about the same things that Schielein and I talked about: family and motorcycles. And I would always talk about Kelly. That was a given.

Captain Rohr found Parker and me and said he was ready to go check out the bridge. We got Master Sgt Hendricks and off we went again to Alpha's position. But this time we went south instead of north. People were being allowed to use the intersection to travel north and south. Somewhere in the middle of Alpha's position they had a shit load of prisoners. Some Marines who were interrogators by trade were talking to them one by one. We drove through Alpha's lines and headed south. We got to two bridges that were side by side. Captain Rohr got a plugger reading for the bridge. He said that they were going to call artillery or air on the bridge to destroy it in order to cut back on the traffic going through Alpha's position. There was a hotel-looking building off in the distance. Someone told me it was a hospital.

At one point I was looking at a stick that was poking out of the water near the bridge. I just stared at it. Day walked up and he was kind of excited for some reason. He looked at the river and said, "yea, that's just a stick poking out of the river." For some reason I went off on him. I didn't know why. I still don't. I just did.

After the Captain got what he needed, we left the area and headed back to the middle of Alpha's position. Master Sgt Hendricks said he wanted to check on the Marines since he had not seen them in a couple of days. There was a building off to the east that looked like a gas station. The Captain and I checked it out. Of course if there had been anything worth a shit it would have already been gone.

When we got back to the Humvee a bunch of Marines from CAAT had gathered around the Mystery Machine and were talking to Day. They were all in a pretty good mood. One of the Marines gave me a pack of Iraqi cigarettes. Hendricks returned and we headed out. The Captain wanted to go to the bridge that went over the Saddam Canal.

We drove over to the bridge and parked just north of it. Captain Newland was there because one of his Platoons had been attached to Tank Platoon. First Sgt Parker was yelling at Platoon Sgts to get their boys to take cover down at the river bank, and he was yelling at a Sgt to stop pulling his whole squad together to pass the word. He was not in a good mood.

There was a two-foot wide water pipe that ran across the bridge. It was cracked and water was spraying all over the place. Captain Newland was telling Captain Rohr that the civilians were bitching about the town not having water, but they kept breaking the pipes to get at the water so they could never get the water to the other part of town. He also said that there were fighting positions along the south side of the river that had weapons in them. Children were being sent to get the ammo out of the holes and go back into the city. He wanted to blow the holes. He didn't want to shoot the children getting the ammo, but he also did not want the ammo to turn around and be used on his men. The two kept talking as I watched everyone around me digging in and setting up their defenses. Parker had all the Platoon Sgts around him and he was chewing their asses again. I saw Jones and he looked like he was the only one not being defensive about what Parker was saying.

I looked into the city and I saw a man (if you could call him a man) walk up to a Marine at the south end of the bridge. The "man" was carrying a child in front of him so that no one would shoot him. What a fuck stick. Off to my east was a small group of people traveling north and south. Hendricks said that Snipers had been taking shots at soldiers in that area for the past couple of days. I was getting bored. We left the area as the sun went down.

Like every other night, I found Leggett and Lt Clayton and we bullshit for a while. We talked about up-coming missions and what everyone else was doing. Leggett and I said we wondered where we were going next. Lt Clayton said, "We don't have to fight the whole war ourselves." At first it kind of threw me a little, but he was right. There was no reason for us to go anywhere. All of a sudden it was nice right there where we were.

Picture of my Baptism at Camp Shoup Kuwait. (L to R)  My Godfather Lt Barnhart, me, LCpl Thornton, Doc Sabilla and Father Hoedl.

The gardens on the north side of Al Kut. (L to R) LCpl Cross, my radio operator, and our platoon Corpsman Doc.

One of my Marines of 2nd Platoon who came down with a late case of dysentery from the Iraqi Army Camp.  He is at the gardens in Al Kut.

Last day as CAAT Plt Sgt. Going through my gear before I step off to Bravo Company.

Master Sgt Hendricks at Camp Shoup inside our Weapons Company office.

Doing my monthly laundry in a MRE box at Camp Shoup.

Ceremony for the fallen Marines of 23 March 03.

Compound with the tree is where the stranded Marines were left behind. The blackened walls are all that remain from the RPG explosions when Iraqi forces tried to take the compound over.

North side of compound.

T-Intersection north of An Nasiriyah after the ceremony for the fallen Marines.

Building where we conducted road blocks in Al Kut. Notice the Iraqi & Kuwaiti flags on the building.

Early morning shave at the Mystery Machine. Doc and Day are eating breakfast in the back. Lt Barnhart can barely be seen standing on the hood. He is looking for Fast Movers (airplanes) that are about to straff an enemy position.

3rd Squad, 2nd Platoon, Bravo Company, 1st Battalion, 6th Marine Regiment that I led in the First Gulf War.

Capt Newland & 1st Sgt Parker on liberty at the wine garden in Spain.

GySgt Ingerson, Amtrak Plt Sgt, and all around moral booster.

GySgt Carrico at the T-Intersection at An Nasiriyah.

Bravo Company (L-R) 1st Lt. Judson Daniels, GySgt Rodney Carrico, Capt. Timothy Newland and 1st Sgt David Parker.

Lt. Beere during a company meeting on our way to Al Raleef.

Lt. Daniels in the Iraqi Army Compound North of An Nasariyah.

Lt. Garlock and me at a company meeting on our way to Al Raleef.

Picture of the 507th Maintenance that had been brought back to the Battalion COC for medevac.

1st Sgt. Parker, GySgt Carrico and Capt Newland at a Company Meeting on our way to Al Raleef.

In the middle is Sgt Lopez. Everybody in the picture knows why only his name is used.

Lt Moxey and me on the USS Kearsarge off the coast of Sierra Leonne.

# CAAT Platoon Sergeant
## Chapter 5

**31 March 2003**

Hendricks called me up on the radio and wanted to see me. I hoofed it on over. I ran into Captain Rohr. He told me that he was moving me over to CAAT Plt as the Platoon Sgt. Roger fucking that! A Gunny, who was the Admin Chief for the Battalion, was getting promoted to First Sgt so they were going to frock him and put him as the First Sgt for Weapons Company. Hendricks was going back to being Operations Chief, something he had not done since last December. He had helped me a lot, especially when it came to working with people outside the Company. Lt Letendre and Schielein already knew about the decision and had told the Platoon. Hendricks told me to send the Mystery Machine over to the Battalion COC. Hendricks, who had been pulling watch in the FSCC, wanted to keep Doc and Day over near where he was working. I walked back over to the Mystery Machine. I told Doc and Day what was going on. They didn't like it. It was not because they did not like Hendricks; they just liked the way I ran things -- I would travel to where the Platoons and Sections were to resupply them, rather than have them come to me. Everyone knew Hendricks would do it differently, not wrong, just different.

I had Day drive me over to the Intersection where Charlie Company was set up, where the Section I wanted to ride with was. CAAT was broken down into three sections of five vehicles each. I had called up Schielein, who was over at Alpha Company, to meet me over at Charlie's position.

He showed up before I did even though I was closer. The first thing out of his mouth was "What's up boss?" He asked me if I wanted his vehicle, and I told him no. His vehicle had a Blue Force Tracker and you could navigate in it without a map. As a Platoon Sgt I could have taken his vehicle but I could navigate by making my own maps and using a compass and a plugger. I figured I would take the maps that I had, turn them sideways, and number the grid lines in the direction the Battalion would be traveling. I could then plot the checkpoints on the map. Using the plugger, I could plot my position and as long as we headed in the right direction (compass) everything would be okay.

I put my stuff in Martinez and Pulliam's vehicle. Martinez was my driver and Pulliam was up in the turret. By now CAAT's vehicles were starting to fall apart. The rear hatches on the vehicles either couldn't be shut at all or, if you did shut one, you had to crawl underneath it inside the vehicle to open it back up. With all the gear in the vehicle, that was impossible. So the solution was to get rid of the rear hatches. Not all the vehicles had this problem but a lot did. The ones that had lost the rear hatch had a hard time keeping the equipment in the rear of the vehicle clean and dry. The passenger doors on the vehicle had the same problem. The Mystery Machine was a high-back HMMV so the doors were soft skin (canvas) and could be stored in the back of the vehicle. The HMMVs with CAAT were hardback HMMVs so the doors were hard also. The doors were stored either on the rear hatch or discarded at the Motor Pool. Also, CAAT had been issued green camouflaged netting that they had yet to use. The idea was that the when we got farther north where the maps showed some type of vegetation, we might be able to use them. At this point it became obvious the nets were useless and were doing nothing more than destroying the gate on the rear of the vehicles. So I called over to Master Sgt Hendricks and asked if I could get rid of them. He said instead of just trashing them I was to turn them into supply, which we did immediately.

So at this point Schielein's Section was over at Alpha Company's position, which was to our west and separated from the rest of the Battalion by about two miles. Lt Letendre was to our east with Bravo Company, and the Section I was to travel with was in the center with Charlie Company.

The first order I received with CAAT came that night. The next day I was to travel down Ambush Alley to escort a humanitarian team to our side of An Nasiriyah. I told the Section that I was going to work the closest with, what the plan of attack was for the next day. One of the Marines said they had been tasked with this type of mission before and asked if we were going to use the same plan. I asked what plan they used last time. He said that the last Marine to "lead" them through Ambush Alley told them that they were to drive fast, and if any of the vehicles broke down just to leave the vehicle and the Marines in that vehicle behind. I told the Marine no, we would not use that plan. I said we would drive about thirty-five miles an hour, communications would be continuous, and if anyone broke down we would all stop, redistribute all the gear and personnel, and continue movement. If we were being shot at we would do the exact same thing -- except we would fire back.

That night Doc and Day stayed inside the compound with the Battalion COC. I stayed with my Platoon for the first night and Lt Letendre came over to talk to me. He told me what was being done wrong (which was very little) and what he wanted done about it. I listened -- like I said before, he thought before he spoke.

I crashed out on the ground next to my vehicle. The Marines were kind of quiet around me. They knew what they had to do and they did it, but I think they were unsure of themselves around me. I put myself on watch with the Section just like I did with Doc and Day. I always took the watch after midnight, every other night. I did that so I would know how the Marines felt. It was easy to make decisions about things but if you weren't doing what the Marines you led were doing, you weren't their leader. There is a difference between a good leader and a bad master.

It was about two in the morning when I took my watch. I wanted one person up in each of the machine gun turrets and one person in the TOW turret. The TOW had a night vision sight in it that allowed you to pick up thermal images (heat). Whichever vehicle had a radio in it would be the one that had radio watch while up in the turret. The stars, like every night, were bright. It seemed like all I ever thought about on watch was Kelly. I wondered if anyone back home knew what was going on with my Marines and me. I wondered if she knew it was my unit that was out here.

**1 April 2003**
CAAT stood to, just like 81s did. They had some showers going that day. The humanitarian tour took precedence. We got the order to move out at nine that morning. I checked out with Battalion, made my communication checks, made sure weapons were off safe, and headed out, back through Ambush Alley. I was point going across the bridge, leaving Tank Platoon behind us. We picked up speed as we entered the town. I looked out the door and thought the buildings were farther apart than the last time when I was driving out of there with Poma. People were looking at us. They were not looking at us like they were mad or upset. They looked at us like they were surprised we were driving through. The destroyed Amtraks that had been on the road earlier were gone. I wanted to start shooting for no reason. I had not been around this many Iraqis before and I was starting to get mad, like I had no control. I had heard over at Alpha and Bravo Company that they had seen a bunch of orange vehicles with black doors that might be used by the Iraqi Army to move people and ammo around, and to gather

intelligence. I saw a few of those vehicles haul ass out of the area as we drove farther down the street. I could see the southern bridge over the Euphrates. It seemed like we would never reach the bridge. I wanted to be in the rear all of a sudden, making sure everyone made it through okay. I wanted all of us out of there.

As we reached the top of the bridge, there were Marines on guard at the high point and they were letting civilians traverse the bridge. I still did not feel safe. We drove down the road for about another three miles looking for the Regimental Headquarters. We pulled in and found the Regimental Three. Some Captain asked who we were and I told him. He told us to hang on for a second and left his tent. I looked around and saw a coffee pot. I asked some Corporal if I could get a cup. He said no because he only had a half a can of grains left and he did not know when he was going to get more. A Staff Sgt that was sitting at a desk got up, walked over to the Corporal, took the cup out of his hand, went to the coffee pot, filled up the cup, handed it to me, and sat back down without saying one word. I drank the cup and was finishing up just as the Captain returned and told me that we weren't needed anymore. What the fuck. I drove down Ambush Alley for a motherfucking cup of coffee, and I almost didn't even get that.

I went back out to the five vehicles and told my Marines that we were not needed. You could see in their eyes that this whole thing was bullshit. But they just laughed and said it was good to get away from the Battalion for a while. We started to head north again. There was a young man on the side of the road carrying a suitcase. Behind him were two women carrying more equipment than he was. The man put the suitcase down, pointed at it, and yelled at the women. He then walked off. One of the women picked up the suitcase and put it on her head with the other suitcases. Pulliam was laughing his ass off and Martinez thought it was fucked up, and he started calling the guy lazy.

About a mile short of the southern bridge some Iraqi had put himself in the only way to pass through a roadblock. I got out of the vehicle and pointed my shotgun at the guy. As I started yelling at him, some Marine came out and pulled him out of the way. The Marine told me that the guy was crazy and was always doing something, and that he was harmless. I just shrugged my shoulders, got back into my vehicle, and kept heading north.

As we started over the bridge again, one of the Marines that was on guard kind of looked at me, like "it sucks to be you." We kept on driving. We got the same blank stares from the Iraqis as we drove through the second time. I was looking for the house that I pulled the Marines out of. I couldn't find it. We got back over the north bridge and set back up at the intersection, oriented north. I walked over to the Battalion COC and told them that we had not been needed. Captain Greene said that they had gotten the word we were not needed about ten minutes after we left, and they had tried to call us back but could not get hold of us on the radio. No big fucking deal. No harm no foul.

The rest of the day was pretty uneventful except that we got word that we were moving out. Lt Letendre was getting the order. Routine movement. Of course no contact was expected. Lt Letendre moved his Section over to where mine was, and Schielein wanted to leave Alpha and come over to where we were. The Alpha Company CO did not want CAAT to leave till we moved out in the morning. After much debate, Schielein ended up leaving two vehicles behind and as soon as the MEU replaced us in the morning, the CAAT vehicles would link back up with us.

It was great having everyone around. We had a blast bullshitting and acting stupid. There was a shotgun that Master Sgt Hendricks had given me to see if I could fix it. I stripped it down, fixed it, and returned it to him. He asked me if I had fixed it and I said yea I fixed it. He asked, "How do you know you fixed it?" I said, "I know." There's a smile that Hendricks gets when he knows he is right or has a valid point. It is not a smile like he is gloating over you; it is more of a laughing smile. I took two shotgun rounds, the ones with the birdshot, and fired the rounds out into the dirt. I walked back over to him and told him, "I know it's fixed cause I fired two rounds out of it." He said, "Now that's the way to do it."

When I fired the rounds out, I noticed that no one jumped. I gave no warning about firing the gun and I would have expected people to turn quickly around or something. No one moved. I guess the Platoon was numbing to what was going on around them.

The Platoon started to gather back together right before it got dark. I hooked up my MP-3 player to a couple of speakers that one of the Marines had, and we listened to some music. We went to sleep late that night. We were too busy playing around and bullshitting with each other. It was like a family reunion. This much of the Platoon hadn't been together since Kuwait.

### 2 April 2003

The MEU came in and replaced us, but the two vehicles from Schielein's Section never came up. Finally I had to drive over and get them. It looked like a cluster fuck, but a well-organized cluster fuck. There were just a lot of Marines and a lot of vehicles. I ran into a Platoon Sgt from Alpha and he asked me if I knew a Gunny over in the MEU. I told him no. The SSgt said that the "Gunny asked if I knew you and I said yea and he told me to tell you to stop talking to his wife." Talking to his wife? I had not called anyone except my Dad and Kelly. My family and Kelly's family were friends and I knew she wasn't married. I could not imagine who it was. I finally figured out it was probably a friend of mine fucking with me.

I found my missing vehicles and we got out of there. The Battalion was waiting on these two vehicles so it could leave. When we got to the intersection with the rest of the Platoon, the Lieutenant notified higher and we moved out. The two other Sections took point and the Section I was with traveled as rear-end Charlie.

We moved out and headed north. After a few hours of traveling and listening to the radio I was bored out of my mind. I had the grids plotted on the map I had made, like I planned, and it looked like it was going to work out.

I did not know that Headquarters and the Logistics vehicles were falling apart as bad as they were. As we traveled, the logistics vehicles could not keep up so they would start to spread out. Then to compound this problem, vehicles would just break down on the road. We would find these vehicles on the side of the road and have to wait for Motor-T to find them, and then try to get them caught up. By the end of the day I was leading about twenty vehicles. A Lt that was in charge of the convoy said he got ordered to set up for the night. We found a place that was off to the side of the road. I sent my vehicles out in different directions to check things out around our Battle Position for the night. There was an Army unit to our northwest so we set up to the southeast of them, orienting ourselves in the opposite direction.

There was a small bedouin tent out to our east. Martinez, Pullliam, and I drove up to it. A dog came out and was barking at us. A minute later an old man came out. He kicked the dog and it shut up. He came up and shook my hand. He spoke a little English and told me it was "important, that you learn our language" and gave me a small book to learn Arabic from. He was glad we were there and I didn't think he was a threat for the night.

We headed back to where the Battle Position was going to be set up, and I placed everyone in for the night. Just as it started to get dark, the last of the logistics vehicles pulled up and shot at one of my machine gun vehicles that was located to the south. I was watching them approach and tracers went flying around the HMMV. Dumb fuckers -- if they could not tell a HMMV from an Iraqi pick up truck we had problems. I pulled the vehicle in closer to the circle.

Late that night I watched vehicles travel in and out of the Army compound. The compound was well lit and stuck out like a sore thumb. More power to them. I wouldn't do that, but hey, it was their base, not mine.

### 3 April 2003
The next morning we got up early and moved out. I was told we were going to an airport of some sort. At first I thought it was the airport we were supposed to take over before An Nasiriyah, but it was not on the maps that I had.

Along the side of the road there were different types of Army vehicles. Iraqi civilians had stripped all the vehicles down to nothing. The terrain started to turn a little more rugged, with more places to hide behind, and vegetation started to actually appear. I had two of my vehicles to the rear and my other three traveling to the front. We placed ourselves about 500 meters in front of the convoy. Every once in a while I would send one of the two other vehicles to the rear of the convoy just to check on things. Driving a HMMV leading a convoy is much like patrolling: if you are not doing anything but moving in one direction you are probably getting bored and complacent. Sending these two HMMVs back at irregular intervals kept people from getting complacent.

We approached a Marine Air Wing unit. They had blocked the road off and were using the highway as an airstrip. We had to drive down the side of the road to get past it but could only drive down the side of the road when there weren't helicopters flying in. They had helicopters landing so we had to wait. Some female Lance Corporal walked over to talk to us. She was a petite thing and was nice enough. She said that some Artillery unit had dropped some rounds by accident earlier that day and asked if we had "seen any action." I told her we just left the Naz. She said she hadn't heard of it. I was not surprised. I hadn't expected her to. We talked a little more. I was glad she was not acting like a slut. She was a very nice young lady and it was nice to talk to a woman.

The helicopters left and so did we. We followed the dirt road around the airstrip and after a mile or so we got back on the highway. As we got on the highway we went right into the Air Wing's Base Camp. The Marines there occupied both sides of the road. It was about a half mile long and surrounded with barbwire, with the units tightly tucked away. I was sure they did not move around much with all the work they had put into their defense. As we drove through the camp Martinez said that he would go crazy if he was stationed there and stuck in one place; I agreed.

After we drove through the camp I traded out with Pulliam in the turret. I thought it would be cool to ride up in the turret but it sucked -- the heat, the sand, and the wind constantly on you. It was a good way to get a quick tan, though. I was talking to Pulliam as we drove along. He said the Section was pissed cause Gunny Hanson liked to travel to the rear with the logistics train and they wanted to be up front for once. That would explain why Schielein was on the edge. He was taking care of the Platoon and no one was taking care of him, not that he wanted anyone to.

Late that night we pulled up into the airport area. I was dead-beat tired. The rest of the Battalion was already there except for the tanks. The other two sections were on line at the main gate of the airport. As soon as I pulled in, Schielein started bitching about how the Marines running this airport didn't know what they were doing. Lt Letendre was running around inside the airport trying to get everyone set in. I climbed up on the hood of my HMMV and leaned up on the windshield. Schielein sat next to me on the hood and we talked till we both fell asleep. We woke up with the tanks pulling up in front of us. They were too close for comfort so we pulled all the Marines off the vehicles and back away from the tanks. One of the tanks bumped the side of one of the HMMVs before parking across from us. Schielein said he would go talk to the Tank Platoon Sgt. I said fine. My platoon climbed back on their vehicles, I set up security, and we started to rack out as Lt Letendre pulled up.

He said he had the order for tomorrow and would issue it early in the morning. I was so tired that even if he had given the order I would not have remembered it.

**4 April 2003**
We woke up in the morning and the Lt issued the order like he said he would. I told the Lt that I wanted to be up front. He said there was no problem with that. Schielein would take rear-end Charlie and I would take the point with the Lt behind me. I took my Section and the Lts out to the road and Schielein came out with me. His Section would jump in as the logistics vehicles drove by. The Lt was over at the Battalion getting any final word that might change our orders.

As we were standing around waiting, a van pulled up with three older men in it. One of the men approached Schielein and me and said that he needed our help. The Iraqi Army had just crumbled to the ground. No one knew where anyone was. Communications that had been almost non-existent were now completely gone. One of the men who was in the van was looking for his son, who was serving in the Iraqi Army at the airport we were at when the war broke out. Not knowing where he was and being concerned for him, the man had started looking for him with the help of his friends. I told the man that there were no Iraqis inside the base camp, not even prisoners, but if he waited for my unit to leave there might be someone inside who could help him. He said thank you and went back to the van. He was talking to the other two men when one of them started crying. I couldn't help but think this was something my father would have done if it had been me. I hoped he found his son.

We soon left and headed to our next objective, which was about four hours away. On the way up, just short of where we were going, was an eighteen-wheeler trailer with the letters "EOD" sprayed on the side. Guarding the trailer were two very small female Marines.

It took us a couple of hours of driving from the airfield before we arrived where we were going. It was another makeshift airfield on a highway for Cobra helicopters. There were two bridges at each end of the landing zone and a key intersection off to the east. Bravo and Charlie Company got the bridges to guard and Alpha got sent out to the intersection. The Battalion COC set up at a gas station and went straight into a meeting. It was kind of weird. They usually wanted everyone and their mother at these meetings, and while they had a lot of people there, what they talked about was kept quiet. Only Higher knew what Higher was thinking.

I went off to check out the area to see what was going on. One of the vehicles in H&S had a Blue Force Tracker and a radio that actually picked up news. In the American news there was talk about an airport near Baghdad and the presence of some Army units in Baghdad. The Iraqi news was saying that they held the airport and that there were no American troops in Baghdad. The Blue Force Tracker said we were both lying. The airport had friendly units all over it and Baghdad had just a few blue dots around the city. Hearing the news and looking at the Blue Force, I did not know what to think. I wanted us to be in Baghdad so we could go home, but what if we super-imposed those blue marks on the airport as a morale booster or as a media trick? Too much thinking for one day. I headed back to my Platoon. When I got there our orders did too.

One section (mine) would take the south bridge; another section (Schielein) would take the north bridge, and one section (the Lts) would stay at the gas station as a reactionary force. I took my vehicles south to where Charlie Company was. I placed three vehicles facing east and one more vehicle-facing west with mine. Fucking mosquitoes were going crazy on us. It had never been that bad.

Someone told me that Schielein had gotten orders to go somewhere. I remember thinking "bullshit" because he needed to take a break. He had been riding on the edge too long. I needed him to slow down for his own good, but every time a mission came up he wanted to be on it. He was not trying to get his men killed; he wanted to do his job and it was wearing on him. When the Lt had told him he was going to be with the Logistics train on the way up, he knew it was his turn but that was not where he wanted to be. I pulled one of the three vehicles from the other side to mine and Martinez drove me up to where Schielein was. He was in a great mood. I asked him if he had gotten orders and he said no he hadn't. I pulled him aside and told him what I was thinking. He said he did not agree with me but he trusted what I said and thought I could be right. He asked if I thought he was endangering his men and I told him no, he "just needed to slow down." As I was sitting there, two of his Marines came up and cut the sleeves off my t-shirt. I had not realized till then that everyone in CAAT but me had their sleeves cut off. When they did that, I belonged. I was now a part of their brotherhood; they had made room for me. I headed back over to Charlie Company.

When I got there I checked out the east side of the bridge before returning to the west side where I had been before. First Sgt Henao saw me and walked over. He said that I needed to get rid of the t-shirt without the sleeves. I told him I agreed and I would have my whole Platoon corrected by tomorrow. Once I arrived to the west side I sent the other vehicle back over to the east side. We bedded down for the night.

## 5 April 2003

The next morning we got up and the Lt called all the Sections up to the gas station. Even though my Section was farther out we beat Schielein's Section coming in. When the Platoon got there, I got everyone who was an NCO or above in a meeting. I told them that everyone had to put on a t-shirt that had sleeves. There was some laughter but of course, also the question why. They had gone the whole war so far without sleeves. I told them it was because the Platoon had a reputation as a bunch of cowboys. Not in a bad way, but if we wanted to be trusted and look like part of the Battalion we would need to be like everyone else. If we continued to look different and act different, higher would lose faith in us and we would lose a lot of the freedom – and, more importantly, a lot of the missions -- we were being given. No one wanted that last part. The missions were what kept us going.

We ate together as a Platoon that morning, including the Lt who was usually running around being given mission orders. My Section got the next set of orders. The Amtraks down at Alpha Company's position needed refueling and my Section was going to provide security. Around noon, the refueler showed up and we headed south on the highway through the airfield. When we got to the bridge where I had helped provide security the night before, we headed east. The road was made of dirt, the bridge was falling apart, and there was foot traffic all over the place. The people were going on with their daily lives. We pulled up to Alpha Company and pulled over to the side of the road. We parked our vehicles behind their lines while the Amtrakers drove their vehicles up to the refueler to get the gas they needed.

I found First Sgt Thompson over at the CP. Thompson was about six foot two or three and a good 210 pounds or so. He had a great sense of humor and was the most decorated Marine that I personally knew – he had over 25 ribbons and personal decorations. He was a true infantryman. We started to talk and of course, with his sense of humor, he had everyone laughing. He was comparing my mustache to a multitude of things and none of them were pleasant. I told him I heard an Army unit had taken the airport in Baghdad and supposedly had troops in the city. He said he had heard the same thing.

While I was there, a General stopped by Alpha Company's position. He shook a bunch of hands, said we were great guys, and left. I didn't know what his purpose was in coming to visit us. He told us we had troops in Baghdad but we all already knew that. If he had wanted to raise morale he could have brought us cigarettes and dip. Soon after he left, the last Amtrak got done refueling. It was getting close to dinnertime and we could eat back at the gas station.

My Section was on reactionary force tonight and Lt Letendre was taking guard at the southern bridge where I had been. When we got to the gas station we ate and had to clean up the area. One of the other Sections had trashed the area out pretty bad. We were laid in for the night with our security up and things were going quiet and smooth. I was about to go to sleep when I thought I heard a slight popping noise. I asked Martinez, who was in the turret, if he had heard anything and he said no. I started to drift off when the airfield to our south lit up with indirect fire. I sat straight up and waited. Would there be enemy troops that followed or other indirect targets? I just waited for something, anything. Our radios never even lit up with conversation. Everything was just so quiet. I thought I had maybe dreamt it but everyone was up and looking down the road the same way I was. After the initial explosion it was just so quiet -- as if it never happened. We settled back down to sleep.

I had watch around three in the morning. This time it was on a TOW vehicle and not my machine gun vehicle. I climbed up on the vehicle and clipped the radio's handset to my flak jacket. It was uneventful for the first 30 minutes but as I was scanning the tree line and buildings across the highway, I picked up four people moving southward with rifles. I called higher and asked if we had patrols in the area and was told no. I woke up the Section and, using my compass, I gave everyone a direction to the target. The 50-caliber HMMV from my vehicle would go first, and once he was on target everyone else could fire onto where his tracers were hitting. I called the COC and asked permission to engage the Iraqis across the street. I was told to wait because they were still checking with Alpha Company to see if they had any patrols out. I was impressed with their patrolling -- it was a dark night, and their dispersion was really far apart but they were still able to stop and move as one. I got permission to fire but it was too late; they were gone. Alpha Company was told that I had spotted an enemy patrol in the area.

114

## 6 April 2003

The next morning we were all tired. It had been a long night and we had work to do. Lt Letendre's Section, along with mine, was to go look for where the mortars were fired. Battalion said they thought it might be a part of an Iraqi unit that had been bypassed or shot up but not completely destroyed. Whatever they were, they were a thorn in our side. We moved out on the highway up north some and pulled off to the west down a dirt road. I got out of my vehicle along with a couple of others from the Platoon. The roads were small and there were too many places to be ambushed. We headed out into this area looking to pull this thorn out. We pulled up to a couple of houses next to a river. No one was around. There were chickens and a couple of mangy dogs, but no one to talk to.

We found another house and I couldn't decide if it was empty or not. I did not want to break into it, so I walked around to the other side. As I was back there with another Marine, I heard a crash in the front of the house. I ran to the front to see what had happened. Apparently Lt Letendre was not as worried as I was about breaking stuff. The house was abandoned and had nothing in it. We traveled a little farther east when we came across a man who could speak English. He said he had seen nothing during the night but had heard the explosions. We headed north to a Mosque. So far, the Iraqis had had a pretty good tradition of fighting from mosques and hospitals. As we traveled north we would check the fields for imprints from the mortar plates. We found none. We finally arrived at the Mosque. Some Marines went further north a little to check out a home. I checked out the Mosque; there was nothing. Lt Letendre, looking on the map, said that if it had been 82mm mortars we had looked to the limit of their maximum effective range. There was no use going any further. We loaded up and headed back with nothing to show.

We arrived back at the gas station and got an order to go guard a trailer with "EOD" written on the side of it. I knew which one they were talking about -- I had seen it on the way in. I took my Section down to the trailer and set up security around it. There were two large-looking rockets in the back. One of the Marines with me said he thought they looked like SCUD missiles. Hell if I knew. We set up around it and established security.

As we were there, people would walk up and try to sell us stuff or just look at us. It was weird because we were on the side of the road in the middle of nowhere and people would just show up. Two guys in particular came up and wanted to take the tires off the trailer. I told them no. One guy started to walk up to the trailer, and I told him to get away. He smiled at me like I was joking. So I shot a round over his head. He did not think it was funny any more and the two ran off. Later, word came over the radio that we were going to have an EOD team come out to check on the missiles.

Late that afternoon, four EOD Marines came out. Their HMMV pulled up next to ours. One of the Marines jumped out of the back with a hammer and said it would only take a second to defuse the two missiles. One of the other Marines told him to quit fucking around and get to work. A few minutes later a SSgt with the team asked who was in charge. I told him I was. He said that it would be a good idea if we put our gas masks on and moved upwind. I didn't even ask why; the mask went on and we were out of there. The last time I put my gas mask on that quickly was in the last Gulf War. My Marines saw me put my gas mask on and they did the same without even asking why -- but with an "ohhh fuck look on their faces."

We drove north to the southern bridge. Marines that were guarding the bridge asked me what the fuck was going on. I told them and soon they all had on the same Halloween mask that I did. From 200 yards upwind, we sat and waited. A little while later, one of the EOD Marines waved at us to come back. I told every one to wait there. Pulliam asked if he could wait there too. I couldn't tell if he was serious or not, so he came with me. When we got there, the EOD guy had a gas mask on and he told me that he couldn't work on the missiles cause they were leaking nerve agent. He had to call higher and get some Army NBC unit out to work on it. He said it was not leaking enough to be dangerous, but that if he were me he would stay upwind. I called the rest of my section down and we took off our gas masks. I told them what he had told me and called higher with the information. I felt like a kindergartner teaching psychology.

The ground around us had two ponds on each side of the road, and around each pond was flat ground for miles. So the wind kept changing direction. We stayed on the north side and then moved to the south side, then to the west, then to.... We kept moving from the time EOD left till we were relieved the next morning.

116

## 7 April 2003

After wasting a tank of gas trying to stay upwind of the missiles, I was glad to see our relief. It was part of a Rifle Platoon from Alpha Company. The SSgt that was relieving me thought I was joking as I told him about the nerve agent. He started to laugh and I told him again. He did not believe me, so fuck it. My Section started to get ready to move out. Our next mission was to be point for a city that needed liberating. As we started to prep to leave, the SSgt walked back up to me and with a shocked look on his face said, "Gunny, you weren't fucking around about the nerve agent, were you." I told him I wasn't teasing. As we drove off, the SSgt was cussing left and right. I guess he had a problem with being exposed to nerve agent. They moved farther south, upwind, to set up security.

We met up at the gas station again. There were several missions going on at once while we were providing security. So it was decided that Lt Letendre would ride with my Section and we headed north. I did not mind, I mean it was his fucking Platoon. I was his Platoon Sgt, and our job was not to run a Section, but to run the Platoon. That was what we did. The three of us (Letendre, Schielein, and me) each took a Section to lead, but there were Sgts in each Section that were more than capable of doing the job if we had to do something somewhere else in the Platoon.

We left the airport and headed to some other piss-ant town. There were a lot of small towns between the two points. The weather was dry but towards the afternoon it started to cloud up a little. When we saw a vehicle coming from the opposite direction while we were moving, we would call it in to higher. We ended up doing this every twenty minutes or so. I only saw two groups of people. Once during the movement the Battalion wanted to take a rest break, so we ended up stopping in a small town. When we stopped I went between two bushes to piss. When I came out of the bushes, people had come out of their houses. They did not get close and we didn't let them. After a few minutes of just staring at each other we left. The second time we saw a group of people was while we were moving. There was a "bus stop"- looking building made of mud on the side of the road and there were a bunch of old men in it talking. Besides that, just the usual small group of young men who had deserted the Army and were wanting to go home. I kind of envied them; they were going home and I was going to an unknown city.

117

The town was on the edge of the Tigris River. It was small and there was nothing but mud houses on both sides. There were a few houses made of cement that had walled-in courtyards and were painted bright colors. My Section was the first in the city. As we approached, people started to pour out of their houses, children were clapping their hands and dancing, old men were waving at us, women peered over walls and through gated windows. It was everything except the ticker tapes being thrown out of the windows. We drove down the road and it made a hard left. The left went over a bridge to the other part of the city. Schielein was getting the same reception that I was, except he was at a bridge farther north. Instead of making the left, I stopped and turned around. Just as I cleared the thin road, Alpha Company with their Amtraks started to drive down the road. They were going to set up just south of where I had turned around. I had to check out the area between the two bridges to make sure they were secure.

Between the city and the northern bridge was a berm that kept the Tigris from flooding the small houses and fields along the river. It was about fifteen feet high and about ten feet wide; at some points it got a little more interesting. The six HMMVs and I climbed up on the berm and headed north. We took our time and drove slowly. It was an awesome view. After about two miles we found an area to our right that kind of nestled onto the river. I had the Marines pull their vehicles into this harbor. From there we watched another unit kill a T-55 tank with a TOW round. That was the extent of the battle to liberate the city.

We washed ourselves in the Tigris River. I felt like I belonged to a brotherhood of warriors who for thousands of years had done what we were doing at that moment: enjoying the water of the Tigris in the middle of the desert.

I was sitting in some grass when four Iraqi men approached me. Two of the men were not as well dressed as the first two and followed behind them. The two men that walked in front, one was my age and the other much older. As the man my age approached, the older man was trying to stop him by grabbing his shoulder and pulling on it while whispering in his ear. The man my age shrugged the hand off his shoulder and approached anyway. I stood up, barefoot, washed my hands with the water in my canteen, and shook his hand. He smiled. His hand was finely manicured and I picked up a heavy cologne smell from him as he approached. I looked at the older man behind him and could tell immediately this was his father. The man said that his house was not far from where we were, and that he wanted to feed us with a sheep that he would freshly slaughter. The father was uncertain of what his son was doing. I told the man that I could not take his "gracious offer" and that "we should be the one bringing gifts." He smiled at this and told me that the Iraqi soldiers had left the town not more than an hour before our arrival. They had heard we were coming and threw their AK-47s and other weapons into the Tigris River from the bridge in town. At first, just knowing the soldiers had been there that recently freaked me out, but then I thought they would have already engaged us if they were going to be a problem. We saddled up and left our safe haven. We continued to head north.

At one point in the berm the road got really thin -- thin enough that I did not think our HMMVs could pass it, but they did. A few minutes later we arrived at Bravo Company's position. There were over a hundred civilians chanting at the bridge, glad we were there. I checked on my boys and found Parker and Schielein talking. It was a circular defense, not much in the way of buildings or other obstacles, and the ground they had chosen was kind of sunken. It was a good position. Schielein said that when they arrived there, a young kid started telling him that he (the kid) was in charge of the province, and if the Americans wanted anything they would have to go through him. Schielein started yelling at him to get the fuck away and when the kid started to physically go for Schielein, he pushed him away. The other Iraqis started beating the guy and throwing rocks at him as he ran off. They said that he was "evil" and had done a lot of harm to the people there.

Lt Letendre was to stay there so I headed back to Alpha Company. No one had given me orders on where to go that night, so that was as good a place as any. We followed the road back to Alpha Company. From the road we could see a refueler over-turned off the berm. I had heard Schielein over the radio tell higher that a refueler could not make it down the berm, but I guess someone who had not seen it at all had known better.

It started to get dark when I pulled up to Alpha. I checked in with their CO to see if it was okay to stay the night with them. He said why not, everyone else was. There were two other vehicles that did not belong to our unit there; it was a Green Beret team. They had decided to stay with us for the night. Why not? Alpha was covering the Tigris to our back (east) and the building to our north and south. My section covered the open ground to the west. Watch was established and night came quickly. We went to sleep.

Soon after, a truck pulled up with its headlights shining straight toward us. And it was coming fast, right at us. I yelled for everyone to man their guns but hold fire. If my Marines weren't in a turret, they were pointing their rifles at the vehicle. First Sgt Thompson was over by me in a heartbeat. I wanted to get close enough to make my shotgun useful if I could. All of a sudden, the truck stopped. The cab light came on and a guy stepped out yelling, "Look at what I found!" in perfect English. It was two Marines from Alpha Company that had found the truck in a deserted compound. I frantically yelled at my Marines to stand down. Only cause my Marines were disciplined enough to hold their fire and because I wanted to kill someone with my shotgun did those two idiots live. First Sgt Thompson walked up to them and chewed their asses out from top to bottom. The Marines could only get "but" out a few times till they realized what Thompson was saying and what they had done. The rest of the night was uneventful.

### 8 April 2003

Morning came and when it did the town's dogs awakened us and the people began stirring. Women were already walking around before daylight and we all had to piss. We did not want to be pulling out our dicks in front of these people, so we found one area where we could piss in private. We were shaving after stand-to, and the women started to approach us -- of course with their fathers, husbands, or older women. They had fruit; dates mostly, and freshly baked bread. They walked around to each vehicle and fighting hole, feeding us. None of the Marines I saw took more than half a handful of anything. Later that morning we got word to move out.

My Section was to leave early with the advanced party and go back to the airport where the tank had clipped one of our HMMVs. The ride there was uneventful but took forever. Pretty much the same scene leaving the town as we had had on the way there.

When we got to the airport there was no room for us inside, so we had to set up on the side of the road somewhere. That was when I found out that First Sgt Parker was with us on the advanced party. Lieutenants and Company Gunnys were trying to find out where to put their Companies. The Battalion XO, Major Tuggle I think, already knew where he wanted to put everyone but he was a patient man when it came to everyone except Company XOs. While everyone ran around here and there, I sat with Parker and shot the shit. He said that he needed a break from Bravo for a while and thought coming out on the advance party was the way to do it. Parker was a quiet and patient man. Nothing bothered him. So for him to want to take time away from the family was something unusual. We talked a while and he started talking about some pipes for his Harley.

Later that evening the rest of the Battalion showed up. One by one, CAAT Platoon showed up. We set up on line, vehicle next to vehicle, next to a berm running east and west. I could tell you that I didn't know what it was like when a Platoon got together after a separation, but I did know. You hang out together on liberty, carry each other home drunk, fight each other, meet each others' families, visit each others' homes, get punished together, go to the field and bare your soul, and before you know it you're a family. A true family, closer than anyone who ever knew you. They see the best that your paternal family thinks of you and the worst that your mother would never expect. And the kicker is, they still accept you. When you get to spend time together it is nothing less than heaven. We were in a safe area so we acted a little looser than the Marines were used to. But fuck you. We needed it. I ordered three fire watches that night, one fire watch on each flank and one in the middle.

**9 April 2003**
The next morning everyone kind of "stirred to." There was no reason for "stand to." We listened to music off the MP-3, read and wrote letters, some wrestling went on, but mostly a bunch of nothing. I went by to see Parker but something was fucked up over at his unit and he did not have time to bullshit. I walked around to the other Platoons or Companies in the area. They were so laid back and doing nothing that I got bored just looking at them. I headed back to the Platoon where I just wasted away in thought. I thought about getting out, maybe putting in for the Gunner package, how my dad was doing, what my brother was up to, what Kelly and I would do when I got back and like everyone else, I wondered when we were going home.

# Back to a Rifle Platoon
## Chapter 6

**10 April 2003**

FUCK THE WORLD!!!!! I felt this more this day than any other. No particular reason. Just frustration. I wanted to take my kids to a movie. I wanted to tell my son what I felt was important in life. I wanted to go fishing with my dad. I wanted to ask Kelly if we were okay. It was down time. Maybe this is why I felt frustrated. Too much time on my hands left me vulnerable to my own worst enemy -- me.

CAAT platoon, my platoon, was all in one place. We were like a family that does not get to spend enough time together. No stupid misguided missions without support. No over-stretched security positions in the battalion line. There was one guy up on security for every three vehicles. Some of my Marines were crashed out on their HMMVs, some were writing home, some were bullshitting about pussy they never got or they planned on getting. I went over to Schielein's vehicle. He was listening to a Walkman and wearing a pair of shades that someone back in America had sent us. We talked about riding our Harleys -- the poker runs, bike rallies, and people we could probably get to go riding with us. I knew that none of this shit would probably happen, but I really needed to think it would right about then. So I believed the lie. I got called over to the battalion Head Shed for a possible mission coming up.

I walked by 81's Platoon on the way over. They had their guns dug in and ammo ready, but besides that they were like my platoon -- just enjoying the down time. By the time I got to the Head Shed, Lt Letendre was getting an order. He said it was nothing big, and he would get with me back over at the Platoon area.

With nothing else to do and in a Harley mood, I decided to go over and see 1st Sgt Parker at Bravo's position. He still couldn't really bullshit cause something else was going down with one of the Platoons in his Company.

I ended up talking with GySgt Carrico for a little while, even though he had shit to do. The whole time I knew Carrico he never said much. He just didn't. But when he did say something it was either "Gunny wisdom" or funnier than fuck, which is the same thing depending which end of the stick you are on. He asked me if I heard the latest "news" and

I said no. He told me I would find out in enough time -- with a grin on his face that would make small children cry. With that said, I left back for my platoon, wondering what he meant. When I got there Lt Letendre was back and had word about our upcoming movement. Morale was kind of low, so I decided to pick it up a bit.

My vehicle was down at the end of the Platoon while Cavemans was around the middle. I picked up a smoke grenade and threw it at him. He yelled something, picked up a 9mm bullet, and threw it at me. I yelled something and threw a shotgun shell at him. He threw an M16 magazine. I threw 200 rounds of SAW ammo at him. Schielein threw a can of 50 cal ammo. I reached in the back of another vehicle and grabbed a TOW missile and threw it at him. It did not go far but it went far enough to show defiance. Schielein went in the back of a vehicle and pulled out a can of Mk19 and chunked it, having the same effect as the TOW missile. I picked up a rock and threw it. He flipped me off and we went our separate ways. By doing that, we let out a lot of stress that had been building up in the Platoon. Building a bonfire has the same effect.

1st Sgt Parker came over later, around noon, and said he just wanted to give me a heads-up on something. He said that Captain Newland had to relieve a Lt that morning and that he and the Capt wanted me to replace him. Platoon Commander in a combat zone? Damn right I wanted it. He said he was having to relieve NCOs left and right and some of the Staff Sergeants were not doing their jobs. He said that Captain Newland would be talking to Captain Rohr first and then the Battalion Commander. There were other Lts they could put in there but they did not have time to train someone. They needed someone who would kill the NCOs and get them to do their jobs.

About an hour later Lt Letendre told me to pack my shit -- I was going to Bravo Company. I left all my gear that belonged to Weapons Company, except my shotgun, and walked about 500 meters to my new home. I did not want to leave CAAT Platoon, but to be a Platoon Commander, fuck. Those guys were awesome. I had been in a lot of units where I felt like I really belonged and was part of the family, but more so with these guys. If it had not been for Schielein and Letendre, I would have had reservations about leaving. Those two were real leaders and had more than proven themselves a thousand times over in combat. While they were not the type to put their Marines in harm's way uselessly, any temptation to go overboard was gone. Besides, their questions about combat, weapons, employment, tactics or anything else had dropped to nothing. They were absolutely the kind of Marine I would leave my son with in a combat zone, knowing that if anything happened to him, it wouldn't be because of foolishness or war-mongering but because it was his time. I talked to the Marines in my Platoon one by one on my way out -- no use having a formation and saying good-bye. Formations are what you do when you are just ready to leave. I wanted to say good-bye to each one of them to their faces and make an effort in doing so.

I got to Bravo Company and checked in with the First Sgt. He told me again what he had said before, and walked me over to my Platoon: Second Platoon Bravo Company, 1st Battalion 2nd Marine Regiment. My Platoon Sergeant, SSgt Jason Jones, was standing on a meritorious promotion board. 1st Sgt Parker grabbed the Platoon Guide (Sgt Chase), the Team Leader for the SMAW attachments (Shoulder launched Multi Purpose Assault Weapon, good for blowing bunkers and pissing tanks off) (Sgt Shaw), and told them to form the Platoon up. By the time the Platoon was formed up, SSgt Jones showed up. We knew each other but not that well. I recognized him as the Marine who had held my shotgun while I beat in the side of my HMMV with my helmet at An Nasiriyah. He was a former Drill Instructor. He had met his wife while he was stationed in Iceland on barracks duty. She was in the Navy and worked on communications. They married there in Iceland and she left the Navy to raise their two daughters. Jones had always had his head shaved but he said his hair was now the longest it had ever been.

While Parker talked to the Platoon and told them what was going on, I was talking to Jones and asking him why the Lt got relieved. He started to tell me the story when I kind of got the idea that 1st Sgt Parker wanted me over at the formation. I walked over, he introduced me, and he started to walk away. I don't remember word for word what I said to the Platoon but I am sure it had a lot of "fuck y'all," "mother fuckers," "it was bullshit that they were so fucked up that their Lt got relieved," and if they tried that same shit with me, "I would kick their mother loving asses." So we got off on the right foot. I then told them that this was probably the only all-enlisted, Marine Corps infantry Platoon in Iraq. We would get scrutinized harder than anyone else about anything we did. If we fucked up, that would just prove that Enlisted couldn't handle this type of responsibility and that an Officer had to be with us. I told them to go back to their Amtraks and wait for the word while I talked with the Platoon Sergeant.

124

As I was talking, Jones was in the back of the formation smiling like a Cheshire cat. I asked him why the smile. He then told me about the problems he had had with the Lt that had gotten relieved. Jones said that he would try to correct the Marines and they would bitch to the Lt, and the Lt would change whatever Jones had said. To the Lt it was a popularity contest. Leadership is not a popularity contest -- that's called politics, and politics get Marines killed. Politicians start wars; Marines just fight them. I told Jones that he had his grid square and I had mine. It would not do us any good for us to be in each other's grid unless we just had to. When I said this, he just smiled that much more. I asked him what he thought would be good to start off with. He said he did not care -- he was just happy he was not getting screwed over any more by the Platoon Commander and would be allowed to do his job.

We decided that the Amtraks and packs were filthy, unorganized, and looked like a band of gypsy wagons. The First Sgt had fired some NCOs, so Marines had been moved around in the Platoon, and all this needed to get squared away. My only direction to SSgt Jones was that I wanted all the stuff we needed to kill and save lives in the same place on each Marine, on their packs and flaks. He asked if there was anything else. I said no. He tore into those motherfuckers hard. It was payback time for Jones. They had been running amuck for so long, and Jones wasn't going to let them run amuck any more. Now I was smiling like a Cheshire cat. A couple of the Cpls and a Sgt came to me to ask if they had to do what they had been told because they thought their Squad or Team was not the problem. I told them if they thought that then they needed to talk to the Platoon Sergeant. Not one of them went to him. They knew they were wrong. Jones spent the rest of the day inspecting them and tearing into them where they needed it.

I went and found the SSgt that was in charge of the three Amtraks in my Platoon. SSgt Deitz was a taller than average Marine with a lanky build and a Texas accent. We talked for a while and he was open to anything that needed to get done. He told me how they had been running things and I said it sounded good to me. He showed me how the communications were set up in the Amtrak. It was nothing too difficult, even though working with radios was not my strong point. The headset/helmet picked up transmissions from the Battalion, the Companies, and my Platoons all at the same time. So it was like listening to three radio stations at the same time. With CAAT we did not have this problem. Our one radio picked up one station at a time. If you wanted to listen to two radio stations then you had two radios. There was a toggle switch on the side of my Amtrak helmet that let me talk to whomever I wanted to, but I had to be on that station to do it. It wasn't difficult; it was just a pain in the ass.

The Platoon was busy all the way up until the moment I had them stand to as the sun went down. Jones and I were awake most of the night talking about everything the Platoon had done and needed to do and how the Platoon should be run. I knew I was leading the Platoon but I still needed to know what Jones thought.

**11 April 2003**

Jones woke them up for stand-to, thirty minutes before the sun started to show, and that was the red star cluster. They would stay in their bags and maybe sit up and look around. As soon as the sun was up, I gave them a class on how to stand to properly. I told them everything would get packed up, and I emphasized everything. They would put their packs on the Amtraks, put their flak and helmet on, and stand in their fighting holes, alert, till I decided to stand down. Some of the Marines picked up right away about the fighting holes -- they hadn't been digging in either. This was basic stuff they should have been doing. But the Lt they had was letting them do what they wanted, not what they should have been doing. When Jones tried to correct this, the Lt would override him. I could feel Jones's frustration over all this. It also explained why the First Sgt had fired a lot of Squad Leaders.

After all this I headed over to the Company Command Post; I needed to see what was going on. Rumor said we were leaving soon. Lt Daniels was there along with GySgt Carrico and Lt Fanning. Lt Daniels said that the Captain was getting the word right then but it looked like we were moving out. I was introduced to Lt's Beere and Garlock. Lt Daniels seemed cool with having me as a Platoon Commander, but the other three Lts seemed kind of unsure of who I was. Can't be everything to everybody and I really didn't feel like talking at the moment. Captain Newland and 1st Sgt Parker showed up a half hour or so later. The Captain broke out a map and said we were moving to an Iraqi camp that was on the north side of Al Kut. He gave the order of movement by Amtrak numbers. Man, that confused me from top to bottom. These guys had the numbers down to a science as far as what vehicle went to what Platoon and how they moved. I held my tongue till after the order was given. I then went to Parker and asked him what the fuck. He laughed and broke down all the numbers for me. It was simple after that.

I got back to the Platoon to look at the vehicles and figure this thing out and talk to Jones.

We loaded up and moved out. I was in the commander's hatch of my Platoon's lead vehicle with Sgt Chase behind me and then SSgt Jones following trace. SSgt Deitz was in the same Amtrak as me, sitting over in the gunner's hatch. Deitz was cool about everything except talking on the radio when he wanted to talk on the radio. Thing was, no one could hear him when he was talking, so everyone ended up talking when he was talking. We called it "stepping" on someone when that happened. He would go off when it happened though. No one ever tried to explain to him what was happening. We all figured he just needed this thing to be able to vent about. Being stepped on, well that was his thing. Movement was easy. My Amtrak followed the Amtrak in front of me. Felt like we were on parade again -- the Iraqis were waving at us and we were waving back. Every now and then we would drive by three or four males walking on the side of the road in the middle of nowhere. Best bet was they were soldiers who had capitulated as a unit or just deserted. Whatever they were, they did not want to fight.

CAAT Platoon was screening our front while we moved forward. They had come to a bridge and did not know if it would support the Amtraks going across it. It started to get dark so we just stopped on the road, still in movement formation. The Battalion decided to wait till the next morning to find out if the bridge would hold the Amtraks or if we could find a way around the bridge. As far as I could see, the grunts got out of their Amtraks and went into the mud in the ditches on the side of the road. Of course I had my Platoon stand to. I did not know if my Platoon really understood or respected my expectations about what should be done for night security. Jones knew what I wanted and had been thinking the same way I had. He would take first watch during the night and I would take the second. I pulled out my poncho. Still wearing my flak and helmet, I wrapped myself in it and laid down on the side of the road. It was cold that night. I woke up one time; I was hugging my shotgun and Jones was standing a few meters down watching the line of our Marines. I went back to sleep with my head still in my helmet.

## 12 April 2003
I woke up with Jones kicking me in the foot. I asked him if it was my watch he said no, that it was time to stand to. He had taken duty all night -- he must have been beat. I had gotten four hours of sleep and was still dead to the world. One Marine from each fire team was putting up all his

team's gear while the rest were on the line. That way, not everyone would get up at the same time and leave big gaps in the line. I put my poncho up. It was a pain in the ass. My pack, like all the rest of the packs, hung on the outside of the Amtrak. But my pack was in the front left slant and was a bitch getting to. I put everything I used everyday in my daypack and all that I did not use regularly in the main pack. The stuff I used regularly was coffee, my poncho, my toothbrush, shaving gear, and an MRE or two.

The sun started to rise and we got the word to move out. 1st Sgt Parker went by the Platoon Sergeants to get their counts of Marines to make sure everyone was up. The other Platoon Commanders and I called the Captain up and did radio checks. The world was round and turning; we moved out.

We arrived outside the eastern side of Al Kut sometime in the afternoon. Orders came down from Battalion to the Companies, CAAT, and 81s. It started to turn into a goat fuck from Battalion but Captain Newland filtered the bullshit out before it got to us. We ended up setting up a vehicle checkpoint facing south while the rest of Battalion set up in the Iraqi Army Camp. My Platoon had the east flank of the checkpoint while another Platoon actually conducted the checkpoint and another Platoon took the west.

There was an open patch of ground, then a large creek of mud, followed by a 10-foot berm. All of this was no farther than 100 meters from where the Amtraks were set up. On the other side of the berm were scattered berms and clay houses and a few brick buildings. Besides that it was deserted. I initially thought about putting the Platoon on the near side of the mud creek, and then decided to put them on the berm. Yea, the mud creek would slow their movement back to the Amtraks if we were going to get over run, but I did not plan on running from a fight. Jones was crashing out off and on. When he wasn't asleep he was talking to people or checking the line.

I turned in my fire plan sketch to Lt Fanning, the FiST Leader (Fire Support Team Leader, the guy who orchestrated the indirect fire and air support for the Company). Fanning said that he thought the checkpoint was a bad idea because we weren't going to find anything searching the vehicles, and it made us look like the old Iraqi Army -- all we were doing was pissing people off. He was probably right.

128

After we set up the checkpoint, I decided to walk around and see who all was in our Company. The slow stream of Iraqi vehicles moving through the road we were on had one thing in common -- they all had little kids in them. Some Marines were throwing candy to the kids. I had given up looking at them because they just made me miss my daughters that much more. I ran into GySgt Carrico and he wasn't doing much at the time, so we both kind of started walking around till we ran into GySgt Howard.

GySgt Howard was better known as "Father Time." He was the Platoon Commander for the tanks that were attached to us. He stood about five foot six and weighed maybe 150 pounds or so. He had a thick southern accent and spoke the same speed he walked -- real slow. He was wearing tennis shoes because he said his feet hurt. We started talking about An Nasiriyah a little. We were joking about this or that, kind of laughing about things. Then for a brief moment Howard got serious, he looked me straight in the eye and said, "I would kill a million of these fuckers before I let them lay one finger on one of my Marines." He then smiled and asked if Carrico and I wanted some food that his sister had sent him in the mail. We walked about 200 meters over to where the tanks were positioned on the roadblock, and we climbed up on the top of his tank. His sister, he said, had been sending him so much stuff he did not know what to do with it all. Damn if she hadn't been sending him some packages. Not just the regular grandmother candy and letter-writing gear. She had sent him full packaged meals, books, canned food and things a grunt couldn't have cause all we could have was what we carried in our packs. If it didn't fit in our packs it didn't go. I took a pasta meal with sauce. It was getting late now and I knew the word would be coming soon for us to move out.

I headed over to my Amtrak and as soon as I got there the word came down that we were moving out. I pulled the three squads in, except for a fire team for security. For some reason my hay fever was kicking in pretty bad. Doc Hoysock, the Platoon Corpsman, gave me some medicine for it. He told me that the medicine might make me sleepy. I did not pay him any mind. I climbed into the commander's hatch and went through my routine; took off helmet and placed it next to my shotgun to my right. Then put on the helmet with the radio on, and went through the roll call of comm checks. First I called the Captain, then the other two Platoon Commanders, and then Chase and Jones. I could see the line of cars that were held up by our vehicle inspections. It looked like our checkpoint had turned more into a roadblock. I broke out the meal that Gunny Howard had given me and dug in. I was going to save it for later but fuck it, it was different than a MRE and I was starving.

We followed the road up north till we came to an entrance of an Iraqi Army base. We followed the main road of the camp down to where our Company was going to set in, facing east. I don't know which Air Wing did it, but this place had been bombed to hell. Iraq was covered with dogs but this place was the worst yet. They had been having a feast on the dead Iraqi bodies.

First Platoon took our left flank, my Platoon was in the middle, and Third Platoon took our right flank. The Company CP was set up in this small building behind us. My three squads got on line just as they had been doing before. It was getting late by the time we had arrived and I didn't want people digging in at night. The noise would have given away our exact position. We had a berm to our front that we could have used to fight from. Plus, I thought we were going to be there a while so I wanted to get a good look at the land before I had people digging in. Ever since H&S Company unloaded on me while I was trying to get rid of the Iraqi artillery ammo with the help of 81's Platoon, I developed this phobia about walking out in front of friendly lines at night.

I was laying out my poncho to sleep on and Jones, Chase, and LCpl Cross were standing around me. All of a sudden, the medicine that Doc gave me hit me. I sat down and started telling Jones what I wanted done, and as I was talking I realized that my words were coming out slurred. Jones looked at Chase and Cross and said "you heard him, let's get on it." Chase and Cross walked away and I asked Jones if he understood a word I had said. He told me no, but that he got it and that he'd "take care of it." I lay down and the ground was soft and rolling. I thought to myself, I shouldn't take this medicine again. I cradled my shotgun and was out like a light.

### 13 April 2003
I woke up for stand-to. It was still dark out. Everyone but me had slept lightly the night before, so everything was put up quickly. Jones, Cross, Chase, Doc Hoysock, and I were back at our Platoon CP. Jones told me about how I was talking but nothing was coming out of my mouth the night before. I told him I was sorry but the medicine Doc gave me had really knocked me out. He said he knew it was the medicine cause Doc told him about it. I thought it was good that Doc was telling Jones about the medical stuff without him having to hunt the information down.

It started to get light and half-buried bodies were starting to poke out of the ground. Chase had Fairchild dig a straddle trench. Since there were soft sinkholes everywhere, Fairchild started to dig into one of them to cut out some of his work effort and time. Five minutes into it he started digging up body parts. Turns out the sinkholes were graves, which were caused by the decomposing bodies giving way to the ground. So much for the soft and rolling ground I was sleeping on the night before.

I took Sgt Chase with me to scope out the area. Sgt Chase sounded like he was from Boston, but he was from New York City. Big Irish-Catholic guy, his wife was a Marine back at Lejeune and they had a kid that was only a couple of months old. We found nothing that was going to be a problem. We headed back and found Jones. I told him what I wanted and they all started to dig in. I wrote up my fire plan sketch and turned it in to Lt Fanning. While I was up at the Company Head Shed, Lt Daniels told me to stand by for the Captain who would be back soon from a meeting.

The building where the Company CP was located was in good shape but had trash all over the place. Some Marines were sweeping it down, trying to clean it up a bit. The building was also split into two sections. One side looked like it was a rather large office. The other side, which is where 1st Sgt Parker and Carrico were at, was a smaller office space but it also had another area that looked like a cooking area. There were two brick stoves there and several hooks hanging from the ceiling that looked like they were used for hanging meat or used by Saddam's sons to torture people.

There were two Amtraks with the Company CP. One Amtrak had the Captain in it and he traveled with the forward observers for artillery, 60mm mortars and Lt Fanning. The Platoon Commander for Amtraks was also in this vehicle. He seemed arrogant and cocky. I didn't know why -- he was prior enlisted so you would have thought he might have been a little more down to earth. But then I found out he was a Staff Sergeant who was a military postal clerk. The guy had had some run-of-the-mill job and then became an officer -- an officer with a military occupational specialty in the combat arms. So I guess in his book he went from nobody to somebody. Nothing wrong with being proud of what you did, just don't be an arrogant little prick about it. The second Amtrak had the First Sgt, the Company Corpsman, Doc Murphy, and the Amtrak Plt Sgt with his mechanics. The Amtrak Platoon Sergeant was GySgt Ingerson. He played the guitar and made up stupid songs to go with his playing. One song in particular was about how we didn't get mail. He was always quick in pointing out something stupid and even quicker with a remark about it. Some of the truest things are said in jest.

Captain Newland held his meeting and said we would be in the area for a while. Passed a lot of other word but the one thing he did pass down that kind of stuck out was that Battalion was going to have an after-action debrief on An Nasiriyah. I figured that this had already been done, but was kind of glad to hear that they wanted all key billet holders, officers, and enlisted at this brief. I left the new Company Office and started rooting around the pile of trash that had been cleaned out of the building. I found a logbook with some writing here and there but it was mostly blank. This is what I needed though. I had run out of paper a couple of days ago and had not been able to write anyone. So I took the book back to the Platoon area and started writing Dad and Kelly.

I liked writing Kelly. She did not judge anything I said or did. If I wrote something and asked her what she thought about it, she would write that if I had done it, it must have been the best choice of action. She never gave me suggestions or ideas like I should do something. It was always like "have you thought about..." Sometimes she would tell me that she did not understand some of my words but that she wanted to learn about what I was talking about, and even the most boring stories I told her always seemed to keep her attention. She was about me, and I liked that because it made it easier for me to be about her.

After stand-to that night, I told Jones to bring everyone in off the line, to put them in a tighter-knit area, and have two-man patrols walk the front lines. The dogs were getting brave, actually coming up to the Marines and trying to take their food as they ate.

**14 April 2003**
I spent most of the day hanging out with 1st Sgt Parker. We talked about everything under the sun. He and Schielein were a lot alike when it came to bikes; except for the way they approached it. Schielein's life revolved around his Harley, while Parker had other things he was into -- like his family. Don't get me wrong, Caveman was into his kids but they didn't live with him so it was just different. Parker wanted to get new pipes for his sled and did not know what type to get. I told him if he had the baffles taken out of his current pipes, he could just leave on what he had.

This was our conversation for the most of the day. The Marines were on line doing the same thing I was doing, talking about nothing, burning time. A Platoon is a weird animal. No two Platoons are alike. None of the Platoons were farther than a football field apart, and at times they were right next to each other shooting the same target. But they were still not the same.

Carrico gave the Marines a chance to take showers. I had gone to a meeting and missed my turn with the Platoon. Parker heard I missed out, so he got a hook-up from Gunny Ingerson for me to take a shower under the hood of their Amtrak. Nineteen years in the Corps and I had never seen shit like this before. Except for the caged-in feeling I had, it was a great shower. I know this sounds weird but after the shower I felt like I was part of the Company. I had fought "with' them in An Nasiriyah, but in a different part. But someone had to have noticed that I did not get a shower. It certainly was not the smell -- the dead Iraqis and the dogs took care of that. Someone was watching over me. Just like I watched over them. I felt like part of the family.

After stand-to, Jones got the Marines together, set up security on the sleeping area, and set up the two-man patrol along the line. We didn't do much during the day but the heat sapped all the energy out of us, so it did not take long for those who were not on watch to crash out. But as we started to sleep, the dogs started to wake up. All night they would bark and howl. Around midnight that night, two packs of dogs went at it. The fight moved back and forth around our area. The Marines that watched over the others as they slept called for me. I didn't bother putting on my boots. I grabbed my shotgun and ran between the dogs and my Platoon. I didn't want any of the Marines to start shooting the dogs with the rifles because the rounds might have gone stray into another unit, or people would have started thinking we were in a firefight and then who knows what the fuck would have happened. I racked a round in the chamber and I heard LCpl Airhart yell, "do it Gunny, do it!" and then Cpl Gonzalez yelled at Airhart to "shut the fuck up." The dogs started to move their fight away from us. I am glad I did not have to shoot that night -- it would have been a pain in the ass to clean up the mess, and the smell of burning off the dogs bodies might have been a little more than I cared to go for. The dogs were out of our area for the rest of the night, but they were still howling and fighting around us.

## 15 April 2003

The word came down that today that they were having a debrief of An Nasiriyah. I was kind of up in the air if I wanted to go or not.

Instead, I decided to do a little urban patrol training in the compound where we were. Rumor was, we were going into Al Kut to patrol the city as security. I cleared it through the Company XO and while Jones was giving classes on patrolling, Chase and I toured the area to make sure there were no duds or unexpended ammo that the Marines might step on or be tempted to fuck with. The only dangerous thing we could find was inside the buildings, and I did not plan on having anyone go in there. The Iraqis had stores of increments for artillery and mortar rounds. Like I said, I didn't plan on going into the buildings.

The squad leaders were almost done teaching their squads when I got back. Chase took Jones out on the course we were going to have them run. Cross was my RTO (Radio Transmitter Operator) and my thing with him was that I wanted him to follow me everywhere I went. He was not to be out of arm's reach at any time, and when we stopped, whatever direction I was facing, he was to face the opposite. Cross was a great guy, a blonde-haired Marine of average build. He had just met his real dad right before we had left for this little trip. His dad was a Marine machine gunner in Vietnam. He had a couple of pictures of him and damn if they did not look alike, except his dad was stocky and covered in tattoos. Cross didn't get to spend to much time with his father but he liked talking about him. The one thing I liked about Cross was his ability to keep his mouth shut. Jones and I would have to talk a lot about other Marines as far as their personal problems, how they were doing in the Platoon, or how well they were performing their jobs. Cross never told anyone what we said. I am sure his mute mouth made life easier on him in the long run. He would have had to leave our fighting hole every time Jones and I needed to talk if he had run his mouth.

The Platoon did a couple of movements around some buildings and everything, for the most part, came off with out a hitch. Cross got a call from the Company telling us to bring it in, which was fine. I could teach what I wanted about patrol bases back at the Platoon CP.

The reason they called me in was that the CO wanted me to go to the debriefing they were having on the Naz. All the other Platoon Commanders, the XO, and the CO had left by the time I got to the

134

Company CP. Parker did not go to the brief, and when I showed up I asked him if I had to go. He just laughed and said, "yea you got to go -- you think you are something special?" I ended up going to the brief but only stayed for a little while. I thought it might be faster moving than what it turned out to be. It was really slow. It's fine to get everything accurate, but I started to realize how much confusion was going on that day. None of the Company XOs or below really knew what had happened to the other Companies. During the only break I stuck around for, I walked around to the clusters of Officers and SNCOs. The frustration and anger everyone had for the other Companies was fucking weird. Every Company seemed to feel as if the other Companies had let them down. Everyone went back into the brief. I walked in the opposite direction. I ran into Lt Jackson, who was sitting in the back of a HMMV. He asked me if I wanted a smoke, I said yea, and then he offered me something to drink. Of course I said yea. We sat and bullshitted for a while. He said Lt Barnhart had taken off to Regiment for some other bullshit meeting. I left and headed back home to my Platoon.

Later that afternoon we got mail call. Just the sound of mail got me motivated. I got a post card from Kelly that had the Texas flag on it. She wrote that she was at a lake close to San Antonio, drinking a margarita and thinking of me. At first I thought it was cool that she was thinking of me and that she missed me. Then I read the postmark on the card and it was dated 24 March 2003. I lost it. I thought of how I was scraping body parts off ammo cans that day while she was on the lake drinking margaritas. I knew she couldn't have known what was going on, but I was mad. I felt alone. I kept my anger to myself. The more I thought about it, the worse it got. It was Sunday morning for us, and Saturday night for her. She was out having a good time, other people were getting to spend time with her, and the only thing I got to do was think about her. Then it wasn't just her it was everybody. There was nothing to do about it. The only way I could cope with it was by saying, "fuck it" to myself. I did not want to deal with it, so I stopped caring. If no one gave a fuck about me, I didn't give a fuck about anyone else. It was easy to get lost in my work.

Parker called a Company formation after mail call. First Sgt called Carrico and me in before formation and told us what had happened. Three idiots from another Platoon in our Company had found some increments for a mortar inside one of the buildings and had decided to light them on fire. This resulted in one of the Marines getting a burn on his face -- not so bad that he would be deformed for the rest of his life, but bad enough to get him out of the war for a while. 1<sup>st</sup> Sgt Parker didn't think it was funny that a Marine was hurt -- that pissed him off -- but he couldn't help but laugh about what an idiotic thing this guy did. When Parker got in front of the formation and chewed everyone out, though, he acted like nothing was funny. The two idiots who let the Marine burn the increments instead of stopping him caught most of the hell.

Word came down later that afternoon that Major Sosa from Battalion Headquarters wanted me up at the Head Shed for the debrief. I got a ride from the Company HMMV. I walked in and sat next to SSgt Pompos. I had not seen him or anyone else outside the Company much since that day at An Nasiriyah. Someone was giving a brief. When they were through, Major Sosa called me up next. He gave me a stick and had the PowerPoint guy draw a close-up of the area north of the bridge at An Nasiriyah. Major Sosa told me to go over what had happened during the battle. I fucking didn't want to be there, standing up in front of all my peers, my superiors, my friends and brothers, and telling them what I did and what I was thinking. My biggest fear was walking out of there having them think I was a fuck-up or a coward, or having them think of me like everyone else I ever met thought of me, which was a cowboy out of control. I talked as little as I could. Lt Letendre was helping me from the crowd as much as Major Sosa would let him. When I was done, even though I kept it as general as I could, I felt like I had put myself on display to be poked at. When it was over I walked straight out, got in the HMMV, and went home, for the second time, to my Platoon.

Capt Newland came back that night and said we were moving out the next day. We were going on the other side of the Euphrates River, only about two-three miles across the map. There was a bridge to the south and a bridge to the north. If we took the bridge to the south it would take us about thirty minutes to get there but we would have to drive through the city. If we took the bridge to the north it would take a couple of hours but there were few houses and fewer places to be ambushed. I wanted to go the north bridge route. Then the rumor was that the Iraqi leaders in Al Kut didn't want us tearing up their roads with our tracked vehicles – so then I wanted to go the southern route, through their city. Who the fuck were they to tell me where to go? Let them ambush us -- we would lay waste to everything in sight. Fuck them. I was not the only man in my unit to think that way. It was our rebellion against what we could not control.

136

## 16 April 2003

The morning came. We had been sleeping with decomposing bodies, dog shit, and burning trash. The ground was filthy – there was trash and rats everywhere. There had been a couple of sick Marines already, but nothing long lasting or serious. I had a feeling that I was about to join their ranks; I was not feeling well at all.

We moved out of our holes and our tracks moved over to a staging area. It seemed we could never just move out from our fighting positions -- we always had to "stage" somewhere. And we could never stage five or ten minutes ahead of time; it was always 12 or 13 hours. Of course, that was not the rule if higher got a thorn up their ass and wanted us to move out "now."

Tanks were running up and down our staging area. There was a cinderblock wall with Saddam's picture on it. One of the tanks ran it over. Everybody got a kick out of it. I have to admit it was kind of cool.

We laid out our gear for sleeping and Jones established watch. It was not quite dark yet but everyone was already trying to sleep. I went to sleep. I hadn't gotten sick yet but I knew if I didn't get some sleep I was done for. As soon as I crawled under my poncho it started to rain. The other Platoons in the Company took off for the cover of some buildings. Lt Daniels and 1st Sgt Parker came over and asked if I was going to bring my Platoon into one of the buildings, out of the rain. I said no, all our gear was covered and I didn't want to go into a building in the dark and have one of my Marines lay on a dud round or some unexpended ammo. Plus we had settled in quicker than the other Platoons had. All my Marines knew it was going to rain and had prepared that way. Thirty minutes later it stopped raining and I was for sure sick.

## 17 April 2003

The next morning we packed up and got ready to move out. I was feeling better so I decided to eat. Of course that was a bad idea. The new MREs we were getting had milk shake mix in them. It was kind of cool. You put water in this oversized zip lock bag that already had the mix in it, and then you would shake the bag and voila, fucking vanilla (also came in chocolate and strawberry, but strawberry sucked ass) milk shake. I was in the commander's hatch of my track; I crawled out and threw up. Parker came over and started laughing at me, which made me laugh and throw up that much more -- and harder -- which made him laugh... a vicious circle.

I ended up getting put in the back of the First Sgt's Amtrak and having an I.V. thrown into my arm. Doc Murphy tried putting my IV in but he couldn't get the vein. First Sgt Parker was yelling at Doc to hurry up cause everyone was leaving. I wanted to yell "don't hurry up, take your time" but I didn't have the energy to. Doc put something in the IV that sent me off into la-la land. I woke up and we were at our new base camp. The Captain put two Platoons on the line and mine in the reserve. Jones had the Marines set up the camouflage netting from our Amtrak. Everyone started crashing out. We did nothing for the rest of the day. I was the first in a long chain of Marines who came down with dysentery.

### 18 April 2003

I traded out with one of the other Platoons on the line, so they went in reserve and I was on the line. Our positions were on the other side of a bombed-out chain link fence so the Amtraks couldn't go with us; they stayed with the Platoon in reserve. The holes had already been dug in by the other Platoon. They really didn't dig in, though; it was more like they threw rocks up around their position so they could tie their ponchos up and keep in the shade. I told Jones I wanted the holes dug deeper and that they could lay ponchos lower to the ground to keep the shade. Jones passed this word to the Squad Leaders. The holes didn't get dug. I told Jones I don't think the Squad Leaders understood what I wanted.

He gathered up the three Squad Leaders -- Cpl Tapia, Cpl Gonzales and LCpl Marshall. Jones had them start digging a fighting hole so they knew what we expected. As they were digging, I got my first chance to bullshit with them. This whole time I had been either sick or concentrating on the way Jones and I worked together. I wanted Jones to understand what I expected out of him, and I wanted to make sure I did not do his job either. I stayed in my grid, and allowed him to work his. The Marines had to see what the two different roles were so that when they became Platoon Sergeants some day, they would not fuck over their Lieutenant. It would have been easy for me to run both our jobs, but more damage would have come out of it.

I knew what it was like to have a Lt think his job was "everything the Platoon did." It was demoralizing not only to the leaders, but also to those being led. And it usually ended up with the Lt not only being disliked by the Platoon, but also not respected. A young Lt sometimes forgets that all the enlisted joined up because that was what they wanted to do -- they wanted to lead. Besides, enlisted stick with enlisted. There

138

were officers in my past that had let me do my job, and not only did I respect them for trusting me and letting me learn and develop, but I would protect them against all enemies "foreign and domestic."

Cpl Tapia was my first squad leader. He was from California. He had been working in the fields since he was twelve, picking strawberries. He said he joined the Marines to get a college education, a good job, and to get his parents out of the fields. I hope it worked out for him. God, I really do. The Marine Corps was easy work for him. Three square meals a day and a place to sleep. Cpl Gonzales was a small, wiry Marine from the Texas/Mexico border. Gonzo's family lived on a small ranch and Gonzo was not having any of that small-town living. The quickest way to leave was the Corps. LCpl Marshall was from Boston and the least experienced of the three as a squad leader. He was so young looking, I don't think he had to shave, but he was definitely not afraid to put his foot up someone's ass. While they were digging, their squads were digging deeper. They finished digging the hole and Jones told me I needed to explain how I wanted the shade set up on the fighting holes.

The Platoon was dug in deep and had shaded up like I wanted in time for evening chow -- a hot MRE! (That's sarcasm in case you did not pick that up.) Their packs were low to the ground so as not to give our position away. The Platoon knew that we were getting pulled off the line the next day and would take over the other Platoon's position, and that I would make them dig in just as deep. They didn't want to leave. The Platoon to our right flank had not dug in at all. I didn't want them to have to dig in again, but if we moved over there we were going to have to. I went and talked to Lt Daniels and he said that my Platoon could stay on line. I went back and told Jones we were good for a couple of days on line. Dysentery hit a couple more of my Marines. The worst cases were pulled back to my hole so Doc could keep an eye on them.

It had started to get dark, and we were at 100 percent on stand-to. When we finally stood down, we went to 25% alert.

**19 April 2003**
Around 0900 we got the word to come off the line and go in reserve. It sucked. The other Platoon had left the area trashed. Jones went to the other Platoon Sergeant and had him get his people back over there to clean the place up.

Capt Newland called me over and told me he wanted me to take my Platoon out and do a vehicle inspection point. He said he was going to get more information from the Battalion Three, Major Sosa, and he wanted me to pick him up at the Battalion CP in about thirty minutes so we could go out and find a spot. I went back and told Jones to get the Marines ready. Carrico had a vehicle ready for me.

The driver took Parker and me over to pick up Captain Newland at the Battalion CP. We were spread out all over this base camp -- which was cool cause this camp, even though it was bombed out, it was not "trashed" out. So this gave everyone a chance to air out and kind of clean up. Capt Newland was talking to some other officers when we pulled up. He finished and we went to recon possible checkpoints. We headed east to some arches and then west to the far end of our Battalion's area of operations. This was all done on one road that ran across the north perimeter of the base we were on. I was having a good time just running around outside the base. Of course the Captain was ragging on me for having been sick. He said that we should set up at the arches to the east. I agreed. It provided more cover, spread us out so we were not bunched up, and there was enough rubble from destroyed buildings to create roadblocks, as we needed to.

We went through the buildings and I found an Iraqi flag. A few minutes later Parker found one and gave it to the Captain. I was going to give mine to my dad. We headed back out to the base camp.

As we were about to leave a kid of about twelve or so came up with some bread for sale. It looked like cornbread and it was cheap. I think he wanted a penny a loaf. I gave him a dollar for three loaves. I gave a piece to the Captain and Parker didn't want any. I started to dig into the bread and it tasted like the smell of the Euphrates River.

Jones had everyone ready when we got back. At first I thought I would need everyone. I didn't think I could really utilize the SMAW gunners so I told Sgt Shaw that he and his squad were staying behind. The rest of us moved out to the arches. I had to physically stop by the Battalion CP to let them know I was leaving friendly lines. Capt Greene, the Battalion Air Officer, was the Officer of the Day so I had to check out with him. I showed him where I would be and told him I would be back when the Battalion told me to, which I expected to be in a couple of hours. He asked me what kind of roadblock I was setting up. I told him I was setting up a vehicle checkpoint and only searching every ten or so vehicles. He smiled, put his small finger to the edge of his chin (like Dr. Evil in Austin Powers), and asked if it was going to be an "evil vehicle check point." I don't know why, but that was funny. Maybe cause I did not expect that at all. I went back to my Amtrak and we headed out the front gate.

As soon as we were out the gate we banked a left and headed out to the arches, about three miles down the road. My plan was simple. One squad would search vehicles in the parking lot off to the north of the arches (the arches went over the road), one squad would set up barriers to slow down traffic and direct the vehicles to be searched, and the other squad would be put in reserve. I would rotate them between duties at my discretion. I had one Amtrak facing east and another facing west. The third Amtrak was off to the side with the reserve. I was going to put the reserve squad in the building but it was too close to the road. My biggest fear was having one of my Marines shot at with small arms fire. So I tasked the reserve squad to send fire teams into some of the small buildings or prominent terrain features around the area. I told LCpl Marshall to send out one or two teams, to check one building or several places, and to vary his time up. Also, being repetitive two or three times and then doing something different would throw anyone off as far as what we were doing. LCpl Marshall did this well. He was real good with the squad. His biggest problem was LCpl Airhart's sarcasm, but he was quick to tell him to shut the fuck up and do what he was told.

The first couple of vehicle searches were a little rough even though we had gone over it at the Company CP, but things smoothed out after that. Things were working well and I expected to be called in soon because we had been out at the checkpoint for a couple of hours and it was about to get dark. Captain Newland came out to check on us. He said he came out not to really check on us, but to get away for a while. He walked around our set-up. He didn't say much so I figured things were good enough. First Sgt Parker was talking to the Marines here and there. Parker knew his shit but was not an officer, so he had the "liberty" of saying what he wanted without being looked at like a jackass. So I asked him if he saw anything that I could have done better. He said no, it looked fine. Capt Newland told me that my Platoon was to stay out overnight and that I was to call in around 0900 or so and ask permission to come in. I wasn't expecting it, but okay -- in a take-an-order-and-carry-it-out kind of way. Inside I was thinking, "what the fuck, but roger that." He also said that at night, he wanted me only checking suspicious vehicles.

About an hour before it got dark, I moved my Amtraks off the line and put them in this lowland off to the northwest about 200 meters, which Jones had scoped out earlier. I sent my reserve squad down there to hold security on it. I then had the squad that was checking vehicles move down to the low ground. I was going to keep only one squad up on line, so there was one fire team watching the road and two teams in reserve. I wanted one person awake watching the reserve while they slept.

Traffic was down to almost nothing at night on this road. It had been busy all day. Since Saddam was no longer in charge, the different Muslim sects had religious freedom. The sect that was predominant in the area had not been able to practice one of their traditions in a little over a decade. Everyone that day had been traveling to gather together to observe this tradition. But like I said, at night it was almost barren. An ambulance tried to drive through our checkpoint. The road guards stopped it. I went over to see what was going on. They had two guys out on the side of the road while the Marines searched the vehicle. I talked to the two guys who were in the ambulance. They said they were doctors. They offered to shake my hand. Their hands were soft and they spoke better English than I did. I told my Marines to stop searching the vehicle and let them go. Before they went, I commented on the good condition of the ambulance. He said the French had given the Iraqi Army a lot of new vehicles and equipment last January. My fucking temper was about to explode. If you ask me what I think our next military target should be, I would say France. I hope that the terrorists let lose on them. The French would rather appease the terrorists and hope for leniency than fight them. The French have paid the "Dane Geld." That is like a fight in elementary school. The bully comes up to you and before he punches you, you fall to the ground and hold your arms up and pull your legs in to protect your stomach and tell the bully he has won and "please don't hit me." You are relying on mercy that is either temporary or is not there at all. I believed them when they said they were doctors.

Later on, going in a different direction, is another ambulance. My Marines stopped it and started to search it. I walked over to the ambulance. It was two different guys and I expected them to speak English like the other guys, but they didn't. I shook one of the guy's hands and it felt like sandpaper. These guys could have been ambulance drivers. I asked the Marine doing the search what he had found he said nothing. When he said nothing, he meant nothing. No medical supplies, no paper work, no stretcher, nothing an ambulance in the States would have. I had them rip into the ambulance even deeper. I even brought part of the react/reserve force to help. Nothing was found but the two guys seemed a little nervous. I thought about detaining them, but for what? The Battalion was supposed to get a translator two weeks prior to all this, and just like the ambulance, nothing. I had to let them go.

Late into the night our last bit of excitement happened. A motorcycle pulled up with two guys on it. You could hear it screaming in the night from a mile off. When they finally got to the arches I was awake and waiting for them. My two sentries wouldn't approach them because the motorcycle had stopped. Airhart was somewhere in the dark calling the two other Marines pussies for not approaching them. I walked up to the side of the motorcycle. I scared the shit out of the two guys riding it. They were trying to kick start the bike but it would not turn over. I called the two Marines up and told them to hold my shotgun, and I motioned for the two Iraqi men to move to the side. I broke out my flashlight and started looking for two things: a bomb and the reason why the bike wouldn't start. Didn't find a bomb but I found a loose spark plug wire. I guessed that the rattling of the bike had caused it to shake loose. I tightened it and kick-started the bike, which turned over. I was tempted to take it for a ride but if I had I don't think I would have wanted to stop. Like heroine for a junkie. The two guys got on the bike and drove off. I could only imagine how great it must have felt to ride through the desert with no traffic, no helmet, and just ride through the night.

I went back to the parking lot where the other Marines were sleeping; the reserve had just traded out with a squad that was back with SSgt Jones. I lay on the cement and went back to sleep.

## 20 April 2003
Got up early the next morning, as we did every morning. By the time the sun rose we were set up for the vehicle inspection point, just as we were the previous day. The only difference was that I had the reserve sitting behind the building, and I had put two observers above the arches over the road to look out over the area.

I called in around 0900 and asked permission to break down the vehicle inspection point. Higher said to bring it on in. No problem. We broke down everything without losing our security. We entered the gate and went straight to the Head Shed to do my after-action brief on what had happened out there. I knew it would probably take a while, so Jones took the Platoon back to the Company CP and left me to walk back to the Company CP. I told him before he left that I wanted to be able to set up a vehicle inspection point in under ten minutes -- sand bags everything. He said he would get on it.

I saw Capt Greene and he asked me how it went with the "evil road block." I told him it was evil. It was his turn to laugh. I saw Capt Rohr -- he was bored. His job was still to coordinate fires, but there was no enemy to coordinate on. We just bullshited a while. There was nothing really to talk about. I thanked him for sending me to Bravo to be a Platoon Commander. He said he did not want to send me but he knew I would enjoy it. He was right, but I missed CAAT and 81s. I still saw them, I just did not feel like I belonged to them anymore. They did not treat me different. The difference was not on their part, but mine. I did not want them to think I deserted them. I was afraid they did. I headed back to my Company area.

On the way over I was walking by 81's Platoon. They were dug in, the aiming stakes were out, ammo was ready, and a man was up on each tube. Besides that they were crashed out, throwing a Frisbee or a football, and listening to music. As I walked by the Platoon, Marines would get up and say hi to me or come over and talk to me about what was going on back home. I liked it when Marines told me about their homes because it showed that they trusted me and were interested in hearing what I had to say about any problems they had. Made me feel like a dad more than a Gunny sometimes. I stopped by Lt Clayton and GySgt Leggett's HMMV to see what was going on. They had two chairs set out in front of it in the shade of the camouflaged netting like two kings upon their thrones. It was awesome seeing them that way. With the frisbee being thrown around, the music, the sand, the shade of the netting, and the two chairs they were sitting in, I kind of felt like I was on a tropical island. It felt good. We talked a while but it was more like gossip. When we got through the Lt asked how I was doing with my not smoking. I told him fine. He said it was hard to believe I had quit cold turkey like that. He said he would quit when we got back to Lejeune, as he pulled a drag on his pipe. I did think he would stop smoking the cigarettes but not the pipe -- I mean nobody quits smoking a pipe.

I got back to the Company CP and Lt Daniels told me that the other two Platoons were going to stay on line and that I was going to run checkpoints for the rest of the time there. The next checkpoint would be tomorrow morning. That was good and bad news. I felt like they trusted me. I felt that my Marines had done well, but I didn't want my Marines out there getting shot either. Lt Daniels and I talked a while about the awards that were being written up. Captain Newland was spending a lot of time at the Battalion CP writing up the awards using the few computers they had. Lt Daniels was also writing a good share of the awards up himself. His father was a retired Colonel in the Marine Corps. I never saw him use that fact to shirk his duty or not be responsible for his actions. When I first met him at Camp Lejeune, he had looked so young I wanted to ask him if his mom knew he was playing Marine. Now he looked old, tired, beaten and worn out, like a beaten dog. I left the Company CP and the shade of the Company Cap's camouflaged netting and headed over to the shade of my Platoon's camouflaged netting. Jones was finishing up with them. They had sandbags filled and on top of the Amtraks, and he told me how he planed to deploy them for the next checkpoint. After we talked about it, we made a change or two - - not changing anything that he had come up with, just a thing or two concerning the employment of the Amtraks.

Jones left to get with SSgt Deitz on the changes. As he walked out, Lt Fanning walked in. He started asking me what kind of training schedule I had set up. I told him the XO knew what I had going on. I asked him why he was checking on my Platoon. He started to explain, and I told him that the CO and XO had directed my actions and if he had any questions he should ask them.

In the big picture, I did not mind him asking what I had going on and would have had no problem with it. But the way he came across, and in front of my Marines, was wrong. Unless I had a good reason to, I would never have acted the way he did to a junior-ranking Marine in front of the men he led. You don't undermine someone like that, unless someone is about to get hurt. Fanning's approach challenged my decision-making process and gave the appearance that I did not have any control over what or how my Platoon did things. I am sure he did not mean anything wrong with it, but his approach was fucked up.

Captain Newland came by my tent and told me that Battalion had a change in plans. I was to set up a checkpoint that afternoon and another the next morning. Roger that. Anything, just to get away from the bullshit for a while. I just hoped that if anyone got shot it was me, no guilt in that.

I went out with a driver from Headquarters' Platoon and scoped out a few spots. I figured, instead of setting up by the arches like we had just done, I would go the opposite direction -- east. I found a spot between a small market and another abandoned Iraqi Army camp.

When the driver and I returned to our area, Jones told us that everyone was ready to go. I gave him, the squad leaders, and the attachment leaders a quick frag as to where we were going and how we were going to set up. We jumped in the Amtraks, checked out with battalion, got out the front gate, and headed east. The platoon was set up in about seven minutes. There was one squad on the west side of the checkpoint and another on the east. I sent one squad into the Iraqi barracks to make sure it was clear. The only thing they found were looters. I looked into the compound to make sure they were clearing the buildings safely. There were a lot of pictures on the wall. It took me a second or two to figure out what the pictures were. They were "lead diagrams," showing how far ahead of a vehicle you should aim various kinds of weapons to hit the vehicle at different ranges. One of the diagrams showed how to shoot a pilot if he bailed out of his plane. I told Cpl Gonzalez (Gonzo) to leave the looters alone unless they started getting stupid with us. Jones and I met at the center of the two squads of the vehicle checkpoint. Since Gonzo's squad had checked out the building, I put them in reserve and had a fire team from his squad doing the vehicle checks.

Things were pretty uneventful. A dad and what looked like a grandfather were playing soccer with a bunch of kids. They invited some of the Marines who were guarding the checkpoint to play with them. Marshall told them they couldn't because they had to work. The man raised his hand like he understood and went back playing soccer with the kids. A couple of the Marines from Marshall's squad were watching the game but not to the point that they were totally distracted. There was an area southwest of where the kids were playing that looked like a rice field. I kept thinking, someone could really do a number on us from there. Marshall was already on it and had a fire team moving in and around the edges of the field.

We were just about to pull up stakes and go back to the Company CP when a long line of new white SUVs pulled up. Gonzo pulled the first one over and the rest stop. An older fat man got out of the back of the vehicle and started yelling but no one could understand him. A younger man from the second vehicle approached the older man and tried to calm him down. By now Jones had called the react force up to our position.

146

When they arrived, the older man shut up and the younger man was directed to me by one of my Marines. He said they had paperwork authorizing them to meet with some Army general. I read the paperwork over and it looked legit so I let them go. On the way out the older man was yelling something at us. The lead driver floored the vehicle, almost running me over. I turned on the second vehicle and pumped a round into the chamber of my shotgun, aiming it at the second driver. He stopped and I pointed to him to go around me, and slower. He did it and the other vehicles followed his lead.

We packed up just as quickly as we had set up and moved back in. Jones and the Platoon went back to the Company area and I reported to the Battalion CP all that had happened and what we had seen. After all that, they told me to keep on the lookout for new white vehicles, especially SUVs.

Fuck me.

I walked back to the Company CP kind of daydreaming while I was walking. Instead of cutting a straight line to the Platoon I decided to follow the road. There was a bomb crater that must have measured thirty or forty feet deep and a hundred feet wide along this road. There was no rubble around the blast; whatever it had hit had been completely destroyed. There was a 7-ton that had just passed the crater and there were a bunch of Marines acting like idiots. It was Javelin's Platoon. I saw them and they saw me and we acted like we had not seen each other in years. It was great seeing them. The way they treated me, and the way 81s had treated me earlier, I felt the brotherhood. We were baptized by fire together and these Marines had not forgotten it. It was good seeing this. I hoped this would last, and I am sure it did. I left for my Platoon.

That afternoon we were told that the plan had changed, again, for the third time. They wanted us to go back to the arches and set up a block that would prevent traffic from going down the south side of the road. Apparently there was a bomb found and it had to be defused. Blowing it in place would have destroyed the road, which would have impeded our use of the road for supplies. Well, that was what we were being told.

We headed out. Since the area the bomb was in needed its space, we were going to have to make a different plan. I gave Jones a squad and some attachments to set up down east. I had a squad in the middle as a react force and I took a squad and some attachments to the west, back at the arches. The three squads set up rocks and guides to direct the traffic to the two lanes on the north side of this four-lane highway. The squad in the middle used rocks to split the two lanes on the north between the traffic heading east and west. Then security was set up for the night. It should have been easy since we were not setting up any vehicle checkpoints. Just making sure traffic flowed the right way and when they actually got to defuse the bomb, we would stop all the traffic.

Before it got dark I wanted to check all the squads and get a face to face with Jones. I took LCpl Airhart as security with me for the walk down. Airhart was always pissing me off for something stupid but I couldn't help but like the guy. He was a good guy; he just acted like the Platoon Jester sometimes. On the way down we passed the Army fuckers, who were setting up their camp to defuse the bomb. They were wearing clean uniforms and had new weapons with a bunch of magazine pouches hanging all over them. There was this overly-fat Warrant Officer with a bunch of Rambo knives hanging all over him, standing around like he was General Patton or some shit. We were walking down in a gully to the south of their position when Patton yelled at us to walk around. I was tired of people like him -- a fucking pogue who thought that just cause he had rank and a cigar hanging from his mouth, we should give into his every whim or thought. We were already walking around, so Airhart and I kept walking. Airhart started laughing because we were not answering this fat fuck. The Warrant Officer yelled even more and started to walk toward us. Some Private with glasses was guarding the corner that we were walking by, and he didn't know what to do. He could see that we were already going around the area, but his Warrant Officer was spazzing out. By the time the yelling, fat fucker with the cigar got to where we were walking, we were already gone. Airhart looked back and said that the fat man was out of air. Life must be grand if your only problem is worrying about where people walk. (On a side note, I have worked with EOD before, and these guys were not EOD. EOD guys are down to earth, usually older, and will tell you in detail what they are doing before they do anything. These guys were too young, clean, and squirrelly -- my guess is that they were Military Intelligence guys).

As we reached the middle squad, Jones was there. We bullshitted a little but a HMMV pulled up, which cut our conversation short. There was mail and packages, a lot of it, and everyone had a piece. The driver started to ask if I wanted the Platoon to have it now or take it back for later after we got done. I interrupted with a "NOW, WE WANT IT

NOW!" I told him to give the middle squad their mail first, then drop it off over by Jones, and then to my position. Jones and I quickly finished our conversation about watch and react plans. Airhart and I ran back to the arches where our mail was going to be delivered. Mail -- I felt like a kid waiting in line to see Santa Claus.

It was about two hours till nightfall when we got our mail. We set up security and ripped into our packages and letters. I received two packages -- one from my Dad and his girlfriend and another from my Aunt Jenny. Of course I received mail from Kelly. I opened my packages and, after seeing what everyone was getting, decided to have everyone store their stuff in a building off to the side of the road. My Aunt Jenny had sent six boxes of Jelly Beans and my Dad had sent the usual necessities. Every time I had been sent to a hot spot around the world, my Dad would send me packages of things I would need for two weeks. Every two weeks he would send another package with the exact same things: candy, pens, paper, envelopes, duct tape, map pens, alcohol, and lamination paper -- these would be the usual things. That night we ate well from the packages. Canned goods were awesome. We would open the can and eat out of it. It did not matter if it was chili, pears, Chef Boyardee or peas. Everyone knew I was a coffee fiend, so I usually got everyone's coffee packets. These packets were awesome; they were like tea bags. Since I had stopped smoking I needed the coffee.

That night after stand-to, everyone went to sleep rather easy. I know this cause I could not sleep. I had Kelly's letters to read. There was a smaller shack behind the building that my boys were in. I went back there and found a chair in the dark, turned on my red lens flashlight, and started reading her letters. All the resentment I had had towards her melted away. She wrote that she loved me, and that how we met was crazy, and how good I made her feel. Like every letter she wrote me, I had to read it twice. I would read it so fast the first time that I would have to read it a second time just to see what she actually wrote. I placed the letters in the left flap of my flak jacket and went back to my Marines. I found a spot on the cool floor and went to sleep.

### 21 April 2003
The next morning at stand-to we all woke up in a great mood. You could tell that the mail made a difference. The Army unit had left during the night so I called it in to higher. Now all we had to do was wait for the word to return to the Company. We ate well that morning and the Marines were passing out their candy to children in passing cars.

Around 0800 I called Jones on the radio to open the road on both sides. Jones told me that the Marines at his position were passing out candy as well. While we were waiting for the word to leave, I climbed up on a track and pulled out Kelly's old letters. Since the mail was all gagged up, I would organize the letters that were written before or after in the stack of letters that I had already received, so I could follow her thought on the letter I had just received. The Amtrakers were still asleep so I got to read her letters alone, again.

I grabbed my shaving gear and some coffee stuff out of my pack and went to the side of the road where Schell was standing guard. Schell was a big, slow-talking kid -- always volunteered for working parties, always had his hole dug first, and never bitched about anything. Airhart was Schell's evil twin. I started making my coffee and shaving. Schell started talking about what we needed to do to win the war. I let him run his mouth; hell, everyone had an opinion on what we needed to do next. My opinion was, kill what needed to be killed so we could go home.

Later on that morning, we got word to come back to the camp so we could get ready to move out to a different position. We were going closer to Al Kut. Going closer to Al Kut meant doing what we had to do and going home. And the peasants rejoiced.

My plan for retrograding was for everyone to pack up and wait outside the Amtrak till my Amtrak got close to their position. When my Amtrak was almost there, everyone was to load up and keep moving behind me. Of course, something happened at the first pick-up of the middle squad, and we had to stop and get out. Ever since An Nasiriyah, fuck being in a track unless you had to be. There were three Iraqi guys with shovels at this position talking to Cpl Benson. One of the guys spoke great English and said they wanted permission to go on the Iraqi base to dig up a friend who had been executed a couple of years ago. Something about a proper Muslim burial. I told him to go to the front gate and I would make the necessary arrangements. The older man said thank you and I started to walk away. I thought about turning around and asking who he wanted to dig up, but I was afraid he would say it was his son. I would have felt like it was my fault since we did not come here sooner, like during the First Gulf War.

We continued movement back to the base camp and radioed for an interrogator to be at the front gate waiting for this man and his two friends. The front gate was slow letting us back in. They wanted us to

150

clear weapons. Clear weapons? Fucking bullshit games, but apparently some fucker in another Battalion had unintentionally shot a round off. So, the ripple effect -- we had to clear weapons. Jones took half and I took the other half. We checked in with Battalion. While I was there Capt Greene asked me how my evil roadblock went. I don't know why this was so funny. It was elementary school stupid, but it was funny.

I headed back to the Company. We unloaded for a while, loaded back up, and got ready to move out. As we were waiting to leave, I saw the old man from outside the gate and his friends walking across the ground looking for where the body might have been buried. The ground was torn up from bombing; I didn't know how they would find what they were looking for.

The whole battalion was lined up, ready to roll out to our new position, when word came down that there was more fighting in Al Kut and that we may need to hold our position. Carrico and I talked about this new predicament. He said if the fighting was so bad then maybe higher headquarters should move out of their hotel in the city and come sleep out on the ground with the rest of us. From Imperial Rome to modern day battles, great leaders have followed great fights from comfortable positions and have spoken words of poverty.

When I found Parker, he was around the outside of one of the Amtraks. He said he thought we were spending the night. We walked around and found an old motorcycle that was missing everything but a frame and a seat. I took a seat on it and he took a picture. Said he would send it in to *Easyrider Magazine*. We talked about his pipes for his Harley again. I thought he should leave his pipes as they were, but he was dead set on changing them. He acted like the only thing challenging him more than figuring out what pipes to get was getting his wife to agree to it. I think he knew Dawn would not have given him any trouble, but he had nothing but time to figure things out. If that was how he kept his sanity, who the fuck was I to blow it for him.

I ran into some guys from CAAT -- they were having a blast. They had been getting missions to go everywhere and do things. They acted glad to see me. That made me feel good, like they did not think I had deserted them. One of the guys from CAAT gave me a bottle of whiskey that he had gotten from out in town. Life was good. It was a clear glass bottle that was shaped like a flask with that magical brown liquid inside. If the color of the liquid did not give it away, the small white square label that had "whikee" on it with the Arabic lettering under it would tell you what it was. I headed back to Jones and the Platoon.

Word came down that we were staying for the night.

Later that evening the temperature began to cool and it was quiet -- no dogs. The nights when we did not worry about being shot at were awesome. The stars came out every night, but it wasn't every night that we could enjoy them. I looked at the open sky above the fields across the Euphrates River. At first only the strong stars would come out, and then slowly, as the night progressed, the smaller stars would start to show themselves. I found myself looking for the Big Dipper and then the North Star. After finding the North I would look for the star of the South. That would always remind me of night patrols in the Philippines, where we could see the Southern Cross. Different times.

### 22 April 2003
The morning brought us to stand-to. We moved out for Al Kut. We headed east for about five miles and pulled into a fenced-in area on the north side of the road. It was a large area of about two thousand square meters. The north and west sides were open bare ground with no shade. The south and east sides had tall trees, gardens, a small creek (that couldn't be crossed), a house that was completely open, and a large storage building. My platoon got the whole east side along the creek that was running north and south. The squad and attachment leaders and I tripped the line, deciding where the platoon would lay in. We were to tie in with 1st Platoon on our left.

This area was a garden that had different herbs growing in it. Thin nets and tall trees shaded it. There was a small irrigation trench where water from the creek came through. There were two T-55 tanks that had been burned up pretty bad. There was expended ammo everywhere. But time had run its course and the leaves and wind had started to cover the battle that had taken place. There were no dead bodies. I placed first squad there with a SMAW and machine gun team. As we moved north up the river, I could see the open fields being irrigated for hundreds of yards. The creek itself had fish swimming beside us that were a foot to a foot and a half long. I could not help but think my dad would love to live here. The garden slowly died away and the trees began to take over. The wind felt cool in the shade but lacked the dryness it once had due to the irrigated fields.

I placed Second Squad in along the river just as I did First Squad. The trees started to break away from the river when it came time for Third Squad to be set in. Third Squad would follow the tree line and the berm that started to form, and tie in with Third Platoon to our north. The ground was soft and easy to dig in. I found Jones and he had started preparing for the re-supply of the platoon. He had found an area that was shaded but open from the trees. There was a destroyed tank and a command vehicle near our position. I could smell the earth as the Marines dug into the ground. It had been along time since I had smelled that smell. The house on the property had a young man, who did not own the property, living in it. Gunny Carrico made the man move out of the compound. Some snipers set up on the top of the roof. HQ's platoon set up on the far side of the house under a large carport.

I turned in my fire plan sketch to Lt Fanning. We bullshitted for a while. While I was talking to him he was telling me about his daughter and his ex-wife. I chuckled to myself as he started to tell me about the history of the area. I felt relaxed as he was talking. All of Iraq had been a shit hole, but this small part was beautiful. Lt Fanning was a smart man, who was not lazy, who cared deeply for his daughter, and who wanted to do the best for his Marines. He was not the type of man that you liked right off the bat; you had to get to know him. We finished talking and I left back to my platoon.

As always, Jones and I took turns checking the line as the Marines dug in so we could catch any mistakes and correct them before there were any problems. Jones was gone, which left Doc and Cross at our CP. I asked Cross which way Jones went so I could go the other. Jones had gone to the garden side so I went up to Third Squad. Everyone was doing what they were supposed to do. I could pick up a vibe from them. They felt the same way I felt: relaxed. I met Jones halfway along the creek. There were three or four Iraqi men and they looked like brothers, fishing on the other side of the creek in front of their houses. They waved at us and smiled. We were standing next to the SMAW team leader, Sgt Shaw. I told him to mark the two houses on the other side of the creek, and no matter where we got fired on from he was to light those houses the fuck up. Shaw walked down to his two teams and assigned them their mud houses. We were relaxed but there was no use being stupid.

The day was uneventful. I walked around the wooded area, careful not to step on ordinance but enjoying my surroundings. The tanks were burned to shit inside. I tried to take a seat out of one of the tanks so I could maybe mold it and have it put on my bike back home. But then I thought, I didn't want some Hadji crap on my bike. I tripped the line, talking to my Marines and bullshitting with them about going home. Some of the Marines were hitting water at the bottom of their holes. It was kind of funny, considering where we were. It reminded me of Lejeune, and that reminded me of my daughters.

The night was quiet and comfortable again. I thought about that bottle of whiskey, if it was whiskey. I thought about my Kool-Aid packages from my MREs that I had been saving. If I used orange flavor, I would have a screwdriver; grape would have been wine; and lime would have been a kamikaze. I thought when I did drink it I would go for the screwdriver. I wanted to save it for a time I could really enjoy it.

At around 2200 there was a firefight in town; sounded like it consisted of M-16s and AK-47s. I told Jones to put everyone at a hundred percent alert and to be ready to put all their gear on the Amtrak and go. He did that while I checked in with the CO. Capt Newland was awake and had his RTO listening to what was going on. I talked with Parker and Fanning for a while. We were making half-ass estimates on how far the fire fight was from us, how little it affected us, and how little we could do to help whoever was getting shot the fuck up. We could see where the explosions of mortars and RPGs in the skyline illuminated part of the buildings in the distance. After about five minutes, all the shooting died down to nothing but M-16s. It was easy to tell their rifles and ours apart. Their AK-47s had a louder thud but were slower shooting on rapid fire, while our M-16s had more of a sharp crack and were a lot quicker in firing. After the Skipper told us where the firefight had taken place, I think it was Fanning who had come closest of the three of us in guessing the distance from us to the fire fight.

I went back to Jones and told him what had happened -- that basically some Hadjis had fired at a Marine outpost of some other Battalion that was deeper in the city. The Marines returned fire and had suffered no casualties, but they had killed and wounded a couple of Iraqis. We stood back down to 25% and went to sleep.

### 23 April 2003
We woke up and stood to. Airhart, Sitarek, and one of the SMAW gunners hadn't put all their gear away like they were supposed to, so I followed Marine Corps Order and talked to Captain Newland about some EMI (Extra Military Instruction). I got his blessing and Jones got the

First Sgts. We had them dig fighting holes by the abandoned house, over by where the snipers were. Jones had them break all their gear out and set it up around the newly dug holes. We pulled one squad off the line at a time so the three of them could give a class on how to dig holes. As one squad was getting the lesson, the next squad was patrolling their part of the line. When they were done I sent them back to their holes and Jones chewed their Squad Leaders' asses.

The rest of the day was laid back. Marines stood their watch for their fire teams while the rest of the Marines slept or talked in little groups back off the lines. I walked around to get a better look around at the tanks, command tracks, the abandoned house, and the spice garden. Jones said that Third Platoon was using the area behind our Third Squad as a shit area. Jones went to talk to the Third Platoon Sgt about having them come bury all their shit. Neither one of us wanted our boys getting sick again. About an hour later I saw Third walking over to our area with shovels. Problem solved.

We got the word that we would be leaving the next morning. Our route would be through town. Everyone felt that it was ironic that we could not drive through the town before, but tomorrow morning we would. No one complained about how we should drive where we wanted to, though. Driving through a town was our last heavy fight. We knew that better than anyone, including that Army Maintenance Company in An Nasiriyah. Our ego and pride left and reality had set in.

**24 April 2003**
Since we were leaving early in the morning, Jones had the Platoon get up and had one Marine from each fire team put the packs on the Amtraks. The rest of the Marines were at 100% on line. Things were going good till I heard a Platoon in the building behind me making a bunch of noise. Fuck that. I went over to the Platoon Sgt, a SSgt, and had his ass. I was fed the fuck up. I had my Platoon doing what they were supposed to be doing and he was letting his guys just run amuck. I had his flank covered, but he was not covering my flank. He walked away when I was done with him. I went over to 1st Sgt Parker and told him what I had done. He said he did not have a problem with it. He said that I had just reinforced what he had been telling that SSgt for months.

We left early that morning before the town even woke up, and for once we were really headed fucking south. Like my daughter used to say, "for

155

reals no plays." South was good, because south was Kuwait and there were ships waiting in the Kuwaiti harbor, and ships meant going home.

The town looked dead as we drove through it. All the buildings looked abandoned but we knew there were people in them. The dust rose from the tracks of our vehicles and with the low hanging road lamps and the dim lights that they produced, the area looked like something out of a horror movie. No human or animal was out on the road. If the town had a soul, it was beaten, tired, and was begging for mercy. Our weapons were pointed outboard and some Marines sat on top of the Amtraks, not wanting to be caught inside if an RPG found its way into its side. We drove over the bridge where we had been denied access before, and left Al Kut for good.

We traveled all day and when the Battalion finally stopped we set in the defense right next to a highway. I had my platoon dig in and set up security. Digging in seemed kind of idiotic because we were so close to the highway. We were close enough to get shot at, so why not just go ahead and give them the full deal and not dig in? I figured, though, that because someone had fucked up and put us so close, even more reason to dig in. The Marines were thinking, if you aren't going to do it right, why do it at all?

Jones had had enough of the Platoon coming down with the "run and shit," so he had our trash hole and straddle trench placed out a good 100 meters from the line. Like I said, we were right next to the highway so the newly formed Republic got to learn how we set up our straddle trenches. Given the speed those Iraqis drove by us, in fear of being shot, I really don't think they learned much. One of the Marines was using the straddle trench, and as if some director had yelled "action," an Army convoy drove by. A female soldier stuck her head out and started cheering. I did not care about that, as long as she was not a two-faced bitch who would cry "sexual harassment" if it happened to her -- which she probably would, but then we will never know. One of the Platoons started to set their straddle trench right behind our lines. SSgt Jones let them get finished digging before he told them to get the fuck out of our area. Jones did not look like a mean fucker, but then looks are not everything in this game.

Lt Daniels and my Platoon Guide, Sgt Chase, left the Battalion area to go to the city where our Company was going. The order was kind of still in the forming stages, but I guess enough had been planned out to send

156

people to our next city. The Captain called for me and pulled me aside to show me a map of this smaller city further south. He said that higher thought that there were enemy sympathizers there and that my Platoon would be tasked with providing security on this city. There would be no indirect, air, or direct support except for the attachments I had with me. Like I really wanted this mission -- getting so close to going home that it's the only thing the rumor mill is talking about, only to get whacked at the Alamo.

## 25 April 2003
We picked up from our over-night defense and started to move out. I did not know exactly where we were going but I did have a pretty good idea what we were going to do: provide security and help the Police Force with the public perception of their new government. Maybe even clean up a schoolhouse or rebuild a Mosque. Each Company in the Battalion was assigned a different city to help. I was up for it, though I did not think we were the unit to be actually doing this. I overheard a Captain put it best. His thoughts were that we had been training up to this point to kill and destroy everything in front of us and then had actually put the training to use a couple of times. Now the high command wanted us to hold hands with them and help them clean up their country; it would not be easy. I agreed with the Captain but I was game. We started moving down to our adopted city and took a refueling break. One of my Marines, Sitarek, went down with dysentery. Jones took him out of the Amtrak and put him in the Company Gunny's vehicle. That way they could stop and let him puke all he wanted. His face actually looked green.

We started moving again, with me up in the turret. I felt like I was on parade the whole time, waving at everyone. There were a lot of different sects of Muslims. The one way you could tell if you were entering a different sect's area was by the women. We had just come from an area where the women wore bright clothes and had entered one where the women all wore black and covered their hair, but they could show their faces. There was a group of women on the side of the road and one of the younger women in the back of the group waved at me. I waved back. The mother turned around to see what I was waving at and saw it was her daughter. The mother beat the living shit out of her with three good hits (I know I am ugly but give me a break). Then the mother covered her face and started laughing at her daughter for being a flirt. I hope she did not get in any more trouble, but after that I was really careful about who I waved at. Besides, my right arm was getting tired from also pointing my shotgun at everyone I waved at.

Al Raleef was a city that was built with a highway on the east side and a major river on its west side. Both these obstacles were running north and south and were about two miles apart. There were very few buildings on the outside of these two obstacles. There was a hard-surfaced road that crossed the bridge over the river on the west and went through the center of town to the highway. On the east side of this highway was the village-trading center. This really wasn't a center, more of a flat area of dirt covered with sheep shit. There was a market in the center of town. Lt Daniels, like I said before, had gone ahead of us to scope things out to see what was going on. He said he had gone to the market and was going to buy these large cookies that were covered in raisins. As he walked up to the merchant to buy a raisin cookie, all the raisins flew away. The market was covered in flies.

He also said that it might not be a good idea to occupy any part of the city. They might look at it as if we were establishing ourselves in the city and trying to control them instead of assist them. Capt Newland originally thought of putting a Platoon or so in the city and the rest within arm's reach outside the city, but he wanted to think about it first. He kept the Company together till he got more information. We moved down the highway to the south side of the city to our first large open area. The Amtraks moved in around a busted up dirt building and set into 360 degree security, and we dug in. My Platoon was facing the southeast and towards the Battalion CP, about 200 meters away. I really did not see us shooting up the Head Shed -- not that there weren't times that we wanted to, but we had good fields of fire and as far as fire discipline went, I felt really confident about my Platoon.

Before the first e-tool started breaking ground, rumors started flying around about us going home. We all had an idea that this was our last mission before heading out, but the rumor mill was more than confirming the thought. The only person that I heard deny the fact that this was our last mission was Major Sosa. Of course, he was also saying he thought we should stay longer to do the job right. In principle, everyone agreed with him -- but as far as agreeing with him on any other basis, no one did. Fuck these Iraqi people. The Lance Corporal hotline was saying a lot of things, like we were second in the order of units going home, how we were going to bus back to Kuwait because we were going to lose the Amtraks, that a memorial service was to be held in An Nasiriyah, and

158

most importantly, the rumor of the time line of when we were going home. Major Sosa's reply to all this was, don't plan on leaving Al Raleef for another six months. Even with all this rumor and counter-rumor, we had a mission to do.

## 26 April 2003
I had my Platoon; as we had been doing all along, stand to that morning. I was packing up my gear and something just did not seem right. Then it hit me: the city had lights. We were not so close to the city that the lights did us any good, but the fact that a city had lights meant that they had electricity, and that meant that things might not be as bad here as we thought. After stand-to the Captain called all the Platoon Commanders in and said he was going into town for a recon of the area. He also said that one of the Platoons could be tasked with moving south to guard some stuff by a river. When he said that, I hoped it was my Platoon that went. The Captain left and took 1$^{st}$ Sgt Parker with him along with some bodyguards.

The Amtrakers we were with asked us if we wanted to use the camouflage netting to shade us from the heat. This area was not like the garden we were in at Al Kut; this place was full throttle hot and in the sun. There was no shade anywhere. Jones had the Marines set up the netting and then set up a smaller one for himself, Chase, Doc, and me. He did this for two reasons. First reason was obvious: to provide shade so that the Marines didn't overheat, and so the water they drank could go to rehydration and not just to sweating. The second reason was that Jones didn't think we were going anywhere. So to keep the Marines' minds and bodies occupied, we did things -- we set a routine. Bottom line, it gave them something to do. After standing to in the morning and before it got hot, the netting would go up. As the end of the day started to cool off and before we would stand to at night, the nets would come down. During the day when nothing was planned, we would give classes under the cami-netting and have a Marine walk the line for security. There was no way anything could sneak up on us because there were no obstacles or concealment for a good mile around our position.

The CO and 1$^{st}$ Sgt, with the two Marines they had taken for security, returned later in the day -- and all Parker could say was how fucked up the city was. So much for electricity being a good sign. He did say, though, that they had found an interpreter and his name was Hussein. I thought he was fucking around at first but it turned out that Hussein was a pretty ordinary name, like Brown or Smith.

The Captain pulled all the Platoon Commanders in and went over his game plan. He did not want to rush into the city and set up patrol bases, but he said there were some other Companies that had already moved into the cities that they were responsible for and that they were doing well there. One of the problems was that the unit that had been here before us had promised that they would not patrol the city without the Sheik's approval, and that they would not set up inside the city at all. Capt Newland did not like that and told the village leaders that he was not the same as the other unit -- he was different. He also explained to them that we were not engineers -- we did not build and repair things. We were infantry, and all we knew how to do was fight. They understood that part. The Captain also told us that he wanted to talk to Lt Col Grabowski about some things before he decided anything. He also wanted to get another interpreter. Lt Beere, a first-generation American from Irish immigrant parents, was given the order to move south and guard a point next to a river. Luck of the Irish.

**27 April 2003**
We got up that morning as we always did. Not long after we stood down and got our tents set up to protect us from the sun, the Captain had taken off with Parker for the Battalion COC and then gone straight into town.

Jones and I sat in the hole that held our platoon headquarters and talked. Mostly we talked about our daughters and about his wife and my girlfriend. We both talked about how we were going to physically, mentally, and morally hurt whoever hurt our daughters. I liked to talk and work on the math of starting my own job when I got out. His big worry was getting home to help his wife with moving into their new home. He was sure that she could handle all of it by herself, but he wanted to be there to help her. We talked about these subjects over and over again.

The Skipper and First Sgt returned later in the afternoon. Parker pulled me aside and told me that he wanted me and a few of my Marines to go into town with him tomorrow. He said that they had had a meeting with the town counsel and that there had been some young Iraqi there who kept interrupting the meeting with questions in the form of demands. He had introduced himself as a Sheik but none of the counsel members or actual Sheiks there gave him any respect or acknowledged his presence.

Parker said that he thought the kid was going to be trouble. I said we should kill him. We had killed everybody else, what was one more? Bury him so deep that the dogs wouldn't bother to dig him up. Parker laughingly said "maybe," and said that we should run him out of town and see what happened after that. I agreed, but I jokingly said that it would be a whole lot easier if we just killed him.

I found Capt Newland and he told me the same thing as the First Sgt, but went into more detail about what was going on in town. He never really talked that much but from what I got from him, he really wanted to help these people. His wife was pregnant with their first child and the due date was near. He was stressed to the fucking max. He was older than the Lts so he never looked like a kid, but now he looked like an old man who had been beaten too much. He had to bring us home, do his job, help these people, help his wife, prepare for this child, and then last but not least, if possible, try to make it home alive.

The rest of the day was spent with Parker over at GySgt Ingerson's Amtrak. Ingerson was stupid, in a good way. Some of the shit he came up with. Of course, since he was riding around in an Amtrak all day he had a lot of extra stuff that we didn't have, like a stove, canned coffee, a stack of porn (Mrs. Ingerson, it did not belong to your husband but to one of the Marines in the Amtrak with him), a sack of hard candy, and a guitar. Ingerson would play songs and then make up words to fit our situation. He never sang about something political, but stuff we could relate to, like the mail being fucked up. It was getting late and I had to head back to the Platoon. As I was walking away, Ingerson yelled out, "Doran, for the last time stop coming over here and asking me if you can suck my dick till you have that non-regulation mustache cut off." This threw me off. I had no response. I just turned around and stared at him. My platoon was laughing their asses off. As I walked up, a couple of Marines said in unison, "Hey Gunny, he said your mustache was out of regs!" I told them to shut the fuck up; my mustache was always out of regs. This made them laugh even harder. You think the little bastards are laughing at one thing, and they are laughing at another.

Jones already had the Marines breaking down the cami nets and getting ready to stand to for the night. One of the other Platoons started to do the same thing. I was surprised, for several reasons. First off, stand-to was a bitch. No one liked doing it. You put all your stuff up, just so that when stand-to is over you can go to the Amtrak and break out the stuff you need for the night. Same bullshit problem in the morning. Second reason I was surprised was that they had not been doing it before. So why were they starting now? The reason I had my Marines do it was because the Iraqis didn't have night vision equipment, so I thought they would rely heavily on the nautical twilights. In other words, they would use the sun coming down and getting darker to move into place and throw a few rounds at us, and do the same thing in the morning. I did not want to give them the pleasure of shooting at us, whether their rounds hit us or not.

### 28 April 2003

This was the first day that I was going into the city. I took two fire teams with me into the town with the Captain and First Sgt. We loaded up into two HMMVs and a 7-ton, got on the road, and headed north. There were the usual drivers and such but there was this one Marine I had not seen before. I thought maybe he was from one of the other Platoons or something. Turns out he was an interpreter. He had been with the other unit before us and when they got orders to leave they were told to leave him behind. So he stayed there by himself -- no chow, no water, no orders, no vehicle, no nothing, and he survived till we came along. And come along we did. Parker adopted him and he hung out with us. He had gotten out of the Marine Corps a couple of years before and was changing light bulbs in tall poles. He had been recalled because he spoke Arabic. Roger that.

We passed the trading market on our right and made a left onto a road that headed down to the middle of the city. There were tall buildings made of concrete and short mud houses on both sides of us, and fences lined the street. A great place for an ambush. As I rode shotgun in my HMMV, I looked in the back of the vehicle and I could tell by the way the Marines were holding their weapons and eyeballing the area that they had the same thought. We drove for about three minutes, or a lifetime depending on how you look at it, before we pulled up in front of a fence, which had a large courtyard and a large building set in the back of it.

There were some Iraqis in civilian clothes and some with weapons, dressed as police officers. My Marines got out of their vehicles and provided a half moon security around the HMMVs and 7-ton, with their backs to the wall of the compound. A small generator was unloaded out of the 7-ton and placed by the fence. The Iraqis that belonged to the city council, the chief of police (who had been a Colonel in the Iraqi Army during the first Gulf War), their head teacher, some other cats and dogs, and in the background were some kids who were about twenty -- and one of them called himself a Sheik. Hussein had told Parker the day before that the kid was not a sheik but a thug. He said it took years of training and experience to be a sheik. I just wanted to put my shotgun to his head and kill him. These men were trying to put their city back together -- keep the elderly safe, educate the children, keep the city clean, give the people food, give them oil to keep them warm at night -- and all this punk wanted was to be a big shot for himself. My solution was simple.

Parker, with the help of the Hussein the Iraqi translator, introduced everyone. When Parker introduced me to Hussein he said "and this handsome young devil is Gunny." Hussein looked at me kind of shocked, carefully shook my hand, and introduced me in Arabic to the rest. They did not make an effort to shake my hand. We all went inside the building. There were windows missing and cigarette butts on the floor. Chairs and benches were stacked on top of each other in the hallway. We went into a large open room that was obviously used for city meetings. It smelled musty but it had chairs. I sat down in the back of the room and everyone else went up front. Our guys sat with their backs to the stage and the Iraqis sat in the audience. They all began to talk in English to the Captain and Arabic to themselves. Our Cpl, who was the Arabic translator, kept his mouth shut. He was there to listen to what the Iraqis said and translate it later for us.

The kid I was to watch sat a couple of rows in front of me. He sat quietly and every once in a while he and his little group would turn around and look at me. He lit a cigarette and turned and smiled at me like you do when you want to make sure that the guy with the shotgun is not going to kill you. I ignored his smile from behind my sunglasses. A little later he and his gang left the meeting. I gave him a few minutes and followed after him. I wanted to make sure he was not fucking with my Marines. Schell was one of the guys out on watch and he had said that the group had left the area. I got the Squad Leader, Marshall, and told him to keep an eye open. I went to go back into the meeting and walked up to the fence door when one of the Iraqi policemen opened it for me and said something in French. I just nodded and kept walking. Fucking French.

As I entered the building, Mr. Hussein was there and he stopped me. He asked me if I was really the devil. I did not understand and asked him to repeat himself. He asked if I was really the devil, like the way Parker had introduced me. I said no, I was not, and that was just slang talk where we were from. He smiled and went back into the meeting. Now I knew why everyone was treating me weird. They could comprehend a man being the devil and walking amongst them. Some might say they were backwards for thinking like that -- others might say they're maybe more in tune with things.

Back in the meeting hall, they were still talking. The Iraqis would ask something and then Parker or the Captain would answer it. If we gave them an answer that was maybe not definite, but honest, they would blow a gasket. If we told them they needed to do something, like get their kids back in school, they said they could not because they had not received orders to from An Nasiriyah and that An Nasiriyah was waiting on orders from Baghdad. I may not be an educated man but I knew that was not going to be happening anytime soon. They said that they needed food and if food was to be given out that the Sheiks and council leaders must do it. The last unit just threw food to the crowds and it made Americans look arrogant and wasteful. The people who needed it did not get it. Plus, by letting the leaders pass out the food, they did not lose face and could keep control of what was going on. Some Marine from the last unit had had his pistol stolen during the mayhem of passing out food. Fucking dumb fuck.

The meeting carried on like this for hours it seemed. Finally they all got up and shook hands and we proceeded to leave the town meeting hall. The community leaders, Sheiks, their police officers (who had not stopped working because the lack of pay), and us dumb grunts loaded into our vehicles and drove around town. I felt stupid at first but what the fuck. There were pictures of what looked like the Ayatollah Kohmeni from Iran everywhere. He and these two other guys, they were in car windows, home windows, walls and poles, hell you name it and there was a picture of him. This made me sit a little uneasy in my seat. I mean fuck -- if the whole town was pro-Kohmeni this was going to be a long pacification.

We were at the far north outskirts of the city at a fuel plant that had no fuel when I had a chance to talk to Parker. I asked him what is up with the pictures. He said it was some religious leader who stood up to Saddam so they killed him and his family. The two guys with him were his two sons. The people in that region were not allowed to mourn his death. So when the government fell, they were able to mourn and worship like they wanted. Sure, fine, whatever.

164

After the tour of the town we headed back. I was tired and the heat was killing me. When we arrived back at the base camp, Parker told me that he needed a fire team and me to go back into town tomorrow. I told my LCpl in charge of one particular fire team that he would go into town again with me. He seemed kind of pumped up about it so that kind of motivated me. I went back to my hole with Jones. He told me what happened that day, which was pretty much nothing. I told him what my day was like, which was nothing either, but it was more than his day. I told him I was going back out tomorrow with the Captain and the First Sgt and that I was taking a fire team with me. He said that he would continue with the classes for tomorrow. Good to go.

**29 April 2003**
We stood to that morning as we always did. But I knew something special was going down. I grabbed the fire team and we walked over to the Company CP. Lt Daniels was chilling out with Lt Fanning. Fanning didn't have any Marines cause they were all still attached out to the Rifle Platoons. I bullshitted with the First Sgt and he said that the Captain would be back in a minute. Just as he said that, we could see Captain Newland with his driver coming our way from the Battalion CP.

We loaded up into the two HMMVs and headed out into town. We stopped by the Police Station first and the Captain and First Sgt went into the building. There weren't that many police officers around and kids were running around the vehicle. They walked out of the Police Station with the Chief of Police and the Chief pointed down the road, like he was giving the Captain directions. Parker walked by my HMMV and told me to load my Marines up. I asked him what was up? He said we were going to withdraw some money from a bank. Roger that! I told the Marines to load up.

We drove down the road a mile or so. The buildings were side-by-side, dirty, and two to three stories high. No one was working. The kids weren't in school and women were peeking through the gridiron doors and windows. We drove and the vehicle in front of me stopped. We all piled out. I had the vehicles pull up close to each other and I told the Marines to set up security and when they were done, for the team leader to come in the building. He had the two drivers stay outside with two of his Marines from his Fire Team. He and another Marine came inside the bank and guarded the door from the inside. The Captain and First Sgt were in the office talking to the banker and a couple of town elders. I walked around the bank to make sure it was clear. The office was dirty and in disarray. It looked like it hadn't been used in a long time. The place was clear so I went into the office with the Captain and the others. They were talking about the money in the safe. No one there knew the combination. The one guy who did know the combination was about an hour's drive out. The banker was saying that when someone wanted money from the bank they would have to come in several days early and request it. Then it would have to be approved by, of all places, An Nasiriyah.

The bank wanted a guarantee that they would get the money back. I thought "whatever," it was not like the City Council was taking the money to the local whorehouse to fuck and get liquored up. The City Councilmen said that the city would pay the money back. They talked about the amount of the loan, interests rates, and how the money was to be used. If I was smart enough I would have paid more attention. This was a classic example of a city getting started and a bank investing in the community, capitalism at its best. While all this was going on, a bank teller came in and served us water. There was a rather large pitcher with one small dirty glass. I had seen whiskey with more clarity than the water. By tradition it started off with Capt Newland and then down his guests according to their importance, and then the host would drink and then his group, according to importance. This was all done out of the same glass. Parker had warned me about the water and told me not to insult these fuckers. He said that when the glass came to me I had to drink the whole thing. So when I saw the guy coming I pulled out my canteen and started to sip on that so he might skip me. Parker looked at me with a "you idiot" look on his face. I put my canteen away and the glass came to me. The guy poured some water in it and it looked like something that would have those sea monkeys in it that you buy out of a comic magazine. I drank it down and it had that taste to it, like the breads I had bought in Al Kut. As the pitcher got poured around the room it was decided that the Iraqi Council, the Bank Manager, the Captain, and First Sgt would go get this guy and I would stay behind to guard the bank and bank tellers. Parker said the tellers and the guards were not to leave till they got back.

They walked out and my Fire Team and I waited for them to return. Some Iraqi started cleaning up the bank. I walked outside and a crowd was gathering. Not so much a riot crowd but a "what's up" crowd. I went back inside and we waited. One of the guards brought out more water. I told one of the Marines to wake me if anything started to happen. I smoked a cigarette and went to sleep. I woke up for a brief

166

period and there was an Iraqi woman in the office. She looked good. But she was a muslim woman around muslim men, so there was no way she was going to fuck anyone. I went back to sleep.

About an hour or so later Captain Newland and the rest returned. We looked at the safe, the city leaders got the money, and we left.

We headed back to our Company CP. When we arrived, the Captain told me were going back into town that night on a group patrol along with the town's police department. What fucking police department? He told me to take two squads and leave the other squad back. I told Jones what was going on. It was still daylight and it would be an hour or two before I got ready to leave. Jones looked depressed for some reason and I could not figure out why. We bullshitted a little while but I could not dig it out of him.

Lt Fanning, like I said before, had decided to reinvent the wheel on how mortars were employed. Captain Newland or First Sgt said they wanted me to pull the mortar men in and re-teach them. I said it was not a problem, but they would have to tell Fanning that it was not my idea. Parker laughed and agreed. I guessed that as soon as Fanning heard this he would want to pull his Platoon back together. Tactically it did not make sense. But this was the first day he would start bitching about it.

### 30 April 2003
The day started out the same. The Captain and First Sgt went to town in the morning, as they always did. They took the Company driver, the Cpl who was an interpreter, and the money with them. I began teaching the mortar section the basics all over again. The situation was the same as when I was an Instructor at Advanced Mortar Leaders Course at Camp Geiger. The guy that talked the most knew the least and the guy who kept his mouth shut and did what he was told knew the most. Funny how it always works out that way. While I was messing with the mortars, Jones was taking the Platoon through their drills. The one Rifle Platoon that had not gotten sent to the riverbank for security was not doing anything but sitting and waiting. I thought that training during times like this was productive, but had to be really regulated. Too many times I've had someone of higher rank get over-zealous (usually someone who did not have to participate in the training) and kill morale. The Captain and the others returned later in the evening and as soon as they arrived we left for town.

We went to the Police Station where we had met the city elders earlier. My Platoon set up security for a few minutes while the Captain and his group went inside the Police Station. I could tell that my Marines wanted to talk to the Iraqis but it was kind of like a kid still wanting to pet a dog, even after the dog had bitten him. About twenty Police Officers loaded up in different vehicles than ours and we drove around town. The idea was to show that the Police Department was supported by us, the Americans, and therefore could be trusted. We finished up at an ice cream parlor. We drove up and set up security. As we are walking up, the civilians in the parlor ran off. We walked up and the Chief of Police ordered us ice cream. The Cpl interpreter was passing these small bowls around to my Marines. So, as us big, bad Marines -- loaded down with weapons, ready to kill anything, ready to drink a bottle of anything, and ready to hurt the most experienced of whores – as we ate ice cream, the civilians watched and started to try to talk to us. It was a cool experience.

I was standing next to one of my Marines when Parker, who had been sitting in the ice cream store, came over to me with his uneaten ice cream in hand. He asked me, as I swallowed a good-sized scoop of the sweetest and coldest tasting ice cream I have ever had, when the last time was that I had seen a cow. I thought about it and told him, jokingly, that I hadn't seen a cow since I left Texas. He then asked me how many dogs I had seen? I didn't know where he was going with this, but I said, "a lot." He asked me what the major ingredient in ice cream was? I told him, "milk." Fucking, son-of-a-fucking-bitch-whore shit!!!! They used dog's milk to make the ice cream! As I made this realization, aloud, the Marine who was standing next to me asked if he could have my ice cream since I wasn't going to eat it. I handed it over to him and tried not to throw up.

When we got back to the patrol base, I told Jones what had happened. He was down, and I knew what was bothering him, so I told him he could take the patrol out tomorrow. He had been stuck in that hole since we got there, and I was surprised he hadn't gone crazy by now. I could tell he was relieved to be going out in town. We all hit the rack.

**1 May 2003**
Today was the last day anything exciting would happen. Jones took the patrol into town and while they were at the City Council's meeting place, some kids threw rocks at them. One of the Marines fired a shot in the air to scare the kids off, which it did. But he shouldn't have been firing his weapon at all. What if he had accidentally hit the kid, or the round had landed and hit someone a mile away? It wouldn't take a brain surgeon to figure things out. Rocks hurt but they don't kill. We could take a little hurt versus killing some kid because he was acting rashly. Who knows, that kid could grow up to be wiser some day, and understand the restraint we had used. Then of course maybe not, and we would just bomb the shit out of his city when some chicken-shit President took charge of his country. When they got back, Jones had the Marine's ass. I was so fucking pissed that I didn't say anything. Jones took care of it, the Marine got the point, end of story.

**4 May 2003**
We lost the Amtraks. Life sucks.

**7 May 2003**
Around 0900 we left the bullshit defensive perimeter. 7-ton trucks came to pick us up and take us back to An Nasiriyah for a memorial service before we headed home. Alpha Company didn't have enough vehicles to carry all the Marines they had. Only so many bodies can fit in a 7-ton, and whatever they had, it required that every 7-ton go over by one body – but they wanted another 7-ton. Then I knew we were really going home. Because all the bullshit was beginning again, I was going back to the Marine Corps that I hated – full of rules and regulations that were set in stone that common sense could not over ride. We were not going to get an extra 7-ton in the middle of nowhere, at least not for another two days. No one in the Battalion could leave because Alpha wouldn't load the vehicles to go without getting their one precious extra 7-ton, just so they could follow Marine Corps Order.

Parker was telling me play by play how Battalion was telling them they weren't getting another vehicle and that they needed to load and how Alpha said they were not loading. Finally, the S-3 from Battalion, Major Sosa, drove out to Alpha's position and told them to load the fuck up so we could get out of there. As we were leaving, we were told not to throw any food to the people because children were running out and grabbing the candy, and Regiment was afraid that one of the children would be hit by our vehicles.

We headed south to An Nasiriyah. On the way there, we stopped by Charlie Company's position and waited for them to get ready to follow us south. As we were leaving, some jackass threw food out to the children. In the frenzy for the candy, one kid focused on the food and not the 7-ton vehicle that kept moving. The 7-ton could not stop in time, and it hit the kid. Parker, who was probably the most experienced Marine in First Aid, ran out of his vehicle to try to help him. As he was doing this he was cussing everyone out, telling us we were fucked up for throwing food to the kids. Some Corpsman from another unit started fixing the kid up and got an ambulance to get him and his family med-evac'ed out. We kept moving.

As we were driving out of Al Raleef the Marines were laughing and chatting away, but as we got closer to An Nasiriyah the talking lowered under the roar of the vehicles and Marines started to look more cautiously at their surroundings instead of each other. The fucking "Naz."

We pulled into the same area where we had set up as we had pulled out after the battle. We were south of the Iraqi Army Compound and north of the bridge over the Saddam Canal. We unloaded off the vehicles and everyone got in formation. It seemed that we were naturally changing our ways from tactical to formal, as we got closer to going home. Captain Newland gave each Platoon Commander their sectors to cover and told us where he wanted us to set in. My Platoon was to set into an 800-meter mound that followed along a pond. The mound had a trail following along the top of it that was worn out from the footsteps. I set my Platoon into position as I had usually done -- by leading the Squad Leaders and then having them do their squads. By now this took no time cause the Platoon knew how I wanted them to set in.

After all this was done it was a good time to find my brothers whom I had not seen in a long time. The first person I sought after was Captain Rohr. Captain Rohr acted different toward me than when I first met him. When I first started to work for him, the operation tempo for the Battalion was so high that our conversations dealt only with work. During the war and our ventures into grand theft auto we had more time to bullshit. He was awesome in every way. He could talk about anything openly and honestly and never lose his honor or compromise himself. When I first found him he was just through passing some word to the Platoon Commanders and was about to sit down by his HMMV.

He saw me as I walked up and we shook hands. I had friends that I had known for decades and had not seen for years, and I had never felt like I was seeing an old friend as much as I did at that moment. We talked about what had been happening and what we thought was going to happen. He wanted me to go talk to Schielein, something about him having problems.

I knew what Schielein's problem was -- he was thinking too much. You can't allow yourself to think. Of course, sooner or later you would wonder about what happened and the questions would come in, but it was not yet time for that.

I found Schielein over by his Platoon. Even though the Battalion was setting up security, there was not the sense of urgency there had been when we had an Artillery Battalion, a Tank Company, and Amtraks in support. Schielein didn't care about what we had lost in support; he was still making sure all of his areas were covered and that there were no breaks in his area of responsibility. Schielein didn't see me approach; he was pointing this way and that, yelling at everyone within earshot. I thought when I approached him that he would be glad to see me and would quickly finish up what he was doing, and talk for a while with me. He didn't. He saw me and it seemed like it made him work harder.

When I got within hand-shaking distance he told me to hang on for a second. He finished directing his Marines into place, smiled at me, and we hugged as brothers. I told him I needed to talk for a while. He said he could but that he would need to make it quick. We walked outside the perimeter and sat down on a berm in front of where the Battalion was dug in. I offered him a drink of the Pepsi and he declined. I knew Caveman and I asked him what was on his mind. Without hesitation he began talking. I listened; I could not believe what I was hearing. I will never repeat what he said. I will say this: he talked and as he talked, he reasoned himself into righteousness. He was starting to go over the edge but pulled himself back in. I just hoped he stayed that way. After that, we talked about Kelly, our kids, going home, and a bike rally that was going on in North Carolina about the same time we would be getting home. So far we had figured it would be him, me, Lt Seely, 1$^{st}$ Sgt Parker, and some other guys in the Battalion that I did not know.

It started to get dark out and now we both had things to do. Plus, I had to walk a good click back to my Platoon.

I loved my Platoon. I had chewed their asses, been an asshole over the details, and never gave them a compliment. But I could talk to any one of them about anything. When I got there the Squad Leaders had everyone in position and the security was walking the line. Airhart and Sitarek, "Fric and Frak," had their hole right next to the Platoon CP. Of course Airhart had everyone on the line, within hearing distance, laughing at his rendition of why he was no longer in Charlie Company and was now in Bravo. I had heard this story a million times -- but it was not the story he told, it was how he told it. He was never disrespectful of anyone in the story, even though we knew who he was talking about by his impersonation of them. In his interpretation of the course of events that lead to his demise, he was never to blame. I finally had to stop the show when most of the Platoon had left the line to gather around his hole to listen to his tale. It was usually quiet enough to let him entertain like that but when I had gaps in my line that a Regiment could walk through, it was time to end the show.

The mosquitoes ate us up that night. I guess that's what happens when there is a pond right in front of us.

### 8 May 2003

The next morning felt more like we were at Camp Lejeune than in Iraq. We did not stand to. The security we had walking the line was enough. I found GySgt Carrico and asked him what was going on for the memorial ceremony that day. He gave me a rough idea, so I told Jones and started walking over to the area myself. GySgt Leggett was there with his 81's Platoon before anyone else. We talked for a long while, but we talked about nothing. I had not walked over with anyone for the same reason that Leggett and I talked about nothing. We were remembering our friends. The Companies lined up with the First Sgts in front. Officers from Regiment sat off to the side of the memorial of boots and rifles that were in the ground with helmets on top of them. I stood in the back with the rest of the Platoon Commanders and the Company Commander.

The Sgt Major came out and asked for the report. All was given, with Charlie Company reporting last, 18 KIA. The Colonel came out and ordered the officers of the Battalion to post and take their positions in the front of their Companies. The Colonel gave us a talk and it was honorable and heart-felt. He talked about how when a ship sets out from a port, and, as you watch the port disappear, the sadness you feel. Then he talked about the port that the ship was arriving at, and how the people there were excited to see it coming. Posthumously, 2nd Lt Poorer was

172

promoted to 1$^{st}$ Lt and SSgt Jordan was promoted to GySgt. The mortar section then fired one round for each Marine that had died that day. Before each round was dropped in the tube, the name of the Marine was announced. As the names were read and the rounds fired out, you could see the illumination rounds explode in the air in the distance. The ceremony ended. The First Sgts took their places in front of the Companies as the Company Commanders called them out front. We were led off back to our bivouac sight from the night before. We loaded onto the 7-tons and headed south. Back through An Nasiriyah. Not one shot fired. Not one life lost. Not one word said.

We arrived at some airfield that afternoon. Someone said it was close to where Abraham from the Old Testament was born. How would anyone know where he was born? Whatever. We arrived and set up in this cement hanger. It was hot and it sucked. Parker and I got a 7-ton driver to take us around the airfield to see if we could get some extra hot chow for our Marines. Of course not. The Army would not even give us canned food to take back with us. Fuck sticks.

We were driving around and we noticed all these Army/Air Force fucks were walking around with fresh haircuts and fat stomachs. So we surmised that there must be a PX around there. We surmised right. We stood in line listening to all the faggots behind us bitch about how long the line was. We went through and when we were let into the PX we hogged up some soda, chips, and candy for the Marines. We dropped about $160 or so. We loaded it up on the 7-ton and headed back to the hanger. The Marines drank the soda like they were little kids enjoying it for the first time. Jones established a fire watch with the other platoons and we hit the rack. No stand to, this night.

**10 May 2003**
We got up the next morning at our leisure. No rush, cause there ain't no word. Around 1000 or so, Parker told the Platoon Sergeants to let their Marines run the base for food and haircuts if they wanted. He also said he heard there were phones on the far side of base.

SSgt Jones, a Lt and I headed out to look around. Of course we got lost and the more we tried to find the PX the more pissed off we were getting. We would find these little tent/buildings with different units in them along these streets that ran through the base. They would either give us wrong directions or directions that were so inaccurate that we did not have a chance before we started. We finally found a phone booth. The line was longer than fuck and I was not waiting in it. I wanted to call my Dad and Kelly but by the time I figured I would get near my turn to call I would have to leave cause we only had three hours before we had to be back. So I left the two of them and headed over to the PX.

I had already been through the PX and did not care to go back. But I had some money in my pocket and wanted to spend it so I went and got a haircut. I figured that they would have one of those haircut buzzing things with the vacuum on it keep the hair from getting all over me. I figured wrong. Fuck it. I waited my turn and took off my jacket and sat in the chair. I told the barber I wanted a high and tight. He sprayed my hair wet with water, combed it out and then took out a blow dryer and blew my hair dry. He then commenced to cut my hair. He kept having to stop cutting my hair to clean the sand out of his clippers.

One of my Marines came over and asked if he could borrow some money for a hair cut and I had him grab the money out of the pocket of my jacket. I thought the barber was starting to get a little out of whack because this haircut was taking longer than usual. Could not help it, no one could. He was used to the Army soldiers at the base always being showered and clean. Fuck it. I paid and got my change. Instead of quarters, the "change" they passed out was little brown discs with 25 cents written on one side and a gift certificate "AAFES" on the other.

I saw some of my Marines from my platoon standing over by the PX eating, drinking, and smoking. I joined them. We sat and bullshitted for a while before I asked if anyone knew the way back to the cement hanger. I would have gotten fewer blank stares if I had asked if anyone knew the theory of relativity. So we stepped off back to the Company area, determined to be lost together.

We made it back in time. The Lt and Jones were there; they had been able to make their phone calls before having to come back. Parker pulled me aside and asked if I wanted to go back out. I thought about saying no because of all the walking involved, plus we were about to get a truckload of mail. And I mean a truckload! Parker said he had not had a chance to go out because he had to make sure all the pigs were back in time. So I said yea, I would walk the base with him. He said we would take off when the sun dropped a little lower and it would be a little cooler.

Mail came in. Morale shot through the roof. I received mail, of course from Kelly, and a rosary and Catholic prayer book from my Aunts. Everyone was giving me the coffee they got in the mail. But everyone was giving more than that. Everyone was giving everything they got to anyone who wanted it. Since we were leaving the sand box, Parker decided to give everything extra to the Army and Air Force guys who were going to be there a while. A 7-ton pulled up and it got filled with all the stuff we gave them. They would not give us food but we gave them everything we had.

Later that night Parker and I went walking around the camp to find a phone. I thought I knew where it was, but I didn't. After about thirty minutes of walking around we finally found the phone line. Let me reiterate, LINE. We stood forever -- sometimes the line moved and sometimes it didn't. It was finally our turn to use the phone and we walked into the tent at the same time. The deal was, you had to call a military base near your home and then the base would connect you to your home. Parker called Lejeune and got to talk to his family. I couldn't get hold of anyone. The Air Force clerk who was timing people on the phone let me try for a couple of minutes longer than usual. Nothing. I really didn't care for some reason. As we started to walk back, it started to drizzle a little. It didn't matter. We were going home.

We got back to the bunker where the Company was, I found my gear, and I started to settle in for the night. Jones came over and told me I had to hear Montemayor's ghost stories. Montemayor was racking out in the open like I was, so I walked bare foot over to his sleeping area and we talked for a while. Montemayor was a tall, handsome, well-built Asian kid. He had hung around with the wrong crowd -- to say the least -- before he joined the Marine Corps, and if hanging out with the wrong crowd did him any harm, as a Marine I never saw it. All the Marines looked up to him. He was tough but wasn't a bully or a showboat. Montemayor was Montemayor. His "ghost stories" were pretty good for a last night in Iraq, and whether the stories were true or not they definitely kept our minds off what we had done, where we had been, and the fact that we weren't home yet. That is probably why the more he talked, the more people came over and sat and listened.

The night got darker as he talked, and like little kids at a sleepover, Marines would retire to their portion of the ground to sleep under a poncho and the stars. I could hear the fire watch walking around us as we slept, I thought of the phone call I couldn't make that day, and wondered what my dad, Addie, Jennifer and my girl Kelly were doing.

## 11 May 2003

Reveille was never called that morning. We were to be the last Company to leave Iraq that morning, by C-130. Marines stumbled around doing their morning routine. Some were waking their brothers, thinking they were doing them a favor, and other Marines were waking their brothers by kicking them. Marines ate candy for breakfast from the packages we had received. Some didn't get fully dressed so they could enjoy the morning sun that hadn't turned to scorching yet. It had been a while since I had seen a full Company relaxed like this. First Sgt Parker and Captain Newland were both up and sitting on their iso-mats, leaning up against their packs and just talking sporadically to each other, or looking at what everyone else was doing. Finally the Platoon Sgts started putting things in motion and our day began.

We got our gear assembled as the other Companies marched passed us to the flight line for their flight back home. Parker and the Platoon Sergeants started putting people in the two sticks they would fly to Kuwait on. For some reason I didn't like this flying business. I would have rather trucked out. But as long as I was getting out of there I really didn't put that much effort into bitching about it.

I was the Senior Enlisted guy in the first stick. So I marched them down to the flight line and waited in our little holding area. A short, overweight, Air National Guard woman in the TIGHTEST set of utilities EVER came out to tell us that our plane might be late. As she approached I could hear the snickering behind me and turned around to give the Marines a "shut the fuck up" look, but couldn't help giving them a "what the fuck is that thing?" look. As she walked to us from downwind, her perfume began to reach us. Her hair was perfect for a grandmother who was trying to look her best, and her nails were painted a bright red. She talked in a nasal voice and quickly said what she had to say and left.

Parker had walked up from the cement bunker and asked me what that thing was that I was talking to. I told him I wasn't sure, but if it hadn't shocked me so bad I would have shot it. He laughed and I told him what she had said about the plane being late. He nodded his head like he expected some shit like that, and walked back to where the other half of the Company was.

176

Two hours later the plane landed and we loaded up. Packs got loaded first from the back, and the Marines loaded up from the front. I was the last one on for my stick, which was half the Company and half the gear. I walked up the foldout stairs and looked into the back of the plane. It was crowded. No, you don't understand, it was CROWDED. The military uses a netting for seats and once you sit on this netting with your war belt on or even a small pocket knife on your belt, it gets tangled up in the netting and you are stuck. No one sits down till the guy to the left and right of them is ready to. So it is packed tight. The crewmen on the plane jump around above the "walking cargo" (us) along the frame and poles, like monkeys in the wild, to make sure everyone is sitting as close as homosexually possible. They offered me a spot in the cockpit where they had an extra seat. It was air-conditioned, and the seat was cushioned with some high-speed seatbelts. There was a stack of fuck books next to my seat, so after take off (I mean what is really interesting about a flight after take off?) I picked up the magazines and flipped through them.

The flight was somewhat uneventful except for the comfort of being up front and not packed in the back of the plane like a sardine. About an hour later the plane started to land in Kuwait, so I put the magazines down and watched our descent. For some reason I thought the nose of the plane would kind of rise as we set down, with the horizon in the distance. All I saw was sand. I asked the Gunny, who was a crew chief sitting up front with me, "where is the fucking runway?" He looked at me, pointed at the sand, and with a smile said "that is the fucking runway!" Not only was that NOT a runway, we were headed straight at it. I picked up one of the magazines and started flipping through it. If the end was coming I did not want to see it. I don't know how we landed, but we did.

After we got the plane unloaded, we grabbed some of the same horse cock sandwiches we had in Iraq -- but these sucked -- and we loaded on the buses that were waiting on us. I got a head count from each Staff Sgt that was on each bus and headed back to Camp Shoup. Once we got there, Gunny Carrico met us and told us where each Platoon was to set in for the night. Before nightfall, the whole Battalion was back together again, in one spot. For the whole war, the Battalion had been separated by time or distance. It was kind of kewl being together like that again. But it was not the same without Jordan and the rest.

Someone passed out some T-shirts and baseball hats that said, "I love New York" on them. Mail came in again with a shitload of packages. It was like the postal system had stopped in Kuwait. It was the first mail call ever that I had not received any mail, and I did not mind. I was going home and if there was anything to say, they could tell me when I arrived.

Jones passed some word to me about what was going on the following day, so I hit the rack. I thought about getting out of the Marine Corps and not being with these Marines anymore. I never felt so alone in my life.

# Be Careful What You Wish For
## Chapter 7

**12 May 2003**

Usually Jones would have to wake the Platoon up to get things going, but not that morning. We packed up; the First Sgt was being a prick again about shaving. For once I did not mind being told to shave. No one ate at the chow hall that morning -- we were too pumped up to be leaving. We were actually doing it. We were going home! We had to wait for the other two Companies to load up into the staging area first, so we spent a lot of time sitting around. When it was our turn to put our packs on the road inside Shoup, we got word that the buses were going to be delayed a couple of hours.

Someone from the Battalion Logistics came by with plastic trays of sandwiches, juice, potato chips and fruit wrapped in cellophane. The sandwich was for shit but it tasted awesome to me. There were a couple of extra plates and they were passed out to the junior Marines. They did not want the sandwiches and threw them back in the box. I grabbed them out of the box and ate them. Like I said, they were nasty but tasted awesome.

Word came down again that the buses were really going to be late, not by just a couple of hours. I started to freak out a little; I couldn't keep still. Parker was busy with head counts and stuff but I didn't care. I kept pestering him about when we were leaving. He just laughed and told me to hold on, that when he got done doing what he was doing, we would go find the real scoop. Parker had a knack for that, the real scoop. He could read through the bullshit and tell you what was really going on. We headed over to the Regimental tent, where everyone knew our First Sgt from his Recon days in Okinawa. He found some Corporal who was an admin pogue and asked him what was going on. The Corporal spit out a bunch of info on why the buses were late and when they would be in and how many people we had to put on each bus and blah, blah, blah. Whatever. I was wanting to get the fuck out of there so just tell me what I need to know and leave it at that. As we were leaving, I saw a Harley motorcycle parts book on a shelf and started to flip through it. The mag belonged to the Corporal and he said I could have it if I wanted. The man just went back into my good graces and could talk all he wanted and I would listen till the cows came home, or the buses in this case. Parker and I headed back to the staging area and finally at around 1500 the buses showed up for our ride to Kuwaiti Naval Base, or KNB for short.

The bus ride was quick and as soon as we arrived, the LCACs (landing craft, air cushion) were there to take us to the ship. No waiting around at all. That kind of sucked, but only because of Parker. He had a daughter in the Army and she was supposed to be at KNB somewhere, so if we had time he was going to try to find her. We loaded onto the LCACs and hit the USS Gunston Hall.

I was on the first LCAC to arrive and when we landed in the hull of the ship, Lt Daniels and Sgt Chase were there waiting on us. We started unloading the packs, 782 gear, and the sea bags. I looked up onto the upper decks and saw a bunch of Sailors looking down at us -- there must have been 50 or so. Lt Daniels walked up to me and the first thing out of his mouth was that they were having a problem with the Sailors having sex on the ship. I looked back up at the upper deck and that's when I noticed that the Sailors who were looking at us were all female. This was going to be a longer trip than I thought.

Eventually everyone was on board and had found all their gear and had it staged in the right spot. Parker, Gunny Voorhees, and I went down to the Chief's Mess for some chow. Since Bravo Company had been on this ship on the way over, they all new the Chiefs and had stuff to talk about. Parker told them who had died in the firefights and an RPG accident. They all knew who he was talking about.

The three of us walked over to the chow line and all thought the same thing: "This is a sin." All the food we wanted to eat, as many times over as we wanted. I had weighed myself earlier at 178 pounds; nothing like the 198 I had been when I came over. I wanted to eat to my heart's content, but I couldn't do it. When we sat down, and after we had said our prayers, I felt like crying. Food. It was great. The Chiefs ate like it was no big deal. You could not blame them though; they did not know better.

After chow we went back to the berthing area and squared our gear away for the trip home, putting things we would not use in a locker and everything else in the compartment underneath our racks. There was hardly anybody in our berthing area. Most of the SNCOs from the Amtraks and Tanks had flown back to the world. We were doing it the old fashioned way.

There were two Chiefs from the LCACs and us three Marines in the berthing area that could have held 20 more people. We had plenty of room. Parker said that Tenth Marines had an Artillery Battalion coming on board the next day and we might not be as comfortable. I did not care -- I was going home.

For the last five months I had not slept as well as I did that night. Take it when you can get it.

**13 May 2003**

Woke up early that morning along with Parker. We headed down to the Chief's Mess for some chow. Felt the same that morning as I did the previous night about the food. Parker kept saying, "it's a sin" over the amount of food we were able to eat. In a couple of days Parker would be like an Italian grandmother trying to force food onto my plate.

After chow we headed back to the berthing area and racked out. Parker had gotten with the Captain and worked out some crack deal where the Marines could take the next two days off and do nothing.

The head that connected the Marine GySgt and the Chief's berthing areas had two washers and two dryers. I washed my clothes in a machine for the first time since we hit land. I even washed my "clean" clothes -- they were so filthy that even after the second washing the water came up dirt brown. I had an Iraqi ammunition holder that I had originally thought was light brown, like the desert, but after washing it a couple of times I realized it was green.

Washing my clothes was the most exciting thing I did for the next two days. Of course we got some more Marines in our berthing area. Two more. So we were living large and in charge. We took down the dead-man racks and arranged an appropriated table for cards and TV visibility. It was awesome. A Master Sgt from the Artillery unit had a laptop computer and got some computer geek from the Navy to set up an Internet connection for us. We had Internet capabilities again. I did not get a personal "address." Mine went to the Platoon but Parker let me use his. It was a good life, and we were alive.

**16 May 2003**

The ship had been waiting in the harbor for the rest of the ships in our little convoy home to finish filling up with equipment and Marines. Even before this happened, every day was becoming like the rest. This usually would have killed me but we were heading to Spain for some liberty -- Barcelona, Palma, Rota, and names of cities I can't even remember. All the old salts who had been to the Mediterranean before were telling sea stories about which port was better. The port they usually favored was the one they had gotten laid in or the one that was the only port they had seen in Spain. The younger Marines would listen to them like children listening to bedtime stories for the first time. The only difference between the bedtime stories and the sea stories was that the sea stories started off with "this ain't no shit..." Then, after Spain -- the States, the World, the USA, home. No one needed to hear stories about the States; we had all been there before. We all knew what that would be like.

This was also the first night our nightmares began. Around 0200 in the morning the Marine who slept in the rack next to me started yelling for help. It woke me up and I jumped out of my rack and opened the curtain to his rack. I told him he was all right. His eyes were as big as cue balls and he asked me, where we were? I told him we were on ship. He asked me if I was sure. I told him yes. He asked about some Marine being okay or not? I told him he was all right (he was dead). He calmed down and went back to sleep. Some Marines (me) would toss and turn like they were fighting, and bang into the metal walls that separated the racks -- or they would not be able to sleep at all and would just watch TV all night. Whatever it was, it hit everyone at one point or another.

**17 May 2003**
The daily routine was getting to me, so Parker agreed to do a workout routine with me in the gym on ship. There were designated hours when the Marines got to use it and hours when the Sailors got to use the gym. Sometimes Sailors or Marines would work out during the wrong time, but as long as it was not crowded no one said anything. After the workout we would go to the flight deck and walk in circles and bullshit about everything under the sun: the new command, awards, Marines who were fucked up, Marines who were not fucked up, his wife, my ex-wives, Kelly, his children, my children, high school, Harleys (specifically, pipes he wanted), money, debt, getting out of the Marines, joining the Marines, what I could do when I got out, and a thousand other things. We would walk for about a half hour because we had decided we were too old to run. After this we would grab a magazine, a Walkman (I would grab the MP-3 player my dad had sent me), and our iso-mats, and lay out for a tan.

182

Parker and I were sunbathing and talking a little. We would lie on the catwalk on the fourth deck of the ship. Only officers and senior enlisted walked in that area so it was kind of quiet. I was saying that we would have a lot of drug use, disciplinary problems, and combat stress-related problems when we got back to the States -- unless the Marines were made to feel like they did something, that they were successful, and more importantly that what they did was okay, that the killing was not wrong, it was justified. Parker said that he thought the same thing but that the stress and post-traumatic stress disorder was nonsense. Just as he said this, the Navy opened up with some test firing of their 50 caliber machine guns. Parker, who had been lying down, popped up to his knees and had his hands in position, like he was holding a rifle. He started laughing at himself and started to lay back down to get some sun when the machine guns fired off again. He jumped again to his knees like someone was firing at him. I jokingly asked him if he was going to be okay? He said yes, laughing at himself again.

### 6 June 2003
GySgt Supply from the Artillery Battalion and I decided we would be liberty brothers in port, which was awesome cause we were both single and no one was watching our paychecks. We could spend what we wanted, when we wanted, without a jealous wife bitching about what we spent. That, and we both had the same game plan: get drunk as fuck as soon as possible.

I pulled out and ironed my clothes for liberty the next day, and for each day in port after that. I was ready for liberty. God was I ever. We could see the shore lights from the ship. Some of the younger Marines had been talking with the female Sailors about meeting out in town. I would hear different Marines talking about meeting the same female Sailors at different times in port. Those girls had it figured out.

### 7 June 2003
We pulled into port as soon as the sun broke the horizon. Tugboats pushed us into port. The Navy had their work detail ready with the plank running from ship to shore.

A group of Americans from the Naval Investigative Service, along with some civilians, came aboard and gave the SNCOs and Officers a liberty brief. They went over where to go and where not to, bus schedules, exchange rates, and the political thought of the neighborhood. Of course they said there were a few assholes starting shit, but it was nothing special that any country wouldn't have. SSgt Jones leaned over to me and said, "Like I give a fuck -- I want a beer." He then pointed at a middle-aged Navy Officer about ten feet away from us. He said that the Naval Officer had been rumored to be fucking some female Petty Officer. He had been down in the smoking area and saw a Marine talking to his young beloved. The officer walked by and bumped into the Marine and then started yelling at the Marine for not being careful. That pissed me off to no end. I looked at Jones and said in an overly loud voice that if any fucker bumped into one of my Marines cause he was making headway with one of his fucks, I would kick his punk ass. The Naval Officer heard this and looked at me. I looked back and Jones started laughing. What would he do? He was a punk. If he wanted to fight, bring it on. Write me up and then all the trash gets brought in about her and about him bumping into the Marine.

As the NIS agents continued to talk, they said the best place to get money exchanged was on ship. I thought to myself, ship? No fucking bullshit, I knew this. The Chief standing next to me looked at me and gave me that "what are we doing here?" look. I took some money from Jones and a couple of other Marines and headed to the upper deck to the Enlisted Mess to get the jump on exchanging money. As I got up in front of the guy exchanging money, a voice came over the ships 1 MC announcing that money was being exchanged in the mess hall. I did not even make it through the hatch before the line started to form. The only thing that was stopping them was some young Spanish female jeweler who was catching the younger Marines' eyes as they came into the mess. Couldn't blame them, it had been a while and she was a looker.

After getting my money exchanged I headed back down to the brief but it was over. Jones said it had ended as I was walking away. I gave everyone their money and headed back upstairs to change into civilian clothes. First Sgt Parker wanted a liberty brief in civilian attire to be sure no one was leaving the ship looking like some loser. About a half hour later we were in formation. Fucking smiles everywhere. We could have been told that we were headed back to Iraq after shore leave and the only question would have been, "We get to go on liberty now though, right?" Parker passed the usual shit that all liberty briefs pass, except he always added his little one-liner: "Man rules apply." Basically that meant we were responsible for our actions. Then he gave the time that shore leave expired for the different rank structures. Around midnight Marines had to start coming in, and at 0300 all hands had to be on the ship.

Parker did not fuck around at all. He finished his liberty brief and a few minutes later they sounded liberty for the ship. We were the only Infantry Company on ship; the other Batteries started their liberty brief as we were leaving, which sucked for me because Gunny Supply was my liberty partner and he was in the Battery. We finally found each other and left the ship.

My liberty partner and I debated about getting a taxi or waiting for the bus. The bus won out and after about thirty minutes of driving around Barcelona and figuring out that we were far enough away from the ship to have fun, we jumped off the bus.

It was great! Girls wearing summer dresses, traffic going everywhere, people walking to and from work, buildings that had been built by the Romans, dogs on leashes and not fighting over dead body parts -- I was in heaven.

Supply and I walked over to a shop that sold quick food and spent some of our Monopoly money on a sandwich and beer. Man that beer tasted good. After screwing around with a game machine for a while, we left the store and walked around some more. There was a corner shop that had a lot of foot traffic walking by, so we sat out on the patio and had a couple of beers. They were selling lottery tickets and I won back the money I had gambled away at the game machine. Breaking even is sometimes just as good as winning. I remember closing my eyes and waiting till I got a small sniff of perfume, and I would open my eyes and try to pick out the woman whose perfume I had smelled from the rest of the crowd. I could have sat on that corner for the rest of my life. Supply said he wanted to walk around some more before we hit any bars, and that was fine with me so we left there and headed out. There was a lot to see and even though Doc Sabilla had taught me some Spanish in Iraq, I felt I only knew enough to get by in a whorehouse and order the beers for the rest of the night. Maybe in retrospect that is all Doc thought I would need to know.

We ended up in a small open courtyard that had tall buildings all around the yard. They were apartments and the bottom floors of these tall buildings were shops and bars. I found an Irish pub and ran into one of the guys who had been on ship for the safety brief. I asked the guy where a good hotel was, cause I did not feel like going back that night. Parker said if I wanted to stay out it would be fine, to just call him on ship. He told us and gave us directions. We sat in the Pub and had a few more beers but got bored cause it wasn't even dark yet. I guess this is the point where I should have headed back to the ship, but instead I decided I would just slow down my drinking and sit out in the courtyard for a while. Well, I guess none of the voices in my head had told Gunny Supply that I was going to slow down. As I sat at a table in the courtyard he went into an ice cream parlor and came out with several shots of whiskey. That fucking moonshine in Iraq tasted better than that crap we got from that ice cream parlor.

It was still light out but things were getting dark in our heads so we decided to go find a hotel that we could crash out in, make some phone calls to the ship, and not be the next target for a mugging. We started stumbling down the street when I had to sit down. It was a small one-way brick road with tall buildings on both sides. Supply tried to keep me going but he couldn't even stand up himself without falling into the bushes or onto street behind him. I knew we were done. Then the best thing happened. Captain Newland and some other officer showed up. God I was glad to see him. He looked at me laughed and with a smirk he said, "Hey Gunny, let me give you a ride back to ship." I said the only thing I could say: "Roger that, Sir." We drove back to ship and pulled up to the gangplank. I walked up the plank and went up the three flights of ladder wells to my berthing area. The ship was tied into port but for some reason was rocking pretty bad, causing me to bounce off the bulkheads as I stumbled down the passageway. I reached my rack, crawled in, pulled the curtain shut, and went to sleep. Thank god for Captain Newland, still saving my ass.

### 8 June 2003

I woke up with the worst hangover. I got showered and dressed and put on the sunglasses I had traded out with Schielein the first time in An Nasiriyah. GySgt Supply was still in the rack as I started to head out, when a First Sgt from one of the Batteries told me my liberty had been revoked and I was restricted to ship. All I could do was laugh. I had signed up for a wine tour from the USO and was going to bring that up but I said fuck it, turned around, and went to go sleep for the rest of the day. It did not bother me being stuck on the ship. Why should it? Yea, I just got out of Iraq, a well-deserved rest and blah, blah, blah. I fucked up and got drunker than I should have. A lot of the Marines from my Platoon were pissed that I got restricted. I loved them guys, and the more they showed they cared about me, the more I felt I had to do for them.

Later that night Parker came rolling in with the Captain and asked what the hell I was doing on ship. I told him that the First Sgt from the Battery had told me the Artillery Battalion Commander had restricted me to ship cause I got drunk last night. Parker went haywire. He said that no one had told him that I was restricted and that the "punk sat right next to me on the bus and didn't say a damn thing." Why was everyone madder than me over this? Parker had a saying, that if it didn't have a B by the name he didn't care -- the B being Bravo Company. He told me he was getting me off restriction and went and talked to Captain Newland. He came back a few minutes latter and said that I was off restriction. He said I hadn't started a fight, hadn't robbed an old lady, wasn't disrespectful to anyone, didn't try to pick up a whore in front of the church -- the only thing I did was get drunk too fast. He said next time to try to stay sober "past noon." The Master Sgt who racked out next to me said he was going out tomorrow and I could hang out with him. By now it was late so I hit the rack and got some more sleep.

### 9 June 2003

The ship looked like hell the next morning. I wasn't the only one who was drinking. The 1-MC started squawking that the Sailors who had duty that day should form up at their quarters. Then the ship's XO came on, saying that everyone needed to clean up their areas. That message came on a couple of times. Sometime that afternoon, the Master Sgt and two other First Sgts from the Arty unit and I headed out for dinner. Parker said I could stay out in a hotel that night if I "chose" and I did "choose," so I figured on hanging out with these guys, and when they headed back in I would go to a hotel and stay there till morning. I kind of just wanted to get away from everyone for a while. I wanted time alone. After we ate dinner and had a few beers, I told them I was headed for a hotel and gave them the name of it. The First Sgt who had restricted my liberty the day before said he was uncomfortable with me staying by myself. I told him I had permission and that I was going to call in to Parker when I found out my room number. They reluctantly left me and headed back.

I went into the hotel and got a room. I didn't have any bags so I went to the Internet room and wrote some e-mails to Kelly and dad. Kelly mentioned in her e-mail that she had gotten the ticket for North Carolina and would be there waiting for me as I got off the boat. After that I headed up to my room and was in the lobby when I saw the two First Sgts and the Master Sgt. I asked them what was up. The First Sgt said he couldn't leave me in town alone. I told him I was staying in my room and it was cool with my chain of command. I didn't want to get into a pissing contest. The First Sgt was just trying to do what he thought was right. I could respect that, but the fact was, he really couldn't tell me I couldn't do something when my command had told me I could. He finally asked if the Master Sgt could stay with me. I didn't have a problem with that. The Master Sgt said he didn't have money for a room and I told him the room I had rented for the night had two beds and he could stay in the extra. This turned out to be a better deal than I had bargained for. I had planned to stay in my room all night so no one would ask me where my liberty partner was, but now that I had a liberty partner I could still go out to the bars. This is exactly what we did.

We found a strip of bars close to the hotel that were all run by a bunch of Brits who had retired in Spain. We found one bar that was empty and the Master Sgt started talking to the bartender/owner, which ended up in several rounds of free drinks. We then headed over to a bar that played some Spanish rock. It was fucking great!!! The bartender was a cute little brunette thing and one of my Marines was making some good headway with her, which meant I got to talk to her too. I wasn't trying to cock block my Marine but I was enjoying just talking to her. It made me want to talk to Kelly that much more.

We headed back to the British bar. There weren't but a few people there and it seemed really laid back. We sat and bullshitted a while. The Master Sgt was drunk and was talking more than me, but it was cool cause he was enjoying himself. He needed to unwind. He started to talk about NASCAR and what a blast it was to go out in a RV to party at the races. The conversation then went to Rugby and then to politics and that was when we left. Not that the Brits disagreed with the war, we had just had enough of it. Plus, if Shore Patrol was out running around, we didn't need the problem. Especially me. We headed back to the hotel, turned on the air conditioning full blast, and watched some TV. Within a few minutes we were both passed out.

**10 June 2003**
The next morning we woke up around nine, just in time to look out our window at all the topless sunbathers gathered around the pool. It was awesome. We had planned the day before to meet the other 1st Sgts from the Artillery Battalion at the hotel and then head to the beach. They showed up just as we finished drinking our first breakfast drink and we headed off. We ended up shopping for shorts, towels, and flip-flops on the way there. Once at the beach I did the beach towel changeover and ordered the first round of beers. It was great. You would think that we

188

had had enough of the sand and heat, but if you add females, beer, tanning, ocean waves, and not having anyone shoot at you, it makes it awesome.

The Master Sgt wanted to head down to the water and hit some waves so I went down with him. The water was so cold it felt great. I felt so far away from the war at that moment. Despite the fact I was still hanging out with Marines and our conversations would wander back and forth from Iraq to America, I really felt so far away, and it felt comforting. But I was ashamed that it felt good.

After the beach we went out walking down the strip of stores, looking at the local women and items for sale, and just enjoying the weather. We stopped after a while, for ice cream of all things. There was a menu with pictures of the different types of ice cream and the ways it could be served. The ice cream shop had been family-owned for 150 years. You could say that in that time they had come up with some "unusual" ways to present ice cream. None of us wanted to get an ice cream that looked too over-the-top. We all just wanted a bowl of something, and they didn't serve it that way. So we ordered, in Spanish, what we thought looked like the simplest plate. By the time we were served I had forgotten what I had ordered, and man did my order look like an "Elton John." After I had swallowed a couple of bites of ice cream (and my pride) the waitress came up and said something in Spanish, and then took my plate away and gave me what I had originally ordered. I guess my point about the ice cream is, we were still humble and felt undeserving of things that were nice or a little over-the-top, even something as simple as ice cream. When we left the ice cream parlor I picked up a shirt in a local store on the way to the bus stop. When we got to the bus stop and were waiting for the bus to take us back to the ship, we ran into some Marines from the Artillery Battalion. They were kind of lit and were telling their 1st Sgt about who in the Battery had gotten in a fight, who went to a whorehouse, and who got the same benefits from the local ladies without going to the whorehouse. Everyone was doing their thing and enjoying themselves, whorehouses to ice cream parlors.

We left back for ship on the liberty bus. The shore patrol on the bus was bitching that the guy who was supposed to relieve him had never showed up. Go figure, it was our last day of liberty before we set sail again towards home. The guy obviously thought that the last remaining hours of drinking and whoring were worth the punishment he would get for not showing up for shore patrol. It probably was.

After returning to the ship I checked in with Parker to see what he was up to. We traded liberty stories and before I hit the rack, I told him I would be down at the gangplank that night to help him get accountability of the Company. Liberty was to end at midnight for everyone.

Around 2330, he and I were out on the flight deck watching the Sailors and Marines return to ship. The XO of the ship, drunk, pulled up in a taxi, extended liberty from midnight to 0130, jumped back in his taxi, and headed back into town. Half the people who were checking in off liberty went back into town too. That was fucked up because the First Sgt said he was going to burn anyone that was late checking back in. Now, people who were just barely sober enough to get back to the ship would hear that, drink more, and not be back on time. Plus, surely some jackass would spread the wrong time around.

### 11 June 2003
At 0130 all but two Sailors were back on ship. We were pulling out of port early in the morning. So I went back to sleep. After I woke up, I had breakfast and went out on the flight deck to see the tugboats push us out to sea. Right before the gangplank was pulled in, a taxi drove up and the U.A. Sailors jumped out and ran up onto the ship. They couldn't have timed it any better if it had been Hollywood.

By late that afternoon, the shore was out of sight and we were heading home.

The rest of the sail home was just like the sail from Iraq to Spain. Of course the little relationships that had developed on the ship between the married couples had to be shut down. Married tended to fuck each other, because it was a safety net as far as keeping their mouths shut. For the most part it worked. Besides the Navy Officer who was starting fights with whoever was talking to the Petty Officer he was fucking, there was only one other rumor. A young female Petty Officer had told an Officer she was supposed to deliver a report to, that she would deliver the report when she wanted to. The Officer asked for it several times, and from all rumors he had asked nicely several times. The Warrant Officer she worked for, in her Captains Mast, said that she should not be punished. Everyone had already thought that they were screwing, but no one could prove it and nothing was ever seen -- but people weren't going to try to prove something that wasn't there just because of a rumor. But when he did that for her, the rumors really spread. The Senior Chief of the ship

190

had her moved to a different workspace. The Navy Chiefs were pissed off about her not getting punished. It sent a bad signal across the ship.

As we sailed deeper into the Atlantic the seas got rougher, and as we passed through, the seas got calmer. When we were a couple of days out from porting in America, a team of wizards came on board. They were there to give us some group therapy. They asked us some questions and gave us some advice. One of the psychiatrists asked me in front of my Platoon, "What would you tell someone as you came off the ship and they were about to get on and go to Iraq?" I told him that I would tell the guy getting on the ship, "It sucks to be you." At the end the wizards asked if there were any questions or if anyone wanted some one-on-one individual counseling. What the fuck were they thinking? No one would ever ask a question or ask for help in front of their brothers like that. Doing so would have made them look weak.

I don't know if it was the wizards or some other brain department who was responsible, but there was a sheet passed out that asked a variety of questions. It had questions like, did you hear gunfire, did you see dead bodies, did you kill anyone, did you receive friendly fire, and so on. The questions got progressively deeper. By the time I finished the questionnaire and looked over it, I thought to myself that I really had seen some shit. I mean I knew I was in combat and all but what the fuck. We really, kind of hit a little, or a lot of everything on the sheet. Reading the sheet made me feel a little worse off than when I began.

We were chomping at the bit to get off that ship. No matter what bullshit was said or done to us, it never outweighed the fact that we were about to get home, and those of us that didn't get laid in Spain were about to get laid in America. We were going to go home and see our families and friends. It was going to be a great time. It was even better for me, because I had put my retirement papers in on ship. As soon as we got off leave, I would be retiring from the Marine Corps. Don't misunderstand, I really loved the Corps, but I was done. I wanted to go home. My dad was having problems with his health, I thought Kelly and I could make a go of it, I could work for myself and maybe make a little more money than I was making in the Corps, and maybe do some traveling like I had always wanted. To top it all off, I was tired of the bullshit and games. I just didn't have the heart anymore. The meetings I used to enjoy were becoming a pain in the ass. Fixing problems didn't give me the sense of accomplishment it once did. In my mind I was becoming a liability to the Marine Corps.

**21 June 2003**

We could see the coast of America and somewhere just beyond the coast, Kelly, was waiting for me.

**22 June 2003**

Our ship started to pull into port early that morning. Of the three ships carrying our Battalion back, we were the first to pull into port. The unloading took no time at all. We didn't have the vehicles, helicopters, or heavy armor that we had loaded onto the ship when we had left for Iraq that January. Plus, the other ships were waiting on us. Parker put everyone in a formation and I hung out with Jones. He and I had not been talking on ship like we had done in Iraq, so we did some quick catching up. His wife had moved his home and his children to base housing while he was gone. He had a lot to do and even though he acted like it was going to be a pain in the ass, you could tell he was all about it. He loved being married and being a father. He had the temperament for it. The buses pulled up and we loaded up.

Jones and I sat next to each other in the front of the bus. Airhart was in the middle of the bus cracking jokes and making everyone laugh as he always did. He started performing a little skit that had three characters in it and of course the more we laughed the more he hammed it up. Everyone was in a great mood and was lighthearted. Scattered along the side of the road back to Camp Lejeune were people by their cars with American flags, and they would wave at us as we drove by. The weather couldn't have been better for being out like that. There was not a cloud in the sky, but there was a cool wind coming from the sea that made it seem, so surreal. As we drove on base through the side gate, it slowly grew quieter on the bus. Airhart had now stopped his joking around and my conversation with Jones had dwindled to muttered words. Jones noticed that they had built a new gas station on base and said that they had built it quick. I said we had been gone six months. He had a look on his face as though hadn't realized that we had been gone that long.

The bus pulled up to the Armory and the 7-ton that had our gear in it pulled up to where the families where waiting for us by our barracks. I had my gear in the Company Vehicle along with the 1$^{st}$ Sgts, and it was going to be in the office waiting for me. We loaded off the bus and turned our weapons in to the Armory. It really didn't take that long. I turned my shotgun in to the Weapons Company cage since I had

192

originally gotten it from them. The rest of my gear belonged to Bravo Company. Like I said, the turn-in of all the weapons and stuff took no time at all. It was the count that Lt Daniels had to do that held things up. Not that he was slow in counting; there was just a lot of stuff to count.

During the wait at the Armory, we could hear the kids and the music playing from the Battalion Headquarters building. I looked at Jones and asked him if he smelled the same thing I did. He said he did and smiled. After about an hour 1st Sgt Parker called the Company to formation and gave us our liberty brief. He said that as soon as we marched over to the barracks and he dismissed us, we were off for the next couple of days. He called the Company to attention, had us right face, and march to where our families were. Just like the rest of the Platoon Commanders, I was marching off to the side of my Platoon as the Platoon Sgts were sounding cadence. We came up behind our barracks and were marching up the side. I could see a rope was set up in order to keep the families back as we marched up. I wanted my shotgun back.

I started to look for Kelly out of the corner of my eye. I could see wives crying, children waving their hands, and fathers smiling, but I didn't see Kelly. I wondered if she could see me. I thought maybe she didn't make it on base. Parker gave orders for the Company to halt and left face. I was behind my Platoon now but at least I was facing the crowd. I looked even harder and could not find her among all the faces. People from the crowd were shouting and yelling names. The order came from the 1st Sgt that we were dismissed. My platoon disappeared in a wave of people. I was left standing alone, just kind of looking around. I was looking at the ground -- I didn't want anyone to see me looking disappointed and alone. Then I breathed in the faint smell of Kelly's body oil, her cool soft hand touched the back of my neck, and her leg wrapped itself around my left leg. We locked onto each other. We could have stayed that way forever and it still wouldn't have been long enough. We didn't say a word.

I had to get my bags up to my room. She was holding onto my left arm as we walked. I felt so awkward at first. She walked so smoothly, more of a glide than a walk, while I thought I had two new feet. I grabbed my bags and took them to my room. In the small refrigerator there were some baked goods, Girl Scout cookies, and a six-pack of beer. We stayed in my room for a while before we left for the hotel she had booked on the beach.

As we were leaving we went by to see the Marines in my Platoon. They had already started drinking and the music wasn't from the band that had marched us in, but from radios playing from the rooms. I introduced them to Kelly and they all looked down at the ground when shaking her hand. No one insulted me by eye-fucking my girlfriend.

We left for the beach. The hotel she picked was great. That night we walked along the beach down to a bar that was on the beach. There were two Marines from my Platoon there. It was night when we walked back to the hotel. The weather was just as nice as it had been during the day.

We spent the next couple of days bouncing from hotel to hotel, just to get our fill of the area more than anything else. That, and Kelly couldn't find a hotel that we could get a full booking on for the time we were there.

One of the nights we went to Parker's house for dinner. It was a great time. Food, beer, and the company was great. Besides, someone very important to me was at his house: my motorcycle. The damn thing wouldn't start. A friend of Parkers had been over to his house to start up our bikes every now and then, but he couldn't figure out how to start mine. I messed with it a little while before I said fuck it, and went back to everyone in the house. As we left that night, Kelly told me that Parker had told his wife Dawn that I had done well in Iraq. She said she was proud of me. Bingo! I had the approval of a beautiful woman on the inside and out.

After a wonderful four days with Kelly, she had to return to Dallas -- which was fine, our time off was coming to an end and I was going on leave back to Dallas that Friday anyway.

**27 June 2003**
The Battalion got off early and I headed over to John's Speed and Custom to get my bike out of the shop. I knew that if I spent enough time on it I could get it running again, but with Kelly being in town I didn't want to waste my time. I had dropped it off to have John figure it out and give it the once-over. Besides, I would have had him give it a second look anyway just to make sure I didn't fuck something up.

I returned back to base and after picking up my leave papers I went back to my room in the barracks to get a good night's sleep before I left for Dallas in the morning. I didn't have any packing to do -- I was riding

194

with what was on my back and only enough shit to fit in an Iraqi ammo pouch that I strapped to my handlebars.

## 28 June 2003

I got up around seven in the morning and took off out of town. I had to get moving -- a storm was coming in and I wanted to beat it out of North Carolina before it overran me. I put my helmet on and the red vest that was required to ride a motorcycle on base at Camp Lejeune. I headed west and when I was out of Onslow County I took the vest off without even pulling over.

A couple of hours later I hit the North/South Carolina border and the rain was catching up to me. So I pulled over into a gas station while I waited to see what would happen next.

I ended up eating at a diner next to the gas station and then making a phone call to my dad, to let him know I had left on time. By then the rain had stopped and that southern sun was doing its job -- it got humid fast and the water was already starting to evaporate. I was sitting on the curb when some guy came over to talk to me about my bike. He was waiting for his car to be repaired. He asked me why I cut my fender so short in the rear and pointed out that I couldn't ride anyone on the back. I told him that was the whole point -- I couldn't ride anyone on the back who was going to tell me what to do. He laughed and asked me what I did when it rained; I told him "you're looking at it." He laughed to himself again. We talked some more. Turned out he was a retired Marine Gunny from Vietnam. I told him I had spent some time in the Marines a long time ago. I didn't feel like talking about the Marines or the war. After a good chat about the local raceway, his car was ready and he left.

I went inside to get a cup of coffee and some gum. As I was waiting in line, a woman of about thirty with blonde hair, blue eyes, wearing a short summer dress, slender at about six feet and about six teeth (upper and lower gums), came over and asked me my name. I told her "Jay." She said she was hoping it was Cowboy, because she had had a dream about a cowboy taking her away "and the things he did to me." I told her I was pretty sure my name was Jay and that I wasn't a cowboy. I still didn't want to talk about the Marines and the war, but now for totally different reasons. She left and everyone in the store kind of laughed, but mine was a little more nervous than everyone else was. I went outside and the same woman walked up to me and introduced me to her girlfriend who had the same admiring qualities as her friend. She began to tell me how they worked together, lived together, went fishing together, and started to talk about how they did everything together. The road looked dry enough to me, so I headed to Dallas. I ended up in Atlanta for the night.

There was a bar just on the east side of Atlanta that looked decent enough. I went in and didn't leave for hours. I had a Harley shirt on, with the sleeves cut off, and the lower part of the back was missing from rubbing against the rear tire. Everyone else was dressed in suits and ties but they were really down to earth. I had a good time in that bar.

## 29 June 2003
I left east Atlanta, got back on the road, and headed west again. I was still in Atlanta when a car pulled up next to me with a kid in the back seat pointing at me for his parents to look. All kids like motorcycles, so I was used to it. But the way this kid pointed at me kind of raised the hair on the back of my neck. I looked at my back wheel and it was wobbling from side to side. The belt drive had pulled the rear wheel extension out of the rear wheel. I pulled off at the first exit I found. There was a man standing at the corner of the exit, waiting for the light to change. I asked him if he knew where a garage or auto parts store was. He pointed north and said about four miles. I drove down the road till I pulled up in front of a Napa auto parts store.

I looked at my rear wheel and could tell I was fucked. I kept thinking what kind of tool I could use to fix the wheel. It was around ten and the store wouldn't open up for another two hours. As I was contemplating my situation, a lady walked up to me and asked me if I wanted some crack; I looked at her and briefly and shook my head. She then asked if wanted a blowjob. This time I looked at her and said, "No thanks, I already had breakfast," which was a lie. She walked off, mad, in one direction and I walked in the other to get some coffee. After about ten minutes of really studying it, I realized there was no tool at the parts store that I could use to fix my situation. I was going to have to pull the whole tire off. I found a phone book, but since I didn't know Atlanta, I was lost as to where any of the stores were.

I decided to head west till I found a U-Haul and just put the bike in the back and drive it to Dallas. I was on the highway five minutes when I found a U-Haul. I pulled in and waited for the place to open up. I had found a ball in the parking lot and threw it against the wall while I contemplated my situation. I came to the conclusion there was no use

196

even trying to drive it to Dallas; I would just cause more damage and it wouldn't be worth it. A guy pulled up and said to give him a few because it took him a while to open up, and then he disappeared inside. A few minutes later a guy driving a Home Depot 18-wheeler pulled up and started testing his tires with a bat. For shits and grins I asked him if he knew of a garage near-by. He thought for a moment and said that he thought there was one about six miles down Martin Luther King Rd.

I got on my bike and headed off. I found the place, and just as he said, the mechanic was sitting in the front of the store in a recliner. I pulled in and explained to the guy what was wrong with my bike and after a good five minutes of silence he said, "I don't know nothin' about no bikes." You could have pushed me over with a feather. Then he said I was welcome to use all his tools in the garage if I wanted.

The garage was a mess but the tools were easy to find. He had air-powered hoses so the rear tire dropped easy and the pulley came off and on with no problems. After thirty minutes I was ready to jump back on the road. I asked the man what I owed him and he said nothing since I did all the work. He offered me a beer and we sat around on the front porch of that old gas station till about one in the afternoon. After that I was ready to head back out.

I pulled into a small town just east of Shreveport and found a local hotel. I checked in and turned on the news and found out that a hurricane was headed my way. I got back out on my bike, drove to the beer store, picked up a twelve pack and headed to the restaurant across the street from the liquor store.

I ordered a burger and some fries. The waitress and I talked a bit till her husband walked in. I finished my food and left. I had just pulled my bike inside the hotel room with me when it started to poor down rain. I drank most of the twelve pack and watched it rain. I passed out somewhere in the night.

### 30 June 2003
I woke up early with the mother of all hangovers. I pushed the bike out into the parking lot. The sun had been up a short while and the rain was already starting to look like a memory on the pavement. I started up my bike and I found out my headlight didn't work. I headed to Shreveport for a new headlight and some gambling.

I hit Shreveport and found an auto parts store that had the type of light that I needed. It didn't take a mechanic's garage to fix the light bulb. The guy I bought the light from said the nearest casino was three miles straight down the road. I headed west and found three or four big ones. I took to the one that was farthest west; that way I would feel like I had traveled farther and was closer to home.

Did you know you get your liquor free when you drink and gamble? I parked my bike outside the casino and walked in. It had money on the walls and clothing stores. I walked around for a while before putting twenty dollars into a slot machine. I ordered a Jack and coke and when I tried paying for it, the guy told me it was on the house. I thought maybe since they had security all over the place that they had seen the military base sticker on my bike and so he gave me a free drink. I drank it rather slow and ordered a second. He told me again the drink was free. I asked him what was up with the free drinks and he told me that because I was gambling I got free drinks. I slowed down on pushing the one armed bandit and quickened my drinks. I don't know how much a drink would have cost without gambling, but I am sure I made out in the long run on that twenty dollars.

I had come to play blackjack, so I bought some chips and sat down at ten-dollar table. I played for a while and the guy to my left was raking in some cash. Of course it had partly to do with the way I was playing. He looked at me and told me to keep on doing what I was doing. I looked at him and told him I did not know what I was doing, but that I would try. His face about dropped to the deck. He got mad and left the table. I didn't mind him winning, I just minded him expecting me to play his hand and the one that was in front of me.

I started with about fifty bucks and with 175 dollars in chips, which I bet all on one hand, and walked away. I don't even know if I won. I do know that the fucking drunk ruined my fun.
I left for Dallas again.

Kelly had to be at work in a couple of hours and I wanted to see her before she left. I pulled back the throttle and headed to her house. I didn't think Texas would ever end. After a couple of hours I pulled up in front of her house. I got to see her before she left. I felt really relaxed, like everything was okay. She left for work and I left for my dad's house. At his house there was a package that I had sent to myself from ship. I opened it and gave him the Iraqi flag that I had put in it. After some drinks, I went in the back bedroom and went to sleep.

Several days after I arrived home on leave, my dad held a welcome home party for me, and my family and friends came. My oldest friend showed up with his wife and two kids. As I was talking to him I realized I was cussing, my voice was rising, and there was anger in my voice. I would have known better in any other circumstance not to act this way in front of his wife and children, but I was just doing it.

Later, as my cousin -- a Green Beret from the First Gulf War, Counter Drug Operations, and Somalia -- started comparing our experiences, the more I didn't like being in Dallas. Listening to him I realized he hadn't adjusted yet -- he was still fighting battles that ended a long time ago. It scared me into thinking that the same would happen to me.

At one point my mom tried to get my attention by yelling my name and waving her hands over her head, so I would come in and cut a cake. I wanted to take cover and yell for everyone to get down. I kept my cool, but inside I was ready to fight.

A couple of days later I went and got my stuff out of storage and moved into a duplex. Kelly and I went out shopping for furniture to kind of fill the place up. It was good being with her, looking for furniture, establishing a home that I would not be jerked out of to go fight somewhere else. There were two bed frames we were trying to decide on. Of course she was saying we should pick the cheaper one, but when I said we should get the more expensive one, she smiled. She looked so happy being with me. Kelly moved some of her stuff into the duplex and we started living together.

Things were great. Kelly was totally fun to be with, my dad lived right down the street, everyone seemed eager for me to come home, prospects of getting a good-paying job seemed more than possible. But I still felt something inside me telling me to run. For the life of me, though, I couldn't tell what I was supposed to run from.

My leave was over and I flew back to Camp Lejeune with second thoughts on retiring. I talked to Parker about pulling my retirement papers. He said if that was what I wanted to do he would pull them, but to be sure that's what I wanted to do. I thought about it and decided that the adjustment to civilian life would not be a problem, that I could correct and control my feelings. Besides, I would have to do it some day, might as well be now. I let my retirement papers process through the system.

I drank a lot till my paperwork was processed for my retirement. I wasn't required by the new CO to go to the field; in fact I got the feeling he didn't want me around. I disagreed with his training methods and I wasn't the only one to point this out to him. Parker and some officers had told him that what he was doing was wrong. He didn't listen to us, and after several fiascos, he ended up getting relieved.

## 4 September 2003
I picked up my retirement papers at the Administration Center at Camp Lejeune. I didn't know it but they were all fucked up. The Admin Marines, who didn't even go to Iraq, took the day off to go see a concert that was for the Marines and Sailors returning from Iraq. I went back to the Battalion area and waited for Parker to get off and take me to the airport.

I was called outside a time later, received my plaque from the Battalion. There was no formation or band, which I didn't mind but the new Battalion Commander didn't even come out to greet us and say a few words. The SgtMaj was out there. He said something and since he served with us in Iraq, that meant something. I said a few words to the Battalion and that was it. They returned to training for the day and I went back in the office for my ride to the airport. Parker came in and we left. Like Parker said, "you just come in, turn out the light and go home."

200

# Whose Country Is This?
## Chapter 8

**4 Sept 2003**
I returned home, in uniform, for the last time. My Dad picked me up from the airport. We drove over to a bar called Milos by Greenville Ave. and had a few beers. After an hour or two, Kelly showed up to take me home.

As we got in her car, I felt like something wasn't right. I wasn't for sure what it was. It had nothing to do with Kelly, Dallas, my Dad, or anything else tangible.

I felt this uneasiness inside me. It really didn't hit me till I walked out of the bar -- I was a fugitive again. I felt like, soon everyone would know what I had done, who I had killed and had ordered to be killed. I would soon be judged by those who had no right to judge me. My sins were catching up to me.

**23 March 2004**
I am back in the world and I am not adjusting well, I guess this is my sentencing for my sins. I am easily angered, rash in my decisions, at times incapable of having a conversation with someone that I don't agree with, and destructive physically and mentally. I feel at times no guilt for killing or ordering people killed but I can't say the same about retrieving the dead Marine in the Amtrak or the deaths of other Marines. Here in the world, if I cuss, people stop and stare like I am some sort of outlaw. How would they look at me if they knew I had killed so many people that I had lost count?

Sometimes the smell of burning oil from cars around me reminds me of the burning Amtraks and the feeling and fear that RPG rounds are about to slam into the side of my truck. When I am at St Thomas if the mass begins praying "Hail Mary, full of grace..." then for the rest of the mass, I am in Ambush Alley again, praying for those I am about to kill and for those with me. At night, when I do fall asleep, I dream of the Marine I left behind, sitting in the hatch of the back ramp of the burning Amtrak. He is sitting there, calmly smoking a cigarette, waiting for me to return to get him. Rounds are flying all around him and he doesn't move, he just calmly sits there. At times, I wake at night and feel that if I go into the other room, Jordan or Reiss will be in there waiting to talk to me. They are not mad, just calmly waiting for me.

There is not a time when the morning sun rises or the night falls that my memory does not sort through those days. Some things I pass on quickly so as not to dwell on them for reasons I, at times, cannot comprehend. But at times I bring up the memories on purpose and think about them hard, and I find comfort for our suffering. Children dancing in the street while old men, whose legs had lost the capability to dance, clapped upon our arrival in the city. Iraqi soldiers throwing their weapons into the Euphrates and rejoicing that they are no longer serving in an Army that they were forced to join. Little girls the age of my daughters going to school to learn and to become something more than just married to a man of their family's choosing. Bus loads of men going to worship for the first time in decades. Communities would be able to mourn the death of their leaders and families in ways that were not allowed before. All these memories show up when I hear that the war in Iraq is wrong. It will never be wrong to let a people live free.

I feel at times like an old man crying for his youth. But at times I know it is more than that. I miss standing next to my brothers. A brother is someone who stands next to me and we have no bond but that of being a Marine. My brothers have seen the worst of me in my greatest moments of failure and stand next to me believing only in my achievements. They acknowledge with no words but with action alone that they would stand next to me even when death passed over us. I, too, do these things for them, out of respect, love, and the things I have seen them achieve. They found courage where none could be found, mercy where there was only hate, time for sorrow while carrying the fight to the enemy, giving their hearts equally to both. When they were thirsty and hungry they gave not only to each other but to those that hated them as well. They are the Marines that not only follow the path of their forefathers, but also make it wider and take it farther than before. They will ensure freedom is not lost on the table of chance.

We joined the Marines to prove to the world that we were honorable men; we went to war and proved we were honorable men to ourselves.

### 28 August 2004
Today I was at the Consignment Shop, looking for furniture with my new girlfriend. Schielein called me on my cell phone. Two times we

202

were disconnected, and I finally reached him on the third try. By then I was in my truck going home, headed north on Greenville Avenue.

He told me a Marine that we had served with, who was on his second tour in Iraq, was killed. Schielein said that he didn't want to talk. We hung up. Anger filled me and I punched the windshield of my truck so hard it cracked. Guilt took over because I wasn't there with him. Embarrassment took over for acting out in such a way. Sadness came and I broke down into tears because even though I probably would never have seen him again, I missed him.

I had talked to him on the phone about a month before he left for Iraq. He said he was going to re-enlist one more time and request his second tour to be in California so he could be close to his family. I wished him the best of luck and told him to be careful. He kind of laughed and said good-bye.

That Marine was Sgt Lopez, the Corporal that I wrote about a little over a year and a half ago in the foreword of this book. He was the one in the turret of the HMMV watching over his brother Marines. Sgt Lopez was his "brother's keeper…"